Cents and Sensibility

Cents and Sensibility

*What Economics Can Learn
from the Humanities*

Gary Saul Morson
and
Morton Schapiro

Princeton University Press
Princeton and Oxford

Copyright © 2017 by Princeton University Press

Published by Princeton University Press,
41 William Street, Princeton, New Jersey 08540

In the United Kingdom:
Princeton University Press, 6 Oxford Street,
Woodstock, Oxfordshire OX20 1TR

press.princeton.edu

Jacket design by Karl Spurzem

All Rights Reserved

ISBN 978-0-691-17668-0

Library of Congress Control Number: 2017930423

British Library Cataloging-in-Publication Data is available.

This book has been composed in New Caledonia and Minion.

Printed on acid-free paper. ∞

Printed in the United States of America

1 3 5 7 9 10 8 6 4 2

To our families and our students—
We love listening, and contributing, to your stories.

Come now, and let us reason together . . .

—Isaiah, 1:18

Contents

Acknowledgments

In the early 1980s, economist Gordon Winston proudly presented his newly published book on the treatment of time in economics to the legendary economist Joan Robinson. Professor Robinson was notorious for her cantankerous nature, and Gordon waited anxiously for several weeks until Joan suddenly walked into his office, tossed the book on his desk, and declared "Winston, this is the kind of book that is a lot more fun to write than to read."

Stories are a mainstay of the humanities, but not of economics. After teaching and writing together, we have become convinced that infusing humanistic approaches and sensibilities into economics would make its models more realistic, its predictions more accurate, and its policies more effective and more just.

We have many to thank for their assistance in that quest. David Figlio, Jean Franczyk, Barry Glassner, Chris Hiland, Dan Linzer, Alec Litowitz, Katie Martin, Mike McPherson, Jeremy Mingo, Adrian Randolph, Judi Remington, Thomas Pavel, Paula Peterson, Alissa Schapiro, and Mimi Schapiro provided very helpful comments on earlier drafts. Katie Porter offered her usual wisdom and Joel Mokyr provided insightful suggestions, large and small. We both had the opportunity to learn from the late, great humanist Stephen Toulmin. Geneva Danko was invaluable in organizing countless versions of the manuscript in her always unflappable and extraordinarily efficient manner. Finally, comments from Peter Dougherty and anonymous reviewers for Princeton University Press made this book immeasurably better.

Writing this was an absolute blast, and we hope that our readers can tell how much fun we had doing it. We hope, as well, that unlike Professor Robinson, you will share our enthusiasm.

Cents and Sensibility

Chapter 1

Spotting the Spoof
The Value of Telling Stories
Out of (and in) School

This book creates a dialogue between two fields that rarely have anything to say to each other: economics and the humanities. We mean to show how that dialogue could be conducted and why it has a great deal to contribute.

The best dialogues take place when each interlocutor speaks from her best self, without pretending to be something she is not. In their recent book *Phishing for Phools: The Economics of Manipulation and Deception*, Nobel Prize–winning economists George Akerlof and Robert Shiller expand the standard definition of "phishing."[1] In their usage, it goes beyond committing fraud on the Internet to indicate something older and more general: "getting people to do things that are in the interest of the phisherman" rather than their own.[2] In much the same spirit, we would like to expand the meaning of another recent computer term, "spoofing," which normally means impersonating someone else's email name and address to deceive the recipient—a friend or family member of the person whose name is stolen—into doing something no one would do at the behest of a stranger. Spoofing in our usage also means something more

1. George A. Akerlof and Robert J. Shiller, *Phishing for Phools: The Economics of Manipulation and Deception* (Princeton University Press, 2015).

2. Akerlof and Shiller, p. xi.

1

general: pretending to represent one discipline or school when actually acting according to the norms of another. Like phishing, spoofing is meant to deceive, and so it is always useful to spot the spoof.

Students who take an English course under the impression they will be taught literature, and wind up being given lessons in politics that a political scientist would scoff at or in sociology that would mystify a sociologist, are being spoofed. Other forms of the humanities—or dehumanities, as we prefer to call them—spoof various scientific disciplines, from computer science to evolutionary biology and neurology. The longer the spoof deceives, the more disillusioned the student will be with what she takes to be the "humanities."

By the same token, when economists pretend to solve problems in ethics, culture, and social values in purely economic terms, they are spoofing other disciplines, although in this case the people most readily deceived are the economists themselves. We will examine various ways in which this happens and how, understandably enough, it earns economists a bad name among those who spot the spoof.

But many do not spot it. Gary Becker won a Nobel Prize largely for extending economics to the furthest reaches of human behavior, and the best-selling *Freakonomics* series popularizes this approach.[3] What seems to many an economist to be a sincere effort to reach out to other disciplines strikes many practitioners of those fields as nothing short of imperialism, since economists expropriate topics rather than treat existing literatures and methods with the respect they deserve. Too often the economic approach to interdisciplinary

---

3. Steven D. Levitt and Stephen J. Dubner, *Freakonomics: A Rogue Economist Explores the Hidden Side of Everything* (HarperCollins, 2005); *SuperFreakonomics: Global Cooling, Patriotic Prostitutes, and Why Suicide Bombers Should Buy Life Insurance* (HarperCollins, 2009); *Think Like a Freak: The Authors of Freakonomics Offer to Retrain Your Brain* (HarperCollins, 2014); and *When to Rob a Bank ... and 131 More Warped Suggestions and Well-Intended Rants* (HarperCollins, 2015).

work is that other fields have the questions and economics has the answers.

As with the dehumanities, these efforts are not valueless. There is, after all, an economic aspect to many activities, including those we don't usually think of in economic terms. People make choices about many things, and the rational choice model presumed by economists can help us understand how they do so, at least when they behave rationally—and even the worst curmudgeon acknowledges that people are sometimes rational! We have never seen anyone deliberately get into a longer line at a bank.

Even regarding ethics, economic models can help in one way, by indicating what is the most efficient allocation of resources. To be sure, one can question the usual economic definition of efficiency—in terms of maximizing the "economic surplus"—and one can question the establishment of goals in purely economic terms, but regardless of which goals one chooses, it pays to choose an efficient way, one that expends the least resources, to reach them.[4] Wasting resources is never a good thing to do, because the resources wasted could have been put to some ethical purpose. The problem is that efficiency does not exhaust ethical questions, and the economic aspect of many problems is not the most important one. By pretending to solve ethical questions, economists wind up spoofing philosophers, theologians, and other ethicists. Economic rationality is indeed part of human nature, but by no means all of it.

For the rest of human nature, we need the humanities (and the humanistic social sciences). In our view, numerous aspects of life are best understood in terms of a dialogue between economics and the humanities—not the spoofs, but real economics and real humanities.

4. For an insightful critique of the purely economic approach to efficiency, see Jonathan B. Wight, *Ethics in Economics: An Introduction to Moral Frameworks* (Stanford University Press, 2015).

Twin Crises

Economics and the humanities are both in trouble, though not for the same reason.

Economists wield a lot of power and take a lot of criticism. Sometimes it even seems as if they have two functions: to formulate policies and to take the blame when things go wrong. Should a stimulus fail to stimulate, or very high interest rates prove powerless to dampen inflation, economists are often quick to explain away the facts while newspapers are even readier to skewer them. When a real estate bubble bursts, journalists eagerly point to the economic theory that bubbles are not supposed to exist at all. For many in the public, the face of economics has turned out to be MIT economist Jonathan Gruber telling his colleagues that the health care law was deliberately written "in a tortured way" so that, given "the stupidity of the American voter," its core provisions would be invisible. For others, it is Paul Krugman responding to his failed predictions regarding the timing of the US recovery from the last recession, the future of the eurozone, and the onset of deflation by declaring that he has seldom, if ever, been wrong.

Economists can always tweak their models to account for what has already happened. Their critics, in turn, have the easy job of not taking any risks at all, just looking for inevitable mistakes. As Alexander Pope wrote three centuries ago, it is always easy to poke holes in someone else's paper.

> And you my Critics! in the chequered shade,
> Admire new light through holes yourselves have made.[5]

Can nothing be done? Over the past few decades, economists and social psychologists have announced the supposedly startling discovery that, contrary to economic theory, people do not always behave rationally! They are not mechanisms for optimizing, their choices are not always consistent, and they

---

5. Alexander Pope, *The Dunciad* (Book IV, ll. pp. 125–126) in *Alexander Pope: Selected Poetry and Prose*, ed. William K. Wimsatt (Holt, Rinehart, 1965), p. 430.

often do not act according to their best interests. Inside economics, the result has been heated controversy, but from an
outside perspective, it has been wonder. Surely no one in his
right mind ever thought people are rational to begin with?
Why, the whole heritage of Western literature has described
people as irrational, and the social sciences point to many
factors other than reason that shape behavior. Why would
philosophers since Socrates have been urging people to act
rationally, if they always did so anyway? And why would intellectual historians have spent so much time describing how the
very idea of rationality in the modern Western sense arose in
the first place? And then there is everyday life, where surely no
one was ever moved to reflect on the absence of folly!

With this discovery in mind, traditional rational choice
theory has generated, like yin answering yang, an irrational
choice theory. Behavioral economics, as this flourishing movement is called, has in its own turn generated new policies and
new critics. It purports to come closer to adding the human
dimension to economic models, but as we will show, although
it has made some advances, it does nothing of the kind. The
human beings it imagines behave just as mechanically, only
less efficiently (judged by the same criteria as traditional economists use). They are still abstract monads shaped by no particular culture. You still don't need stories to understand them.
In short, they bear as much resemblance to real people as stick
figures do to the heroines of George Eliot or Leo Tolstoy.

Adding the human dimension to economics in this and similar ways is like deciding that we need air as well as food and so
prescribing a diet of airy food. (Dairy Queen, anyone?) Might
there be a better way to integrate humanistic insights? But here
we come to another problem: the state of the humanities.

The Dehumanities

Go to almost any issue of the *Chronicle of Higher Education*,
consult recent issues of national publications from the *Wall*

Street Journal to the *New York Times*, read reports from
Harvard University and the American Academy of Arts and
Sciences, and you will discover that the humanities are in
crisis. No one seems to value them anymore. Enrollments in
humanities courses plummet, and majors in humanistic disciplines diminish. If it were not for the recent phenomenon of
double majoring—fulfilling requirements in two disciplines as
a sort of employment insurance—figures for humanistic disciplines would doubtless look still worse.

Like a delicatessen owner who sells rancid meat and then
blames his business failure on the vulgarization of customer
taste, humanities professors account for their plight by fault-
ing their students. "All they care about is money." "Twitter has
reduced their attention span to that of a pithed frog." Critics
of literature professors respond that for at least a quarter
century, they have themselves argued that there is no such
thing as great literature but only things *called* great literature
because hegemonic forces of oppression have mystified us into
believing in objective greatness. If this idea was once bravura,
it is now just boring. The most commonly taught anthology
among literature professors, *The Norton Anthology of Theory
and Criticism*, paraphrases a key tenet of the dominant movement called "cultural studies": "Literary texts, like other artworks, are neither more nor less important than any other
cultural artifact or practice. Keeping the emphasis on how
cultural meanings are produced, circulated, and consumed,
the investigator will focus on art or literature insofar as such
works connect with broader social factors, not because they
possess some intrinsic interest or special aesthetic values."[6] We

---

6. *The Norton Anthology of Theory and Criticism*, 2nd edition, ed. Vincent B. Leitch
et al. (Norton, 2011), p. 2478. For a recent, spirited critique of this volume and similar
thinking, see James Seaton, *Literary Criticism from Plato to Postmodernism: A Humanistic Alternative* (Cambridge University Press, 2016). See also Mark Edmundson, *Self
and Soul: A Defense of Ideals* (Harvard University Press, 2015) and Edmundson, *Why
Read?* (Bloomsbury, 2004).

shall have more to say about this passage later, but it is worth noting that cultural studies did not invent, but adapted, an already established orthodoxy denying any sort of intrinsic literary value.[7] If Shakespeare and Milton are no more important than any other "cultural artifact or practice," and if they are to be studied only "insofar as" they connect with other social factors and not because of "some intrinsic interest or special aesthetic values," then why invest the considerable effort to read them at all? Reading *Paradise Lost* is not like strolling through a field! Could it be that students don't take literature courses because they are responding rationally to what their teachers have been telling them?

The language about "how cultural meanings are produced, circulated, and consumed" gropes for the prestige of something hard, unsentimental, materialistic—in short, for economics, as a literature professor might imagine it. It appears that humanists' key strategy for saving their disciplines has been to dehumanize them. And so we have a host of new movements, announced with the breathless enthusiasm appropriate for discovering the double helix. Sociobiological criticism has shown us how emotions and behaviors described in literary works arose to serve an evolutionary purpose. What's more, you can now recognize why you love Dante (or Danielle Steele) by turning to neuroaesthetics. And at the Modern Language Conference of 2009 it was discovered that "the next big thing" was the digital humanities. Before anyone else thinks of it, we hereby coin the term, and claim to have founded the discipline of, "the nano-humanities." We don't yet know what this

7. See Barbara Herrnstein Smith, *Contingencies of Value: Alternative Perspectives for Critical Theory* (Harvard University Press, 1988). Smith argues: "All value is radically contingent, being neither a fixed attribute, an inherent quality, or an objective property of things but, rather, an effect of multiple, continuously changing, and continuously interacting variables or, to put this another way, the product of the dynamics of a system, specifically an *economic* system" (p. 30). It is crucial, she argues, to avoid reinforcing "dubious concepts of noncontingency: that is, concepts such as 'intrinsic,' 'objective,' 'absolute,' 'universal,' and 'transcendent'" (p. 31).

cutting-edge criticism will do, but we are sure that it will *not* involve real engagement with major literary works or a deep appreciation of what makes them great.

Each of these dehumanities offers something of value. Undoubtedly, the digital humanists have contributed to making good texts available and easy to comment on. It is interesting to learn how the human capacity to make and appreciate art evolved, and it would be curious to know "what happens in the brain when we laugh at Mark Twain."[8] For that matter, the economics of novel publishing could be informative, and so could the chemistry of papermaking, the physics of bookbinding, and the physiology of reading poems aloud. But each of these contributions would matter only if we already had an appreciation of great art and literature, which you can't get by de-aestheticizing, de-literizing, or dehumanizing them.

Humanomics

All attempts to overcome the dualism of cognition and life, of thought and singular concrete reality *from inside theoretical cognition* are absolutely hopeless ... like trying to lift oneself up by one's own hair. —MIKHAIL BAKHTIN[9]

Rather than attempt to save the humanities by dehumanizing them, why not see what great literature genuinely has to offer

---

8. For an important collection of articles from this school, see *The Literary Animal: Evolution and the Nature of Narrative* (Northwestern University Press, 2005). Despite some important contributions by sociobiological critics, a key problem remains: whatever evolutionary process made literature possible applies generally, but great literature is important precisely when it is *not* general but different in a way that makes it great. It is hard to see how evolution or neurology could reveal what makes Shakespeare's seventy-third sonnet a truly great poem, not just a poem that he evidently evolved to be able to write in a way that provokes some pattern of neurons firing in some people.

9. M. M. Bakhtin, "K filosofii postupka," in *Filosofiia i sotsiologiia nauki i tekhniki: Ezhegodnik 1984–85* (Moscow: Nauka, 1986), p. 86; trans. Gary Saul Morson, "Prosaic Bakhtin: Landmarks, Anti-Intelligentsialism, and the Russian Countertradition," in Amy Mandelker, *Bakhtin in Contexts: Across the Disciplines* (Northwestern University Press, 1995), p. 63 (italics in the original).

other disciplines? We have written this book to illustrate one way this can be done.

We believe that economics can benefit by considering key ways of thinking, cultivated by reading great cultural artifacts. To anticipate our conclusions, let us say that economics could benefit from understanding people better. We have three distinct ways the humanities could help in economic thinking.

First, people are not organisms that are made and then dipped in some culture, like Achilles in the river Styx. They are cultural from the outset. A person before culture is not a person at all. This idea of a person before culture resembles a Zen koan, like the sound of one hand clapping. To be sure, economists are not the only thinkers who typically treat culture as an add-on rather than as essential—some political philosophy does the same.[10] But whether we are speaking of mainstream economics or (as we shall see) behavioral economics, the temptation of claims aspiring to universality, and of models reducible to equations, makes the idea of acultural humanness especially appealing.[11]

Second, to understand people one must tell stories about them. There is no way to grasp most of what individuals and groups do by deductive logic. Understanding Robespierre or the French Revolution is not at all like proving the Pythagorean theorem or calculating the orbit of Mars. Human lives do not just unfold in a purely predictable fashion the way Mars orbits the sun. Contingency, idiosyncrasy, and choices—all of which

10. Social contract theories by their very nature involve this kind of thinking, which is present in Hobbes, Rousseau, and, in our time, Rawls. We return to Rawls later in the book.

11. Over the past few decades, a number of scholars have instead turned to culture's importance in economic issues, especially with regard to economic development. We discuss some of our favorites later. But to our knowledge, none of these thinkers has recommended the study of literature, or the humanities generally, to economists. In chapter 7, we argue that including the insights of great novels would help complete Adam Smith's project as he understood it.

allow for alternatives—play an indispensable role. That is why, as the great novelists recognized, personhood and sociality demand biography and history. Novels are a distinct way of knowing; and the very shape of the stories they tell—what sorts of events are represented as plausible, effective, or important— conveys vital, if elusive, information.[12]

Third, economics inevitably involves ethical questions, not reducible to economics itself or, for that matter, to any other social science. Economists often smuggle ethical concerns into their models with concepts like "fair market price" in which unacknowledged ethical questions are treated as unavoidable givens. As we shall see, there are many ways to make these covert issues overt and argue about them explicitly. And as several recent thinkers have pointed out, these questions can be addressed in terms of different ethical theories.

As we conceive them, these questions often invite a distinct perspective best learned from the great realist novels. The works of Tolstoy, Dostoevsky, Turgenev, Chekhov, George Eliot, Jane Austen, Charlotte Brontë, Edith Wharton, Henry James, and other great psychological realists share a sense that ethical questions are often too complex and too important to be safely handed over to any theory, existing or to come. It requires real, but ultimately unformalizable, sensitivity and the ability to express what is sensitively perceived. As we explain in chapter six, this distinctly *literary*

12. See Bakhtin's famous study, "Forms of Time and of the Chromotope in the Novel" in M. M. Bakhtin, *The Dialogic Imagination: Four Essays*, ed. Michael Holquist, trans. Caryl Emerson and Michael Holquist (University of Texas Press, 1981), pp. 84–258. He develops the idea that each narrative genre conveys, by the sort of plot it favors, a sense of how events happen, the role that social conditions play in shaping individual action and vice versa, and the nature of human initiative, in his uncompleted study of Goethe and others, translated as "*The Bildungsroman and Its Significance in the History of Realism (toward a Historical Typology of the Novel)*" in M. M. Bakhtin, *Speech Genres and Other Late Essays*, ed. Caryl Emerson and Michael Holquist, trans. Vern McGee (University of Texas Press, 1986), pp. 10–59.

and *novelistic* approach to ethics may itself be regarded as a sort of theory, of course, and if one does so one can find theorists, like the Russian philosopher Mikhail Bakhtin, who have endeavored to articulate it.[13] But it is not a theory in the sense of a comprehensive system somehow extracted from the great novels that one can learn apart from reading them. That is because the very experience of reading these works is part of what one has to have in order to think ethically in the novelistic way.

As novels understand ethical decisions, they require good judgment, which, by definition, cannot be reduced to any theory or set of rules.[14] Sometimes familiarity with multiple theories—ethical pluralism, as Jonathan Wight has persuasively argued—helps.[15] Such pluralism above all inculcates a sense of modesty about the ability of theoretical reasoning to address the most important questions. As Stephen Toulmin, whose favorite book was Tolstoy's *Anna Karenina*, has argued, good moral judgment is a matter not of theoretical reasoning (what Aristotle calls *episteme*) but of practical reasoning (*phronesis*), which comes from sensitive reflection on a great deal of experience and close attention to the unforeseeable and unrepeatable particularities of many individual cases.[16] As

13. The prominence of so many women writers in this list of authors favoring sensitivity to particulars over theory in ethics was widely remarked upon at the time. It also led some male writers—like Tolstoy—to make his ethically wisest characters women whom men overlook because their thought is insufficiently theoretical and too grounded in particulars.

14. On judgment, see Philip E. Tetlock, *Expert Political Judgment: How Good Is It? How Can We Know?* (Princeton University Press, 2005). We discuss Tetlock's fascinating book in detail in the next chapter.

15. Wight, *Ethics in Economics*, pp. 17–19 and 210–230.

16. See Albert R. Jonsen and Stephen Toulmin, *The Abuse of Casuistry: A History of Moral Reasoning* (University of California Press, 1988); and Stephen Toulmin, *Cosmopolis: The Hidden Agenda of Modernity* (Free Press, 1990). On two occasions, Toulmin and Morson cotaught a course on *Anna Karenina*. Toulmin traces the importance of *Anna Karenina* and other works of Tolstoy for his teacher, Ludwig Wittgenstein, in Allan Janik and Stephen Toulmin, *Wittgenstein's Vienna* (Simon and Schuster, 1973), pp. 161–166.

we shall see in chapters 6 and 7, Toulmin regards his call for
this sort of thinking as a summons to revive the tradition of
casuistry, that is, case-based reasoning, shorn of the abuses to
which casuistry was often put. And as both Toulmin and G. A.
Starr have argued, the realist novel developed from casuistry
by offering particularly rich cases for ethical reflection.[17]

What's more, reading great literature is unlike any other
university-taught discipline, in that it involves constant practice in empathy. Theories of ethics may or may not recommend empathy, but learning those theories does not require
practice in empathy, as reading great novels necessarily does. If
one has not identified with Anna Karenina, one has not really
read *Anna Karenina*.

When you read a great novel and identify with its characters, you spend hundreds of hours engaging with them—
feeling from within what it is like to be someone else. You see
the world from the perspective of someone of a different social
class, gender, religion, culture, sexuality, moral understanding,
or countless other factors that differentiate people and human
experience. And as characters interact, and you identify with
each in turn, you see how each perspective may look to those
with another. You even learn to understand misunderstanding.[18] Tracing the heroine's thoughts as she thinks them, you
get inside her head, which you cannot do with people in real
life. If she makes a foolish decision, you wince. You live her life
vicariously, and in doing so you not only feel what she feels
but also reflect on those feelings, consider the morality of the

17. See G. A. Starr, *Defoe and Casuistry* (Princeton University Press, 1971). Defoe is
often considered the founder of the English realist novel; as Jonsen and Toulmin note,
"Defoe's stories, notably *Robinson Crusoe, Moll Flanders*, and *Roxana,* are filled with
'cases of conscience,' fleshed out in the characters and plots of eighteenth-century English life. For a while the conception of a novel as a case, or series of cases, dominated
English literature" (Jonsen and Toulmin, p. 164).
18. This was Chekhov's great theme—see, as a brilliant example, his story *Enemies*—but
it is present in realist novels generally.

actions to which they lead, and, with practice, acquire the wisdom to appreciate real people in all their complexity.[19]

Theoretism and Literature

Here then are three areas where the humanities could supplement economics: with stories, a better understanding of the role of culture, and a healthy respect for ethics in all its complexity.

By using stories, we don't mean that they should be employed simply to illustrate the results of behavioral models, but instead that they be used to inform the creation of the models themselves. We discuss the importance of stories, and when they are a required form of explanation, when we consider narrative and narrativeness later in this chapter.

Economics has a hard time dealing with culture because it cannot be mathematized. And it tends to replace ethical questions involving noneconomic ways of thinking by substituting other questions easier to handle in economic terms.

The neglect of culture has inspired Richard Bronk's critique *The Romantic Economist.*[20] Bronk's idea of supplementing economics as presently practiced with insights from Romanticism, a movement so heavily invested in nations and particular cultures, brings with it a sense that "national institutions and history matter to economic performance, and that there is no

---

19. In her book *Particularities: Readings in George Eliot* (Ohio University Press, 1982), Barbara Hardy observes: "The novelist invents characters in order to produce what the Victorian realistic novel is expected to produce: characters who are made to seem complex and changeable, to interact with each other, to be determined by environment, to possess bodies, minds, passions, and to speak an appropriate language.... She is like a natural scientist who judges and loves her specimens, and finds her cases hard to classify and impossible to stereotype. George Eliot's classifications and generalizations are dynamic and tentative, and her cases are used to investigate a number of problems simultaneously" (pp. 12–13).

20. Richard Bronk, *The Romantic Economist: Imagination in Economics* (Cambridge University Press, 2009). Bronk offers a critique of rational choice economics and a suggestion for how to remedy it. Chapter 6, Economics and the Nation State, begins: "Most Romantics were sceptical of any attempt to reduce human thought and social behaviour to a set of universal laws" (p. 149).

such thing as a universal template for economic competitiveness or economic growth" because "history matters."[21] Our difference from Bronk, with whom we are also quite sympathetic, derives from his stress on Romantic poetry and ours on realist novels, which, of course, express different senses of experience. But both literary schools stress *particularity*, along with the need for multiple perspectives and the irreducibility of human experience to any single theory.

The third area—ethics—has attracted the attention of a number of interesting recent thinkers. We are particularly impressed with ideas long promoted by Deirdre McCloskey, who argues for an ethics based on the virtues, a way of thinking newly important among philosophers. We also appreciate Wight's defense of a pluralist perspective, including consideration of virtue-based, duty- or rule-based, and consequentialist approaches. Our own approach is closest to Wight's, as one might suspect from the fact that both he and we develop ideas of Isaiah Berlin.[22]

Nevertheless, there is a difference, or perhaps an extension, based on an interpretation of Berlin. Berlin's idea of "foxy" pluralism was originally developed in his book *The Hedgehog and the Fox: An Essay on Tolstoy's View of History*—that is, in a commentary on what is arguably the world's greatest novel, *War and Peace*, by the world's greatest novelist, Leo Tolstoy.[23] The focus on a novel is important. Throughout this study, when we speak of "the humanities," we think, first of all, of great literature, understood as a repository of wisdom. Philosophers and social scientists sometimes imagine literature as sugar-

---

21. Bronk, pp. xii and 2.

22. Berlin's pluralism and appreciation of romanticism, with its sense that no single scale of values is possible, also inform Bronk's *The Romantic Economist* as well as Tetlock's *Expert Political Judgment*.

23. Isaiah Berlin, *The Hedgehog and the Fox: An Essay on Tolstoy's View of History*, 2nd edition, ed. Henry Hardy (Princeton University Press, 2013). This famous essay was originally copyrighted in 1951 and is now most easily available in Isaiah Berlin, *Russian Thinkers*, ed. Henry Hardy and Aileen Kelly (Penguin, 1978). We discuss Berlin's distinction throughout this book.

coated philosophy, as if Proust were just Bergson made into a story, with the real ideas to be discovered in the philosophers. No great writer has ever thought that way. Quite the contrary, the best that philosophers can do when paraphrasing great literature is to create some inadequate representation, not entirely useless but much cruder and less nuanced than the original. In a letter about *Anna Karenina* written to the critic Nikolai Strakhov, Tolstoy explained, as any great writer might:

> If I wanted to say [directly] in words all that I had in mind to express by my novel, I should have to write the same novel which I wrote all over again ... In everything, in almost everything that I have written, I was guided by the need to bring together ideas linked among themselves.... But every idea expressed by itself in words loses its meaning, becomes terribly debased when it is taken alone, out of the linking in which it is found. This linking is based not on an idea, I think, but on something else, and to express the essence of that linking in any way directly by words is impossible, but it is possible indirectly, with words describing images, actions, situations.[24]

Or as Bakhtin argues, the critic and philosopher seek to "transcribe" some of the inexhaustible wisdom of the great work, a task ultimately impossible to accomplish but nevertheless supremely useful so far as it goes. The good critic or philosopher who enters into dialogue with a work can articulate some of its potential meanings.

Bakhtin saw great literature, and especially great realist novels, as shaped by the sense that people and moral questions are too complex to be captured by any theory. Rather, they require a deep appreciation of all those particularities that no theory could ever capture but that can make all the

---

24. Leo Tolstoy, letter to N. N. Strakhov, around April 23, 1876, in the Norton Critical Edition of Tolstoy, *Anna Karenina*, 2nd edition, ed. George Gibian (Norton, 1995), p. 750.

difference—whether in understanding a specific person or in coming to a wise decision about a difficult ethical situation.

Bakhtin referred to the opposite assumption, that literature exists to provide vague stories for critics and philosophers to elevate with a rigorous theoretical formulation, as "theoretism." To be sure, some literary works can be adequately paraphrased, but that is precisely what makes them third rate. There is little difficulty in paraphrasing Ayn Rand or the sort of heavy-handed didactic works favored by many journalists and politicians. Some high school English teachers (or college ones who want to use literature to convey a simple lesson known from theoretical works) often assign such books. They are easy to teach precisely because they have a simple "message." But if that is all they have, who needs them? Why not just teach the message? It is usually a lot briefer than *War and Peace* and a lot easier to read than *Remembrance of Things Past*.

Like Tolstoy, Berlin, and Bakhtin, we approach literature as a source of wisdom that cannot be obtained, or obtained so well, elsewhere. There is an obvious proof that the great novelists understand people better than any social scientist who has ever lived. If social scientists understood people as well as Tolstoy or George Eliot, they would have been able to describe people as believable as Anna Karenina or Dorothea Brooke. But not even Freud's case studies come close. Surely the writers must know something! For reasons we will see, the same may be said about how the great novelists present ethical questions: with a richness and depth that make other treatments look schematic and simplistic.

When we speak of bringing economics and literature together, therefore, we emphatically do not have in mind the way it is done when economists use literature to illustrate economic lessons. Not that this approach is without value, but in no sense does it take seriously the notion that stories could actually *improve* economic analyses rather than merely clarify what traditional economics teaches. Consider the well-known anthol-

ogy edited by Michael Watts, *The Literary Book of Economics*.[25]
Watts treats "literary authors," as he calls them, as people who
"write so well" that they can conveniently illustrate truths
economists already know (Watts, pp. xxi–xxiii). They can be
useful "both because they are well written and memorable and
because they introduce variety into the economics classroom,
compared to the typical steady diet of textbook prose, graphs,
tables of numbers, and math" (Watts, p. xxii). And so, Robert
Frost's "The Road Not Taken" illustrates "choice and opportunity cost," while his "Mending Wall" teaches—God help us!—
about "property rights and incentives." Shakespeare's *Merchant
of Venice* can provide a memorable illustration of "government
regulation and the legal and social framework for markets."
Anyone who knows these works in their complexity will wince.
What's next, a course on international affairs making similar use
of the Sermon on the Mount ("if a hostile power take one of thy
provinces, yield to him also another")?

Nowhere does Watts entertain the possibility that great
writers may teach economists something valuable that they do
not already know.

Dialogue, Not Fusion

> What have I to gain if another were to fuse with me? He would
> see and know only what I already see and know, he would only
> repeat in himself the inescapable closed circle of my own life.
> Let him rather remain outside me. —MIKHAIL BAKHTIN[26]

Economists could benefit from drawing on all three of
these humanistic capabilities: an appreciation of people as
inherently cultural, of stories as essential forms of explanation, and of ethics in all its irreducible complexity. To do so,

---

25. Michael Watts, ed., *The Literary Book of Economics: Including Readings from Literature and Drama on Economic Concepts, Issues, and Themes* (ISI Books, 2003).

26. M. M. Bakhtin, *Estetika slovesnogo tvorechesva*, ed. S. G. Bocharov (Moscow:
Iskusstvo, 1979), p. 78.

economics does not need to abandon all its great achieve-
ments, any more than the humanities should dehumanize
themselves. Economists don't need to spoof anyone. They
should not hanker after some sort of fused discipline analogous to "behavioral economics." Instead, they need what we
call a "humanomics," which allows each discipline to keep its
own distinctive qualities.

Rather than fuse economics and the humanities, humanomics creates a *dialogue* between them. What we are after is not
a set of theoretical propositions but an ongoing conversation.

To preclude any misunderstanding: the dialogue we have
in mind is not between the two of us. After numerous conver-
sations, and teaching a class together several times, we have
arrived, more or less, at substantial agreement. Rather, we have
in mind a dialogue between the two *disciplines* understood as
distinct approaches to knowledge.

A Return to the "Real" Adam Smith

In creating a dialogue between economics and the humanities, we think of ourselves as going back to the most important
source of economic thought, Adam Smith. Smith's wisest commentators have remembered that he was also a moralist. That
double identity makes all the difference. The way in which
economics textbooks typically represent *The Wealth of Nations*
bears little resemblance to its overall spirit. Far from thinking
that it is desirable or possible to describe economic activity by
formulas or other ahistorical ideas, Smith devotes a substantial portion of the book to purely narrative explanations.

Rather than imagine human behavior can be modeled in
terms of rational choices, Smith refers time and again to rationality as exceptional. More often people are guided by mere
folly. Speaking of the pernicious influence of "the constitution
of the Roman church," for instance, Smith observes that it was
"in no danger from the assault of human reason.... Had this

constitution been attacked by no other enemies but the feeble efforts of human reason, it must have endured forever."[27] In this case, as in so many others, purely contingent historical factors, which must be narrated to be understood, accomplished what no principle of reason ever could.

Above all, Smith is far from reducing ethical questions to those modeled by today's economists. As those who have promoted the importance of asking ethical questions have stressed, Smith was the author not only of *The Wealth of Nations* but also of *The Theory of Moral Sentiments*.[28] Indeed, moral argument occurs frequently in *The Wealth of Nations* itself. Not only does Smith reject the idea that all human action is guided by perceived self-interest—an idea that in his time was represented by Hobbes—he argues quite the opposite, that a concern for others, as well as for ourselves, lies at the core of human nature. *The Theory of Moral Sentiments* famously begins: "How selfish soever man may be supposed, there are evidently some principles in his nature, which interest him in the fortune of others, and render their happiness necessary to him, though he derives nothing from it except the pleasure of seeing it. Of this kind is pity or compassion, the emotion which we feel for the misery of others, when we either see it, or are made to conceive it in a very lively manner."[29] And Smith is clear that our inclination to pity and compassion cannot be reduced to an indirect kind of self-love or self-interest, as a rational choice theorist might suppose.

Smith evidently regarded the sort of thinking that laid the foundation for modern economic theory as necessary but not sufficient, either to understand how people do behave or

27. Adam Smith, *An Inquiry into the Nature and Causes of the Wealth of Nations*, vol. 2, ed. R. H. Campbell and A. S. Skinner (Liberty, 1981), p. 803. Originally published in 1776.

28. See Wight, pp. 5–8, 134, and 153–157.

29. Adam Smith, *The Theory of Moral Sentiments*, ed. D. D. Raphael and A. L. Macfie (Liberty, 1982), p. 9. Originally published in 1759.

to recommend how they should. One needs economics and more. We heartily agree, and hope to show just how two kinds of thinking can work together.

We discuss Smith at considerable length later, but here it is worth observing that in chapter 7 we will argue that the realist novel in effect extends and deepens Smith's ideas, with regard to both ethics and psychology, as outlined in *The Theory of Moral Sentiments*. The psychological realist novel is, in effect, a distinct approach to moral sentiments, and it, like Smith's treatise, places special value on sympathy. If philosophers have not regarded realist novelists like Jane Austen and George Eliot in this light, perhaps it is because they tend to turn to philosophy proper and are not used to reading novels as philosophy of a special sort.

The Value of Telling Stories
Out of (and in) School

Humanists love to read and to write stories; economists do not. In the humanities, stories inspire, they explain, they teach us empathy. In economics, they distract from the impartiality expressed in mathematical models and interfere with the disinterested analysis of data. They are disparaged as mere anecdotes.[30]

Of course, there is some rationale behind this difference in disciplinary approach. Economists are trained to trust not what people say, but to observe what they do. Someone might purport to love opera above all but, despite an increase in income or a change in relative prices making opera less expensive than rival consumption goods, never choose to attend a

---

30. There are some economists, however, who believe that stories might help us understand human behavior. Robert Shiller, "How Stories Drive the Stock Market," *New York Times*, January 22, 2016, extolls the virtues of narrative psychology in arguing that popular narratives drive motivation. In his words, "Most economists generally do not refer to such popular stories or assess their emotional appeal." Yet, "such popular stories are serious matters. They can lead to revolutions, or to market collapses."

performance. Does that person truly gain satisfaction from opera, or are his preferences best revealed through his behavior? An economist would say that this person's actions bring his statements into question. A humanist, on the other hand, might say that while this person perhaps does not love opera in the sense that he wants to attend one, he loves to think he loves opera. He gets pleasure not from attending a performance but from thinking, or talking, about attending. And indeed there are many activities we fantasize about but would not really choose to do. Or what's a library for?

If a person sincerely professes one belief but acts as if he believes something else, what does he really believe? For a humanist, this is an interesting philosophical question, and he might turn to the stories in great literature for insight. For an economist, the answer would be to rely on what people actually do.

To an economist who succeeds in teasing out a person's preference structure—understanding whether the satisfaction gained from consuming one good is greater than that of another—explaining behavior in terms of changes in underlying likes and dislikes is usually highly problematic. To argue, for instance, that the baby boom and then the baby bust resulted from an increase and then a decrease in the public's inherent taste for children, rather than a change in relative prices against a background of stable preferences, places a social scientist on slippery ground. As Gary Becker put it, that would be equivalent to saying that a rise in mortality, followed by a fall, could be attributed to an increase in the inherent desire for death followed by a decline. For an economist, birth rates rise and fall due to changes in income and prices rather than changes in tastes. When income rises, for example, people want more children (or, as you will see later, more satisfaction derived from children), even if their inherent desire for children stayed the same.

But might stories inform an economist's models, allowing her to better anticipate the results of policies? Could stories, and associated theoretical and methodological approaches, help us better understand our data, without biasing our results? Could they help us see issues or understand moral implications we might otherwise overlook? We believe they can, and argue that incorporating not just narratives but a variety of techniques and methods from the humanities and other disciplines will make the "Jewel of the Social Sciences"[31] more relevant in addressing the world in which we live and better able to predict the future that awaits us.

We began to think about this topic in the context of an undergraduate course we have cotaught for several years: Alternatives: Modeling Choice across the Disciplines.[32] After examining material from a wide variety of subjects— economics, literature, philosophy, history, psychology, sociology, theology, evolutionary theory, and urban planning—it has become very clear to us that economics has much to learn from its sister fields. While we do not question the significance of economics as a discipline, neither do we question the payoff from a dialogue with other approaches.

Of course, we are the not the first to critique the often narrow and imperialistic nature of "economic science" (that term speaks for itself), but we hope our readers—economists and others—will be inspired to think more broadly about the field. Are we sure this is needed? Some might point to the advances made over the years aimed at creating a more nuanced, and perhaps more humble, version of traditional economics. In fact, in the chapters that follow we celebrate numerous contributions in that direction. But take a look at any of the top economics jour-

---

31. A label, while rarely used, that is favored (by economists) over a much more popular one, the "Dismal Science."

32. This course inspired us to coedit *The Fabulous Future? America and the World in 2040* (Northwestern University Press, 2015).

nals. Even when the topics explored seem interdisciplinary, how often are other fields actually taken seriously? There might be occasional references in bibliographies to the literature in psychology, sociology, political science, anthropology, philosophy, and even the humanities, but they are typically notable by their absence. The norm is economists writing for other economists, using the usual tools of economics. If the article focuses on theory and mathematical modeling, that isn't all that unexpected. But many articles conclude with a policy section, and that raises the stakes. Is a narrow economic view really going to get it right? The world is complex, and so are its actors. Effective policies demand more than a limited approach can produce. We give examples of this in the chapters to follow and discuss next how we came to this belief.

Two Stories

In line with our emphasis on the human, we would like to tell our own stories about how we came to appreciate the importance of dialogue between two very different kinds of thinking. We think it would be helpful to explain how we were driven to write about incorporating the humanities into economics, making its analyses both more realistic and more useful. We will then set out our goals for the chapters that follow.

Morton Schapiro

By the time I left graduate school in 1979, I had completely bought in to the view that "getting the prices right" was almost always the best economic policy. While my focus was on micro- rather than macroeconomics, I had little doubt that governments generally undermined the optimal functioning of the free-market system. But my experiences in the developing world in the 1980s gave me pause, leading me to question the appropriateness of some market solutions. The first instance was in Cairo in 1981. A few years earlier the government had succumbed to the pressures of international agencies and agreed to reduce subsidies that had long led to the cost of bread being well below its market clearing price. I sat with a group of economists who were thrilled that the government had agreed to get that key price "right" and were hopeful that this was the start of an era of reduced Egyptian government interference in domestic markets, even though the government had already reinstituted some of the subsidies. It seemed like a convincing story until someone mentioned the number of people who had died in the riots that had ensued and another talked of the prospects for widespread malnutrition.[33] The argument was resolved with the overriding feeling that the policy was nonetheless for the greater good. But it stayed with me.

How do you properly weigh the cost of death? Would we have been so quick to justify those actions if we had actually known some of those casualties (collateral damage, one might say) or their families? Might other considerations have been relevant in determining whether those policies had indeed been optimal? I suppose those were the dark days of IMF/World Bank arrogance, but some have argued that development policy hasn't evolved all that much over the subsequent decades.[34] A problem, of course, is that the narrowly defined economic cost associated with the loss of life, or with ill health, does not amount to all that much in a society with short life expectancy, low education, and high unemployment.

Why is this the case? The economic value of life is most easily measured by the sum of future earnings, discounted back into today's dollars (with the higher the discount rate, the less

---

33. Many large cities in Egypt experienced the "bread riots" of 1977. Seventy-nine people died, over 550 were injured, and more than 1,000 were arrested.

34. See, for example, Joseph E. Stiglitz, *Globalization and Its Discontents* (W. W. Norton, 2002), William Easterly, *The Tyranny of Experts: Economists, Dictators, and the Forgotten Rights of the Poor* (Basic Books, 2014), and Angus Deaton, *The Great Escape: Health, Wealth, and the Origins of Inequality* (Princeton University Press, 2013).

valuable the money earned in the distant future). A thirty-year-old investment banker with an MBA can expect much greater future earnings than a fifty-year-old waiter who never attended college. For this reason, settlement offers made as part of the September 11th Compensation Fund—a loss-of-life case that not surprisingly attracted widespread popular scrutiny—varied widely based on age, education, and job category. While there was some public outcry about the range of offers, there was nothing there that would surprise an economist. Still, there is the more difficult question of the consumption value of life. What is the value of a year of healthy living, independent of any money earned in the workplace? When there is a market for certain health improvements (for example, one might ask what people pay to improve their eyesight or their mobility), at least we have some notion of how to price this out. But it is far from perfect and often moves economists well outside their comfort zones, leaving them with a traditional economic loss calculation based simply on the present discounted value of the forgone earnings stream.

That reality hit the public eye a decade later in the context of the infamous World Bank/Lawrence Summers memo.[35] Summers, at the time the chief economist for the World Bank, signed a memo arguing that there were a number of reasons why the Bank should encourage greater migration of dirty industries to the developing world. One of those reasons reminded me of that conversation in Cairo: relocating toxic waste to areas with already high morbidity and mortality and with low wages implies a minimal economic cost. A second rea-

---

35. For several accounts and commentary, see "The Memo," December 12, 1991, as published by the Whirled Bank Group, 2001; "Toxic Memo," *Harvard Magazine*, May–June 2001; David N. Pellow, *Resisting Global Toxics: Transnational Movements for Environmental Justice* (MIT Press, 2007); and Daniel M. Hausman and Michael S. McPherson, *Economic Analysis, Moral Analysis, and Public Policy* (Cambridge University Press, 2006). See Hausman and McPherson, pp. 12–23 and 265–273, for a particularly thoughtful analysis of the ethical implications of the economic approach employed in the memo.

son was the assumption that there is a high income elasticity for a clean environment, that is, the richer the nation, the greater its appreciation of clean air and water and improved levels of health. Summers later apologized for signing the memo (quoting former New York City mayor La Guardia, "When I make a mistake, it's a beaut"), even though a subsequent article in the *New Yorker* argued that a young economist had in fact written the memo and that Summers only signed it to provoke debate.

And debate it provoked! The Secretary of the Environment in Brazil, for instance, wrote the following: "Your reasoning is perfectly logical but totally insane.... Your thoughts [provide] a concrete example of the unbelievable alienation, reductionist thinking, social ruthlessness and the arrogant ignorance of many conventional 'economists' concerning the nature of the world we live in."[36]

In my mind that says it all. At its extreme, while it might make perfect sense for an economist to recommend that the cost of reducing years of life is less in a place where the economic value of that life is limited, is that all that is relevant? What about the moral issues at stake? Going outside the limits of traditional economic theory is pretty scary for most economists. Give us the world of Pareto optimality (where we search for actions that improve someone's condition without hurting anyone else) and we are very happy to suggest some policy. But the real world usually involves the kind of trade-offs that economists like to avoid. Someone gains; someone else loses. In a classroom it is easy to shunt aside the question of interpersonal utility comparisons, avoiding altogether the question of whether the decline in someone's utility is justified by the gain by others. But not in Cairo in the late 1970s/early 1980s, or when discarding toxic waste in the 1990s, or today for that matter.

One more story. After spending some time lecturing about development issues in and out of Africa during the rest of the

36. As quoted in sources in preceding footnote.

1980s, I was asked to be part of a team to produce a new pub-
lication for the World Bank. Since 1955 the Bank has had its
Economic Development Institute (EDI), whose mission is to
train officials in development planning, policy making, project
implementation, and investment analysis through its courses,
seminars, and workshops. While many of its participants were
from Africa, most of its teaching materials were about Asia. Why?
Not surprisingly, the EDI preferred to teach success stories: cases
where international organizations had set up programs and projects that were justified by substantial rates of economic return.
And the success stories then, and still probably now, were much
more likely to be found in Asia than in Africa.

So when African officials asked for such success stories
from Africa, the Bank agreed to commission a volume entitled
Successful Development in Africa.[37] It turned out that picking
a title was easier than filling its chapters. A group of us were
hired to scour the continent, exploring a number of intriguing leads. Unfortunately, many of those leads turned out to
be not exactly the types of projects anyone would want to see
replicated—some had only fleeting benefits, others only limited returns. But we eventually found seven cases to include in
the book. My chapters were on the production of horticultural
commodities in Kenya and on the development of an export
zone in Mauritius (the fact that we had to go off-continent to
find a seventh topic worthy of inclusion in the book is evidence of how difficult it was to find African success stories at
that time). But the chapter that has stuck with me described
the Onchocerciasis Control Program (OCP) in West Africa.[38]

Onchocerciasis (river blindness) is a dreaded parasitic
disease that was endemic to West Africa, leading many mil-

---

37. *Successful Development in Africa* (EDI Development Policy Case Series, Analytical
Case Studies, Number 1, World Bank, 1989).

38. Stephen D. Younger and Jean-Baptiste Zongo, "West Africa: The Onchocerciasis
Control Program," chapter 2 in *Successful Development in Africa*.

lions of Africans to lose their eyesight. In 1974, in an unusual example of regional cooperation, seven West African nations banded together and reached out to the donor community to create an integrated approach to wiping out this terrible scourge. The resulting OCP was overseen by the World Health Organization and sponsored by numerous bilateral and multi-lateral aid agencies, including the World Bank.

Its impact was outstanding. After just a decade in place, over 90 percent of the program area had shown substantial progress. The World Health Organization trumpeted the success of the program in helping "to eliminate onchocerciasis as a public health problem and an obstacle to socioeconomic development" (Younger and Zongo, p. 27). The local population certainly agreed. One of the authors told me that when he landed in Burkina Faso, all he had to say was that he was with the OCP and he was treated as an honored guest—even while going through customs! Moreover, a quick investigation showed that the project was operating at (or under) budget. So if there was ever a worthy project for a volume on successful development in Africa, this was clearly it, no? Well, not when success is defined by approaches economists typically rely upon.

It turns out that the Cairo/Summers memo problem was front and center. What is the economic value of millions of Africans keeping their sight? If you count value in economic terms—changes in earnings discounted back to the present—the answer is, alas, not all that much in areas with high unemployment and low educational achievement. When the authors did a classic cost-benefit analysis, the results were "inconclusive"; in other words, the economic returns were only high enough to justify the costs given certain generous assumptions about the economic value of sight. It was acknowledged that "there are humanitarian benefits associated with reducing the blindness and suffering caused by onchocerciasis" but that "these benefits are inherently unmeasurable, and we will not account for them here, despite their importance, especially to donors" (Younger and Zongo, p. 38). Here, a humanist would ask, mystified: But isn't the very point of economic development to help improve people's lives? Sure, an economist might respond, but we are much more comfortable limiting our analyses to what we can measure. When sticking to the economic benefits, "by valuing a year of life saved at the very low marginal product of poor workers in the OCP area (US$57 to US$107 in 1978 dollars), we automatically force the estimated benefits of the OCP to appear small" (Younger and Zongo, p. 39). However, their conclusion would warm the hearts of many humanists, even if it may be an unusual acknowledgment from economists: "Using income figures to judge the value of a life saved inherently biases a project evaluation against the poor. Yet, in debates about social welfare, experts often argue that we should attach more weight to the benefits of public programs that accrue to the poor than to the wealthy. In fact, this is one of the features that makes the OCP especially attractive: its beneficiaries are largely the rural poor" (Younger and Zongo, p. 39).

Is there a lesson here? This is a case where a traditional cost-benefit analysis could easily have led to the discontinuation of a project widely viewed as being among the most successful health interventions in African history. Would interviewing beneficiaries and similar qualitative research have provided additional insights? How about the story of their lives? Should economists step back and think more broadly about the greater good differently conceived? Perhaps. Or at least we argue so in the chapters that follow.

Gary Saul Morson

From 1996 to 1997, I spent a year at the Center for Advanced Studies in the Behavioral Sciences in Palo Alto, California, as one of a few token humanists among many social scientists. The Fellows interacted daily, and it wasn't long before I became so fascinated with how the social scientists thought that my own project swerved to include a history of how the social sci-

ences came to be. Why do social scientists think so differently
from humanists?

Rational choice theory predominated among not only the
economists but the political scientists as well, and it exercised
considerable sway among other social disciplines. At first
I found this difficult to believe. Wasn't this the same view of
people that Dostoevsky had parodied so successfully in *Notes
from Underground* and other works? Surely no one could really
believe that people always acted in accordance with what they
considered to be their best advantage. Could anyone with the
slightest familiarity with people—or with the least introspec-
tive ability—imagine that they never act self-destructively or
against what they regard as their best interests? Psychiatrists
and novelists would be out of business if that were so.

I thought repeatedly of the passage in which Dostoevsky's
underground man sarcastically paraphrases this idea, which
I thought had died long ago. Then it would have been called
utilitarianism:

> Oh, tell me, who first declared, who first proclaimed, that
> man only does nasty things because he does not know his
> own real interests; and that if he were enlightened, if his eyes
> were opened to his real normal interests, man would at once
> cease to do nasty things ... [because] he would see his own
> advantage in the good and nothing else, and we all know that
> not a single man can knowingly act to his own disadvantage.
> Consequently, so to say, he would begin doing good through
> necessity. Oh, the babe! Oh, the pure innocent child![39]

The "babes" I was encountering were people of exceptional
intellectual gifts. Yet somehow they managed to combine their
impressive analytical abilities with a psychological naiveté that
made me wonder if they could really believe what they were

---

39. Fyodor Dostoevsky, *Notes from Underground* and *The Grand Inquisitor*, ed. Ralph
Matlaw (E. P. Dutton, 1960), p. 18.

saying. How was such a contradiction possible? I felt as if the Center had itself set a problem in social psychology for me to solve.

After numerous discussions, I found one key to this paradox. My colleagues began with *theoretical* premises, axioms like those of Euclidean geometry, and reasoned down from them. Axiomatically, it made sense to imagine a principle dictating that people chose what they think best for themselves. Why would they choose anything else? More important, if one began with such axioms, it was possible to construct a remarkable picture of human behavior. The entire edifice of modern economics demonstrates how far one can go with such reasoning.

Economics was then the prestige discipline among the social sciences, not only because its professors were paid more but, more importantly, because it had come closest to resembling what was taken to be the model science, physics. "Physics envy" led to "economics envy." People would wryly comment that on any campus you could always find the economics department by looking for the most attractive building, and the foreign languages by looking for the ugliest. Economics as practiced for the past half century has required a lot of math, and its propositions could all be stated as equations. So it was natural that political scientists would seek to imitate its methods.

And yet I could not help thinking of the underground man's way of refuting this top-down approach. He cited countless specific examples that contradicted its conclusions. "Why, in the first place," he begins, "what is to be done with the millions of facts that bear witness that men, knowingly, that is, fully understanding their real advantages, have left them in the background and have rushed headlong on another path, to risk, to chance, compelled to this by nobody and by nothing ... and stubbornly, willfully, went off on another difficult, absurd way seeking it almost in the darkness" (*Notes from Underground,* p. 19). He offers numerous instances of distressingly familiar behavior, including those in which we all indulge, which contradict the model. He also presents historical examples in which people collectively have acted contrary to what they know to be their best interests. Stand back: Would anyone not already committed to rational choice theory who looked at the Crusades, the religious wars of the seventeenth century, or the endless strife in the Balkans, conclude that people behave rationally? If so, what would irrational behavior look like?

Shouldn't a scientist respect the empirical facts above all? Theories suggest hypotheses to test, but if the facts contradict them, the facts prevail. Or should. It is always possible to disregard inconvenient facts. As the underground man observes, "Man is so fond of systems and abstract deductions that he is ready to distort the truth intentionally, he is ready to deny what he can see and hear just to justify his logic" (*Notes from Underground,* p. 21).

This argument about the empirical facts did not seem to impress my social science colleagues, and one after another they repeated the same responses:

First, when pressed, they redefined their terms so that every choice was *by definition* rational. That is, when they wanted to predict one kind of behavior rather than another—so their work would be useful—they defined rationality narrowly, making sure that prediction of something specific would be possible. But when the model was challenged, they redefined rationality as a tautology, that is, a statement that is true by definition. Whatever one does is rational or it wouldn't have been done; and if it looks irrational, that is because it is rational according to criteria we have not yet identified. Reasoning like this makes counterexamples impossible, no matter what the facts might be. Such a formulation would be entirely useless for making specific predictions, since no matter what happened, one could not be wrong.

It was as if a weather forecaster, when challenged about the basis of his science, should switch from a prediction like "tomorrow it will rain" to "tomorrow there will be weather." I dreamed up a discipline to be called "irrational choice theory": everything people do is contrary to what they regard as their best interest, and if an action seems rational, then it is irrational according to a set of criteria we have not yet identified. This reasoning is just as powerful as the same reasoning used to justify the opposite conclusion, so there must be something wrong with it in both cases.

For a proposition to be meaningful, let alone scientific, it must in principle allow for circumstances in which it could be tested and so proven false. But if it is true by definition, it can't be tested. Those who argue this way literally play fast and loose—a phrase in which the word "fast" is used in its older sense of "close" or "tight," as in the expression "hold fast." When they want to make a prediction, they use a tight definition so they can make one prediction rather than another; but when the wolf is at the door, they switch to a loose one so they cannot be wrong.

These objections did not convince the social scientists. I guessed it was because they seemed like some sort of logical trick. And they were never made from within the field. This guess was based on my observation that all fields respond dismissively to challenges from outsiders.

Second, sometimes my colleagues responded to empirical objections by arguing that economics was a young science, analogous, let us say, to what chemistry was in the eighteenth century or physics in the age of Galileo. Every science has to start somewhere and of course there are things it cannot yet explain. But that just shows the science has a future.

This answer would be persuasive if it could be shown that the discipline had indeed become a science. I thought of a period in literary criticism when it was claimed that it had achieved scientific status.[40] Of course, literary scientists could not yet explain everything, but that, it was argued, is what research to come will do. Reasoning this way, any body of thought, from astrology to dianetics, from alchemy to phrenology, would claim to be a beginning science. But that would not make it one.

Finally, I received a third response—the most sophisticated—from Henry Aaron, who had just completed his service as director of economic studies at the Brookings Institution. Henry referred me to Milton Friedman's celebrated 1953 essay, "The Methodology of Positive Economics."[41] Friedman conceded that the rational choice model might be based on implausible psychology, but that would not matter if the model led to good predictions. This answer struck me as quite powerful. After all, we use a lot of simplifying assumptions we know to be false because their consequences work. That's what models are for. Schematic diagrams and thought experiments often help us draw fruitful conclusions. Why not in this case?

The only answer I could give to Henry was a question: "How good are economists' predictions?" I remember Henry thinking for a few seconds and then saying, "You have a point." And the more I thought of this honest answer, the more I wanted to

40. The claim was made, for instance, by the Russian formalists, who bequeathed it to the structuralists. See Boris Eichenbaum, "The Theory of the Formal Method," *Readings in Russian Poetics: Formalist and Structuralist Views*, ed. Ladislaw Matejka and Krystyna Pomorska (MIT Press, 1971), pp. 3–37. Eichenbaum relies on the "young science" argument: "There are no ready-made sciences. The vitality of a science is not measured by its establishing truths but by its overcoming errors" (p. 4). And then, as we have noted, there are the more recent spoof literary sciences. Computers have inspired one attempt at a hard science of literature. See Joshua Rothman, "An Attempt to Discover the Laws of Literature," *New Yorker*, March 20, 2014, http://www.newyorker.com/books/page-turner/an-attempt-to-discover-the-laws-of-literature. Others have attempted to base a science of literature on evolutionary theory or cognitive science. See "The Next Big Thing in English: Knowing They Know That You Know," http://www.nytimes.com/2010/04/01/books/01lit.html?pagewanted=all.

41. Milton Friedman, "The Methodology of Positive Economics," in Milton Friedman, *Essays in Positive Economics* (University of Chicago Press, 1953), pp. 3–43, reprinted in *The Methodology of Positive Economics*, ed. Uskali Mäki (Cambridge University Press, 2009), pp. 3–42.

defend economics: surely, many of its predictions, especially those offered by microeconomics, are pretty good.

When I offered my reasons for thinking economics was not a hard science, the social scientists at first presumed I was saying that economics was useless or groundless. For a humanist, this did not at all follow. I have never believed that literary interpretation or art criticism could be a science, but I don't think them useless. There is no science of violin playing, but it can be better or worse and we still go to virtuoso concerts. For me, what the humanities are about, and what the great writers offer, is wisdom, and wisdom by definition cannot be formalized into anything resembling a mathematical model. If it could be, it could be taught as just another proposition.

We all know people who are brilliant scientists, mathematicians, or engineers whom we might trust to design a machine but not to decide how it would be used. Might that not be true of economists as well? In that case, couldn't they profit from humanistic wisdom?

Aristotle argued that young people readily learn mathematics but not wisdom because wisdom requires experience, and experience demands time. He cautions repeatedly that different subjects allow for different *kinds* of knowledge. In some cases, precision is out of the question. It is as wrong to impose mathematical reasoning on ethics as it would be to think about geometry humanistically (or, as he says, "rhetorically"): "Our discussion will be adequate if it has as much clearness as the subject-matter admits of, for precision is not to be sought for alike in all discussions ... for it is the mark of an educated man to look for precision in each class of things just so far as the nature of the subject admits; it is evidently equally foolish to accept probable reasoning from a mathematician and to demand from a rhetorician scientific proofs".[42]

---

42. Aristotle, "Nichomachean Ethics," *The Basic Works of Aristotle*, ed. Richard McKeon (Random House, 1941), p. 936.

It seemed to me that economics and other social disciplines could be, and doubtless were, valuable without being sciences. So conceived, they would have to present their claims differently, but they would still offer insight. To me, it remained an open question how far economics could go "mathematically" and at what point it might benefit from thinking "rhetorically" or humanistically.[43]

Sometimes the social scientists turned the tables and quizzed me about the shortcomings of the humanities. They were puzzled that literature scholars still wrote about psychoanalysis as if it were an established science (and did not seem to know that in psychology departments it was a thing of the past). How was that possible? And how could literary scholars think of a discipline that either could not be falsified, or had been falsified, as a science?

The famous Sokal hoax had just taken place, and the social scientists were equally puzzled by it. Alan Sokal, a physicist, had managed to publish in the prestigious, cutting-edge journal *Social Text* a piece of scientific balderdash allegedly showing that the sciences enjoy no special "privilege." He called for a postmodern science that would serve "liberatory" purposes by dispensing with the notion of "truth." Mathematics would have to be reformulated according to socially progressive principles. For example, Sokal wrote the following: "Mainstream Western physical science has, since Galileo, been formulated in the lan-

---

43. For a classic study of economic argument as a form of rhetoric—rhetoric in the sense of persuasive argument—see Donald N. McCloskey, *If You're So Smart: The Narrative of Economic Expertise* (University of Chicago Press, 1990). McCloskey's book begins: "It is pretty clear that an economist, like a poet, uses metaphors. They are called 'models'" (p. 1). McCloskey stresses the role of metaphors not appreciated as such. Economists also use stories, some of which are "unbelievable, really." "The literary solution to this literary problem," he concludes, "is to use the stories and metaphors to criticize one another.... The combination yields truth for science and wisdom for policy" (pp. 3–4). We are also sympathetic with McCloskey's ambition: "The argument here is a moderate, pluralistic argument against monistic immoderation (most of the good arguments since Plato have been monistic and immoderate)" (pp. 4–5).

guage of mathematics. But *whose* mathematics? The question is a fundamental one, for, as Aronowitz has observed, 'neither logic nor mathematics escapes the "contamination" of the social.' And as feminist thinkers have repeatedly pointed out, in the present culture this contamination is overwhelmingly capitalist, patriarchal and militaristic: 'Mathematics is portrayed as a woman whose nature desires to be the conquered Other.' Thus, a liberatory science cannot be complete without a profound revision of the canon of mathematics."[44] Despite containing sentences that were complete nonsense, and scientifically illiterate, Sokal's submission managed to pass peer review. Only after the article appeared did Sokal reveal it was a hoax, concocted just to see if the humanists would publish any nonsense so long as it reached the right conclusions and cited the right people.

The incident focused the social scientists' attention on humanists' assertions that there is no such thing as facts, that what we call facts are what is in our social interest to regard as such, that science is just another form of "discourse," and that no body of supposed knowledge is intrinsically superior to any other. Surely, the social scientists asked me, they can't mean what they seem to say. Doubtless, what they really mean is that we have to be on the lookout for the often unsuspected bias that creeps into our work, and that science is often shaped in part by social forces. I had to reply that if that were all that was claimed, it would hardly be revolutionary. No one in the humanities had ever doubted either of those more modest propositions. What was worth claiming was the extreme version and that, yes, that was the orthodox, if not universal, position. That was precisely why Sokal conducted his hoax.

But most of the social scientists could not believe that anyone could be a relativist in that extreme sense. If all knowledge

44. See Alan Sokal, "Transgressing the Boundaries: Towards a Transformative Hermeneutics of Quantum Gravity," http://www.physics.nyu.edu/sokal/transgress_v2/transgress_v2_singlefile.html.

were equally good, how could the humanist scholars claim to be experts in something? Since this objection must be obvious, no one could maintain such a position.

It was at this point that I understood the idea of "two cultures." When C. P. Snow wrote his celebrated book by that title, he had in mind the gap between the humanities and the hard sciences; but I was seeing an equivalent gap—or gulf—between literary studies and the social sciences.[45] I concluded that a real gulf exists, and we genuinely have two distinct cultures, but not when disciplines hold different beliefs. They always do. We have two distinct cultures when neither can believe that the other believes what it says it believes!

When the humanities were challenged in this way, I realized that, if forced to choose, I would pick the disciplines that at least presumed the possibility of meaningful knowledge. But my hope was that each could learn from the spirit and specific insights of the other.

The more I spoke with the social scientists, the more it seemed to me that the key issue was the role of narratives or stories. One of the social scientists maintained that in a true science stories are unnecessary. Physicists do not prove theories, or mathematicians theorems, with stories. Social disciplines will have achieved true scientific status, he explained, when they can entirely dispense with narrative explanations. To be sure, it would still be admissible to illustrate a law with a specific course of events, but one would never have to resort to narrative to explain why something happened, the way historians routinely do.

Having once intended to be a physicist, I got the point right away. Although one could give a narrative explanation about the orbit of Mars—first it was here, and then it moved there,

---

45. Charles Percy Snow, *The Two Cultures* (Cambridge University Press, 1959 and 2001). For a more recent treatment of the two cultures problem, see Stephen Jay Gould, *The Hedgehog, the Fox, and the Magister's Pox: Mending the Gap between Science and the Humanities* (Harmony, 2003).

and then it skidded in over here—it would be absurd to do so because Newton's laws already allow one to derive its location at any point in time.

So I left the Center with a new concept in mind, which I called "narrativeness." Narrativeness, which comes in degrees, measures the need for narrative. In the example of Mars, there is zero narrativeness. On the other hand, the sort of ethical questions posed by the great realist novels have maximal narrativeness.[46]

When is there narrativeness? The more we need culture as a means of explanation, the more narrativeness. The more we invoke irreducibly individual human psychology, the more narrativeness. And the more contingent factors—events that are unpredictable from within one's disciplinary framework—play a role, the more narrativeness.

So the question arose for me, how much narrativeness is there in economics? Could economics be improved with more stories? When I began teaching with Morton Schapiro, this question, which I first formulated in my last weeks at the Center, was very much on my mind.

Gary Saul Morson and Morton Schapiro

We became convinced that economists and humanists do not just arrive at different conclusions; they also pose different questions, perceive various facts differently, and favor explanations that for the other would not count as explanations at all.

Too often, "interdisciplinary" means approaching the subject matter of other fields with methods of one's own, but genuine interdisciplinarity includes a *dialogue of approaches*. Let us say again: what it requires is not a fusion—a spoof of one discipline or the other—but a conversation, in which each side maintains its own outlook while respecting and being pre-

---

46. See Gary Saul Morson, "Narrativeness," in *New Literary History*, vol. 34, no. 1 (Winter 2003), pp. 59–73.

pared to learn from the other. "I know you better than you know yourself" is not the beginning of dialogue. "Each of us can help the other achieve its own goals" might be. That is the sort of dialogue we hope to create in this volume.

We focus on one side of this dialogue: how economics can be made more powerful in conversation with the humanities. We do not doubt the value of moving in the opposite direction, that is, applying economic ways of thinking to humanistic problems.[47] From time to time, we do just that, but only opportunistically and occasionally. On the whole, we leave that part of the dialogue for a future study, by ourselves or others.

We stress that this is not an attack on the intrinsic value of the discipline of economics. We don't doubt the extraordinary power of economics: its rigor, its focus, its interest in policies aimed at improving the human condition. We do, however, think its narrowness undermines its usefulness. Is it possible that economists could predict the future more accurately? Could they produce more effective policies? Could they better understand human behavior? We grapple with these and related questions below.

If we are successful, our argument will make a difference to three audiences: economists, humanists, and, perhaps most important, the general reader.

For economists, it may sharpen their sense of when economic problems demand more than economic solutions. Especially when policy recommendations are involved, questions regarding values, meaning, and other topics familiar to humanists are likely to prove dangerous to ignore or to address in purely economic terms. Good economics involves more

---

47. We mention in chapter 7 how humanists could benefit from a better understanding of the concept of scarce resources and its implication for making choices. Reflecting on that part of our manuscript, one reader remarked about humanists: "They don't understand budget constraints. Nor for that matter basic ideas such as comparative advantage, opportunity costs, positive sum games, incentives, selection bias, and many other basic concepts in economics." We return to this point in that chapter.

than just economics. We expect that position will unsettle some economists, even if our goal is not to attack the discipline but to expand its scope and its power.

If someone were to argue that to understand human society and behavior one needs more than biology, that would not diminish biology. To say that technological problems cannot be approached in terms of technology alone, but must include their effects on human users and bystanders, is not to be a Luddite. By the same token, to create a dialogue between economics and the humanities should make economics more, not less, useful in its goals of understanding human events and recommending sound policies.

Humanists, too, will come to appreciate where their disciplines can make more of a difference. At a time when the value of the humanities seems increasingly in question, that may give them renewed value. To be sure, this approach runs directly counter to all those attempts on the part of beleaguered humanists to save their disciplines by trying to transform them into some sort of putative science or social science—that is, by creating spoof humanistic disciplines. You can't save the humanities by dehumanizing them. The premature claim of scientific status often generates not a future science but a pseudoscience, and in the process, marginalizes what the discipline is genuinely good at. If humanists renew their faith in their distinctive ways of knowing, and in the wisdom of great literature, they have much to contribute to areas they have usually overlooked and that have overlooked them.

Above all, we hope to interest the general reader, not just by the overall argument but by the specific case studies. Perhaps to their dismay, these readers will learn how some colleges and universities admit students and award financial aid. They will also see why they should be more suspicious of those who rank institutions of higher education, an activity that seems to be expanding rather than improving. Beyond that, readers may be troubled by how little we know about why one nation grows more prosperous than another, or by insights about how people make decisions regarding intimate matters, like marriage and family life. But even those who reject these insights entirely will in the process clarify their understanding of matters close to home for everyone. And in a world of global issues and many cultures, readers may recognize how multiple points of view, including those from perspectives they have not imagined, may prove illuminating.

Today, intelligent readers are called upon to respond to disparate social problems. They are offered endless solutions by supposed experts in many fields. All solutions seem to be tendered with supreme confidence but often contradict one another. How are readers to evaluate them? After all, they cannot be an expert in all fields and in most cases must evaluate recommendations from outside their professional competence. It will not do to take all such recommendations on faith. Readers are not really thinking if they accept only those solutions that accord with their prior inclinations. And it also will not do to imagine that their prejudices—a term usually applied only to others—are enough of a guide.

As Deirdre McCloskey has pointed out, economic argument, like that of many fields, relies on rhetoric often unrecognized as such.[48] In each historical period, there is always a set of terms that add unearned plausibility to a claim. "Studies have shown," "computer models prove," "brain scans demonstrate": these are the magic words of our time. Like social Darwinism in the late nineteenth century, this phraseology seems persuasive because it is new, and it is ours.

If you say "people like sweet things and will expend effort to taste them," it seems like a truism hardly worth saying at

48. Deirdre McCloskey, *The Rhetoric of Economics* (University of Wisconsin Press, 1998) and *Knowledge and Persuasion in Economics* (Cambridge University Press, 1994). With these books, along with the earlier *If You're So Smart: The Narrative of Economic Expertise* cited above, McCloskey has pioneered the creation of dialogues between economics and other disciplines.

all. But say "brain scans show that the pleasure neurons of the such-and-such region of the cerebral cortex light up in the presence of substances with a sweetness index as high or higher than 1.0, and that oxytocin is released when neurons associated with anticipation and focused attention are activated" and it sounds more scientific without adding any real information. Say with wonder "do you know that some forms of learning actually change the brain?" and people forget they always knew that. What else could learning change, the kidney? By such rhetoric, those who would mystify us—or have mystified themselves—may lend unearned authority to weak ideas, or unwanted significance to trivial ones. Economists and other social scientists are not immune to such self-mystification. We need to recognize when that is the case. The present volume offers some tools for recognizing signs that increased skepticism is in order.

Sometimes bold thinkers formulate systems to explain vast domains of human activity. These "hedgehogs," to use Isaiah Berlin's term, may export models from a hard science, say, ecology or evolutionary biology, to some domain of human affairs. In much the same way, economists may extend their characteristic way of understanding to areas that have hitherto seen to resist such thinking. Spoofs proliferate. When a broad enough claim is made, it seems revolutionary. The media will hail the breakthrough and contend that, at last, a scientific solution to intractable problems has been found. Much as professional journals favor positive results, and rarely publish negative ones, so reporters rarely understate a supposed discovery's import and basis. The professional need to attract attention, combined with the sincere hope of social improvement, lead many journalists to paint an all too rosy picture.

Skeptics, however well supported their doubts, struggle to be heard above the applause. They are unlikely to be praised for doing what responsible scientists and scholars are supposed to do—test purported solutions against logic and evidence. They are more likely to be condemned as antiscientific! Nobody likes to have her hopes discredited. If she did, promoters of new diets would have a harder time.

The general reader, without expertise in many fields, may be drawn into accepting whatever supposedly revolutionary claims proponents make, so long as those proponents sport proper credentials. And since sometimes those who object do indeed use shoddy logic, or seem inclined to reject even the best-supported claims because they happen to have unpleasant implications, it is always easy to imagine that any given objection is indeed antiscientific. But how is the reader supposed to distinguish well-founded skepticism from curmudgeonly disgust? This book offers no infallible method, but it does show some red flags to look for.

Every comprehensive theory is based on some set of data that it fits exceptionally well and explains better than its rivals. The temptation arises to extend that theory to data it fits somewhat less well and then, step by step, to data it fits only with Procrustean force. Everything resembling the theory's original domain is seen, and everything radically different from it is overlooked, dismissed, or explained in terms of the theory itself. There are always ways to make a set of claims more vague but less subject to falsification, more extensive but less open to any conceivable counterevidence. Eventually, the claim seems to explain everything but only because, whenever fatal counterarguments arise, key terms are redefined to preclude refutation. We hope that readers can learn to recognize when this happens. They can appreciate the seductive fallacies of all-embracing systems. We examine a number from economics and related fields that have commanded considerable attention.

At the same time, readers can be wise enough not to reject these all-embracing economic theories in their entirety. Even if exaggerated, the value of such theories may be considerable. One can learn not to throw the baby out with the bathwater, while also learning that not all bathwater is baby. For everyone, not just parents, it is important to distinguish between the two.

This book offers several case studies in such discrimination. It also cites wiser alternatives, deeper if less sexy explanations that depend on combining multiple ways of seeing and creating a dialogue of disciplines. We hope to show the general reader what good versions of such dialogues sound like.

Of course, the dialogue between the humanities and economics is only one of many possible interdisciplinary dialogues that we also hope to foster. Perhaps they, too, will aid us all to make intelligent decisions about expert advice. Everyone is a nonspecialist in something, and so democracy demands that nonspecialists can evaluate how good expert advice is. The alternatives—either entirely ignoring all expertise or turning over decision-making power to anyone aspiring to it—both give rise to disastrous results. That is why we hope to show one way in which intelligent citizens can evaluate what an expert may have left out, how her claim looks from the perspective of other disciplines, and how to recognize when ambition has likely gone beyond possible evidence.

Genuine dialogue never ends. It always generates new insights that, a few steps before, could not have been anticipated. Interlocutors, responding to these insights, continue to generate ideas that surprise the interlocutors themselves. We hope to create such a dialogue between economists and humanists and between ourselves and our readers. With them we aspire, most of all, to keep the conversation going.

Chapter 2

A Slow Walk to Judgment

Hedgehogs and Foxes,
Wisdom and Prediction

Justifying government pricing policies on narrow economic grounds while ignoring the resulting death toll. Arguing that it makes perfect sense to export dangerous waste materials to areas that already have low life expectancy, based on the fact that people die early there anyway. Questioning a health intervention that all but wipes out a dreaded disease, on the grounds that there is minimal economic value provided by those who are saved. Formulating behavioral models that not only fly in the face of what we know from other academic disciplines but border on the absurd, given a cursory examination of human nature.

What do these examples call for? In a word, judgment.

Humanists might not have figured out all there is to know about understanding and instilling judgment, but they sure think more about this subject than most economists.

When do we need judgment? This question turns out to have pretty much the same answer as, when do we need stories?

As mentioned in chapter 1, you don't need either stories or judgment to predict the future positions of Mars. You just need Newton's laws and some initial conditions. Nor do you need the sort of experience that makes for better craftsmen, artists, or evaluators of complex moral problems.

If someone were to say that to calculate the position of Mars at some future date we need someone with special experience of Mars contemplation and a lifetime of engagement with the Red Planet, we would probably imagine that he did not understand much about natural laws. Orbit specification requires knowledge and mathematical ability but not judgment. As Aristotle would say, this is a task that young people would be good at.

By contrast, if someone were to tell us there is a hard science of child rearing—take this course and you will know just what to do at each moment from birth to maturity—one would imagine that he had never been a parent. Did he even remember much about his own childhood? We might say the same thing when a person faces a difficult ethical decision or an urgent choice between two courses of action offering no clear guidelines. A political leader might have to decide, in the face of imperfect knowledge, which policy to follow or which warlord to trust. Whether war, sanctions, inaction, or something else might be an appropriate response to a dangerous enemy's provocations is not something one can decide by applying a formula. If it were—if such a formula existed—then the enemy himself would know it and, knowing our decision in advance, would take advantage of that knowledge. The very existence of the formula would defeat its purpose.

In short, we require judgment in situations of radical uncertainty. By that we mean not just those with risk, which sometimes can be calculated mathematically, but ones in which the likelihood of outcomes cannot be known or the outcomes themselves are too difficult to define. Could anyone specify what technology will be like in 2040 and how precisely we should prepare for it?[1]

---

1. Not an easy question to address but one that nonetheless is discussed by John Kelly III in chapter 8 of *The Fabulous Future? America and the World in 2040* (Evanston, IL: Northwestern University Press, 2015), 113–127.

Judgment is required when our values, and therefore our preferred goals, may never have been identified. Sometimes those values come into being only in the course of making the decision in question. It is also required when contingency prevails, that is, when causal factors that cannot be imagined in advance might intervene. What if the outcome of an economic situation depends on factors exogenous to economics? As we shall see, sometimes what look like exogenous factors may be endogenous, but sometimes exogenous causes truly prevail. The same is true in other domains. Linguistics is not enough to determine the future of a language, nor biology the future of medicine.

In all such cases, we need good judgment. We know that however helpful scientific knowledge may be, it is insufficient. We turn to those with wisdom.

Wisdom cannot be formalized. To find it, we look not to hard science but to religion or, in a secular age, to great literature. No writer understood the difference between science and wisdom better than Leo Tolstoy. He devoted his masterpiece, *War and Peace*, to that theme.

At the time the book was written, the thirst for a hard science of society was intense, and throughout Europe there were numerous breathless claims that it had at last been achieved. Russians were particularly drawn to this dream, which seemed to promise a path to universal happiness. Marxism was far from being the only putative science that offered utopian hopes, for once the causes of social arrangements were understood, they could presumably be altered at will. In Russia, such messianic dreams drew upon the intensely messianic character of the Russian Orthodox church, and so the claim to a social science promising utopian outcomes preoccupied the intelligentsia. Tolstoy regarded all such claims as sheer nonsense. In *War and Peace*, he uses a purported "science of warfare," accepted by many European generals, as a proxy for any possible social science.

The novel's hero, Prince Andrei, imagines that Napoleon conquered because he had mastered that science and had the courage to apply it consistently. Having read numerous accounts of battles, it was natural for the prince to think of them as similar to a game of chess. Like the German generals in charge of the tsar's armies, he imagines such broad eventualities as the movement and countermovement of whole flanks, and reasons as if there were an algebra for calculating the best disposition of regiments. At the council of war before the battle of Austerlitz, most generals are convinced that they have placed Napoleon in a position scientifically guaranteeing his defeat, and that any action he might take to escape is sure to make his defeat all the more mathematically certain. In fact, the Battle of Austerlitz turned out to be Napoleon's greatest victory.

Because the tsar trusts his generals' advice, the skeptical commander-in-chief, General Kutuzov, has to go along. Kutuzov knows that there is no certainty in battle, that unforeseeable contingencies allowing little time for reflection arise, and that the morale of the soldiers, which cannot be algebraicized, matters. Kutuzov, in short, has experience, wisdom, and good judgment of both situations and people. After dozing through the council of war, he at last calls it to an end: "'Gentlemen, the disposition for tomorrow—or rather, for today, for it is past midnight—cannot be altered now.... And before a battle, there is nothing more important, ...' he paused, 'than a good night's sleep.'"[2]

Not strategy, not scientifically based plans, but a good night's sleep: a good night's sleep matters when alertness to unforeseeable contingencies makes a difference and when one has to decide on the spot a matter requiring judgment. If everything could be scientifically calculated a day in advance, then alertness would change nothing.

2. Leo Tolstoy, *War and Peace*, trans. Ann Dunnigan (Signet, 1968), p. 323.

When the Russians are indeed defeated, Andrei learns that Kutuzov is right. The next time he listens to the German generals expound their science he reflects:

> What theory or science is possible where the conditions and circumstances are unknown ... and the active forces cannot be ascertained? ... Sometimes—when there is not a coward in front to cry "We are cut off!" and start running, but a brave, spirited man who shouts: "Hurrah!"—a detachment of five thousand is worth thirty thousand, as at Schöngraben, while at other times fifty thousand will flee from eight thousand, as at Austerlitz. What science can there be in a matter in which, as in every practical matter, nothing can be determined and everything depends on innumerable conditions, the significance of which becomes manifest at a particular moment, and no one can tell when that moment will come?[3]

There can be no science because too much is always unknowable and what is unknowable cannot be disregarded or factored out. It is obviously impossible for general laws to determine which soldier will be at a particular place when his morale makes a difference.

Presentness matters. In calculating the orbit of Mars, time is just "t" in an equation, and each moment is entirely determined by its predecessors. It is an automatic derivative, and no moment has more weight than any other. But in a battle—and by extension in social life generally—some moments are truly momentous. Sometimes something takes place that no knowledge of past moments or general laws could anticipate. The night before the all-important Battle of Borodino, Andrei's friend Pierre presumes "a skilled commander" who has mastered the science of war can "foresee all contingencies." Andrei replies dismissively: "... what are we facing tomorrow? A hundred million diverse chances, which will be decided on the

---

3. *War and Peace*, p. 775.

instant by whether we run or they run, whether this man or that man is killed."[4] What can truly matter is what happens "on the instant." This sense of "the instant" is characteristic of situations in which no hard "science" can be sufficient.

Such situations demand experience, alertness, and good judgment. Andrei insists that is the case "in every practical matter." In Tolstoy's view, that is what we mean by a practical matter: one in which theoretical knowledge is inadequate and judgment is required.

What qualities make for good judgment? Is there a way to test it? The French aphorist La Rochefoucauld famously observed, "Everyone questions his memory, and no one complains of his judgment."[5] The reason is that a failure of memory does not harm one's status or self-esteem. And so it can be a convenient excuse for more serious lapses that do. But one's identity is tied up with the quality of one's judgment. Bad judgment does indeed make one a lesser person and to admit to it is hard on one's vanity. How often have you heard political pundits admit that a celebrated prediction they made, now shown to be mistaken, reflected bad judgment?

In his celebrated study entitled *Expert Political Judgment: How Good Is It? How Can We Know?*, Philip Tetlock poses questions that apply to all judgment, not just political.[6] Very few people accept the extreme relativist position that no one's judgment is better than sheer chance, and it is hard to evaluate how good someone's judgment is, so it makes sense to ask what makes for good judgment. Even in everyday life, we

---

4. *War and Peace*, p. 930.

5. In *The Oxford Dictionary of Quotations*, 6th edition, ed. Elizabeth Knowles (Oxford University Press, 2004), p. 469.

6. Philip E. Tetlock, *Expert Political Judgment: How Good Is It? How Can We Know?* (Princeton University Press, 2005). For recent extensions of Tetlock's ideas, see Nate Silver, *The Signal and the Noise: Why So Many Predictions Fail—but Some Don't* (Penguin, 2012), and Dan Gardner, *Future Babble: Why Expert Predictions Fail and Why We Believe Them Anyway* (McClelland and Stewart, 2010).

turn to people with more experience when making difficult decisions and regard the accumulation of experience as often worth the effort. Of course, experience is not enough, and we can ask what it is that people with good judgment learn from experience that other people with similar experience do not.

Not all judgment involves making predictions—moral questions may involve something entirely different—but many practical questions do involve intelligent guessing about likely outcomes. One might suppose that with such questions it would be relatively easy to assess judgment. Is the predictor right or wrong?

In practice, matters are rarely that simple. If a person's prestige is at stake, he rarely admits to having made a mistake, no matter how often he makes them. To be sure, not everyone is like the Nobel Prize–winning, celebrated *New York Times* columnist Paul Krugman, who wrote that "I (and those of like mind) have been right about everything," and in response to those who objected to his characterization of people with different opinions as "knaves and fools" declared:

> Maybe I actually am right and maybe the other side actually does contain a remarkable number of knaves and fools.... Look at the results: again and again, people on the opposite side prove to have used bad logic, bad data, the wrong historical analogies, or all of the above. I'm Krugtron the Invincible![7]

It has, of course, been easy for critics to point to cases in which Krugman (or virtually any economist, for that matter) made explicit predictions that turned out badly wrong: his repeated assertions that the euro would collapse in 2011 ("this is the way the euro ends"), or his recommendation to

---

7. As cited in Niall Ferguson, "Why Paul Krugman Should Never Be Taken Seriously Again," *Spectator*, October 13, 2013, http://blogs.spectator.co.uk/coffeehouse/2013/10/niall-ferguson-paul-krugman-gets-it-wrong-again-and-again-and-again-why-does-anyone-still-listen-to-him/.

Alan Greenspan in 2002 that we need to create a "housing bubble." And opponents have pointed to cases in which he called people fools for asserting exactly what he had asserted on earlier occasions.

Or consider the well-known case of Paul Ehrlich who, in his 1968 best seller, *The Population Bomb*, in testimony before the US Senate, and in countless appearances on television and other venues, categorically insisted that overpopulation would cause a billion people to starve to death within ten years.[8] He based his prediction, which he regarded as scientifically proven, on his field of expertise, the population of butterflies. Together with Zero Population Growth, the Club of Rome, and books such as *The Limits to Growth*,[9] Ehrlich contended that humanity was exhausting its resources and had already reached the point at which catastrophe was inevitable. The *New Republic* accepted his arguments and proclaimed that "world population has passed food supply. The famine has started."[10]

Of course, the exact opposite proved to be the case. Not only did mass starvation fail to take place, but food production grew dramatically due to the "green revolution." Famine was soon confined to areas like North Korea and Somalia, where the causes were political rather than a shortage of resources. In response, Ehrlich and his wife, Anne, did not admit error, but, quite the contrary, intensified their claims. In their 1990 book *The Population Explosion*, they wrote: "Then the fuse was burning; now the population bomb has detonated."[11] Humanity,

8. Ehrlich is discussed in more detail in the introductory chapter of *The Fabulous Future?*

9. Donella H. Meadows, Dennis L. Meadows, Jorgen Randers, and William W. Behrens III, *The Limits to Growth: A Report for the Club of Rome's Project on the Predicament of Mankind* (Macmillan, 1979).

10. As cited in Paul Sabin, *The Bet: Paul Ehrlich, Julian Simon, and Our Gamble over Earth's Future* (Yale University Press, 2013), p. 23.

11. Sabin, p. 197.

they maintained, "was breeding itself into a corner." No matter how often their predictions proved mistaken—what they claimed to be "inevitable" did not happen—the Ehrlichs never confessed to error. And they retained followers. Ehrlich even continued to garner prestigious awards.[12]

Mystified by this imperviousness to counterevidence, economist Julian Simon asked, "How often does a prophet have to be wrong before we no longer believe that he or she is a true prophet?"[13] Simon publicly challenged Ehrlich to a bet in which Ehrlich could pick five metals he expected to grow increasingly scarce over the ensuing decade. If resources were to be exhausted, their price would go up, and Simon would pay Ehrlich the actual purchase price for those metals. If their prices, on the other hand, went down, Ehrlich would pay Simon $1,000.

The bet strongly favored Ehrlich because he got to choose the metals, and his losses were limited while, depending on price increases, Simon's could grow indefinitely large. Ehrlich hastened to accept the terms. By the specified date, all five metals had declined in price. Ehrlich paid off, but never admitted he had been refuted. All he had gotten wrong, he maintained, was the timeline; it would just take a little longer for the prices to rise dramatically.

---

12. Dan Gardner lists the following: the Gold Medal Award of the World Wildlife Fund International; the John Muir Award of the Sierra Club; the Volvo Environmental Prize; the Blue Planet Prize of the Asahi Glass Foundation; the Heinz Award; the Sasakawa Prize from the United Nations; a MacArthur Genius prize; and the Crafoord Prize of the Swedish Academy of Sciences, sometimes considered the Nobel Prize of environmentalism. Gardner notes that while some of these honors stemmed at least in part from Ehrlich's research as a biologist, they often were given for work like *The Population Bomb*. The Crafoord Prize citation specifically mentioned such work. In 2009, the Programme for Sustainable Leadership at Cambridge University surveyed its alumni network of "over 2,000 senior leaders from around the world" to ask them to choose the best books written about sustainability, and in the resulting list of fifty books, *The Population Bomb* still ranked number four. See Gardner, *Future Babble*, pp. 174–175.

13. Sabin, p. 134.

Ehrlich called opponents "idiots" and "morons" and characterized them as "the ones who have to take their shoes off to count to twenty."[14] Apparently, the more counterevidence mounts, the stupider opponents become. Where does such a sense of certainty come from?

Tolstoy notes a similar phenomenon. Austerlitz does not provoke the leading believer in military science, General Pfühl, to reassess. "In the outcome of that war he failed to see the slightest evidence of the fallibility of his theory. On the contrary, to his mind it was the departures from his theory that were the sole cause of the whole disaster."[15] When he wins the science is vindicated, and when he loses it is because his orders have not been perfectly carried out, as indeed, must be the case with orders that complex.

Tetlock cites Ehrlich's defiant comparison of Simon to a man who jumps from the Empire State Building and, as he passes onlookers on the fiftieth floor, announces "All's well so far." If this excuse is allowed, then, as with General Pfühl, no prediction, no matter how explicit and unqualified and no matter how much it is contradicted by the evidence, could ever be proven wrong. It would be immune to falsification.

In fact, as Tetlock notes, there is always a panoply of excuses readily available. If a recommended policy fails to improve matters as predicted, one can always say that without the policy, matters would have turned out still worse. If an opponent's policy proves successful, one can always say that it involved unacceptable risks of catastrophes that easily could have happened. If a predicted event failed to materialize, one can say that it almost did, or that it didn't precisely because people heeded the prediction and acted accordingly. And it is true that low-probability events sometimes happen and high-probability events sometimes don't. As these examples show,

14. Sabin, pp. 176 and 207.
15. *War and Peace*, p. 771.

predictions typically involve counterfactuals—what didn't happen but could have—and it is impossible to get evidence for events that did not take place.

Many complications can make it hard to assess predictions. Explanation is possible without prediction and vice versa. One can have a sound theory without knowledge of the antecedent conditions. One can be right that the radiator will freeze if the temperature goes below 32 degrees, but not know the atmospheric conditions. Conversely, ancient astronomers who held what we would regard as absurd ideas about celestial bodies were often good at specific predictions. Tetlock wryly observes, "The explanation-is-possible-without-prediction argument surges in popularity when our heroes have egg on their faces" while "the prediction-is-possible-without-explanation argument catches on when our adversaries are crowing over their forecasting triumphs."[16] By the same token, no one ever says that he or she was proved right only by sheer luck or that one's opponent may have been wrong but almost proved correct.

As Tetlock set out to examine what qualities make for good political judgment, he needed a way to handle these objections. It is relatively easy to assess beliefs for internal consistency but much harder to score a prediction that the Soviet Union has a 60 percent chance of breaking up within the next ten years. The core of Tetlock's method—if we may risk simplifying his complex and subtle argument—is to rely on the law of large numbers. Someone who consistently predicts events as highly likely, but who is wrong 90 percent of the time, could not plausibly say he was unlucky or almost right in every case.[17]

Tetlock's empirical research led to some surprising but important conclusions. It turned out that better predictions and judgment do not depend on whether one is an optimist like Simon or a pessimist like Ehrlich. Nor does one's place

16. Tetlock, p. 15.

17. For Tetlock's further methodological techniques—specifically, about how to score predictions—see his pages 11 to 13.

on the political spectrum seem to matter. Neither does one's professional background or status make much of a difference. What did prove important was one's style of thinking. "Foxes" consistently outperformed "hedgehogs."

Tetlock adapts these terms from the previously mentioned seminal volume of Isaiah Berlin, *The Hedgehog and the Fox: An Essay on Tolstoy's View of History*.[18] The ancient Greek poet Archilochus wrote: "The fox knows many things, but the hedgehog knows one big thing" (Berlin, p. 1).

Whatever this saying may have meant, Berlin takes it as marking "one of the deepest differences which divide writers and thinkers, and, it may be, human beings in general." A chasm lies between the great systematizers and the skeptics, between the monists and the pluralists. On the one hand, the hedgehogs "relate everything to a single, central vision, one system less or more coherent and articulate, in terms of which they understand, think, and feel—a single, universal, organizing principle in terms of which all that they are and say has significance." On the other, the foxes "pursue many ends" and "entertain ideas that are centrifugal rather than centripetal, [as] their thought is scattered and diffused, moving on many levels, seizing upon the essence of a vast variety of experiences and objects for what they are in themselves without ... seeking to fit them into, or exclude them from, any one unchanging, all-embracing ... fanatical, unitary inner vision" (Berlin, p. 2).

When hedgehogs confront a multiplicity of phenomena, they presume that somewhere, under all the apparent diversity, a simple set of rules governs, the way Newton's laws underlie the amazingly complex motions of the planets. By contrast, the foxes associate a single comprehensive vision with paranoia.

18. Isaiah Berlin, *The Hedgehog and the Fox: An Essay on Tolstoy's View of History*, 2nd edition, ed. Henry Hardy (Princeton University Press, 2013). The essay originally appeared in shorter form as "Leo Tolstoy's Historical Scepticism" in 1951 and was reprinted under its present title in 1953. For a recent work inspired by Berlin, see Stephen Jay Gould, *The Hedgehog, the Fox, and the Magister's Pox: Mending the Gap between Science and the Humanities* (Harmony Books, 2003).

As hedgehogs see complexity as an illusion concealing an underlying simplicity, foxes see just the opposite.

Plato represents the archetypal hedgehog, Aristotle the perfect fox. As Plato looked to the world of mathematics, Aristotle was fascinated by the amazing variety and complexity of biological organisms. Plato composed the first utopia, Aristotle surveyed existing constitutions and examined how they fared in practice. Dante, Leibniz, Hegel, Marx, Freud, Bentham, Einstein, and Skinner exemplify hedgehogism; for foxiness we turn to Montaigne, Erasmus, Shakespeare, Hume, Darwin, George Eliot, William (and Henry) James, and Wittgenstein. The hedgehogs sound like Leibniz: "God does nothing which is not orderly, and that it is not even possible to conceive of events which are not regular."[19] Wittgenstein speaks for the foxes: Don't say something must be the case but "look and see."[20]

Since for hedgehogs the truth is one and unchanging, they are known for categorical dicta: "Nature has placed mankind under the governance of two sovereign masters, *pain* and *pleasure*. It is for them alone to point out what we ought to do, as well as to determine what we shall do.... They govern us in all we do, all we say, all we think: every effort we make to throw off our subjection, will serve but to demonstrate and confirm it."[21] "The history of all hitherto existing society is the history of class struggles."[22] Their language admits of no exceptions, any more than do the propositions of mathematics. Aristotle liked to qualify his comments about politics and ethics with the phrase "on the whole and for the most part," but no one would say, "On

19. Gottfried Wilhelm Leibniz, *Discourse on Metaphysics, Correspondence with Arnauld, and Monadology*, trans. George Montgomery (Open Court, 1989), p. 10.

20. Ludwig Wittgenstein, *Philosophical Investigations*, third edition, trans G. E. M. Anscombe (Macmillan, 1958), p. 36e.

21. Jeremy Bentham, opening to *An Introduction to the Principles of Morals and Legislation* (Macmillan, 1984), p. 1 (italics in the original).

22. Marx and Engels, *The Communist Manifesto*, Karl Marx and Friedrich Engels, *Basic Writings on Politics and Philosophy*, ed. Lewis S. Feuer (Doubleday, 1959), p. 7.

the whole and for the most part, the angles of a triangle total 180 degrees." For the hedgehog, that form of mathematical certainty is the only truth worth having.

For the fox, such certainty is a sign of self-deception. Some sleight of hand has probably ruled out the very possibility of counterevidence or made it invisible before it could be considered. The aphorisms of foxes stress ultimate unknowability, complexity, tentativeness of judgment, and the need for endless revision: "The causes of good and evil ... are so various and uncertain, so often entangled with each other, so diversified by various relations, and so much subject to accidents which cannot be foreseen, that he who would fix his condition upon incontestable reasons of preference, must live and die inquiring and deliberating."[23] "Good and ill are universally intermingled and confounded; happiness and misery, wisdom and folly, virtue and vice. Nothing is pure and entirely of a piece ... the draughts of life, according to the poet's fiction, are always mixed from the vessels on each hand of Jupiter."[24]

Why should foxes outperform hedgehogs most of the time? One clue is that their advantage is greater in the long run. Tetlock surmises, "The foxes' self-critical point-counterpoint style of thinking prevented them from building up the sorts of excessive enthusiasm for their predictions that hedgehogs, especially well-informed ones, displayed for theirs."[25] Their willingness to revise in the face of counterevidence also helped, as did what Tetlock considers the key ability favoring better judgment—"'the art of self-overhearing.' Good judges need to eavesdrop on the mental conversation they have with themselves as

23. Samuel Johnson, *Rasselas, Poems and Selected Prose*, ed. Bertrand H. Bronson (Holt, Rinehart and Winston, 1971), p. 642.

24. David Hume, "The Natural History of Religion", *Principle Writings on Religion including "Dialogues Concerning Natural Religion" and "The Natural History of Religion,"* ed. J. C. A. Gaskin (Oxford University Press, 1993), p. 183.

25. Tetlock, p. 21.

they decide how to decide."[26] They habitually perform "a turn-about test," a sort of thought experiment: If an opponent were to handle counterevidence as they are doing, how would they react? Do they apply the same standards of logical consistency to themselves that they do to others? When counterexamples are presented, do they find themselves asking not whether what they believe is true, but how an objection might be countered?

Nevertheless, foxes have their own weaknesses. If hedge-hogs are subject to hubris, foxes can sometimes be *too* tentative. Or they can assign too much likelihood to too many scenarios. "There is nothing admirably open-minded about agreeing that the probability of event A is less than the compound probability of A and B, or that x is inevitable but alternatives to x remain possible," and foxes are more vulnerable to such confusion than hedgehogs.[27]

Tetlock could have gone a step further. The very way he has set up his experiment stacks the deck in favor of the foxes. The domain that favors hedgehogs is the one in which a hard science has been achieved. But that is precisely when judgment is not needed and so is not considered in Tetlock's tests. Hedgehogs in the social sphere are typically those who claim to have at last put a discipline on a scientific footing, a claim still confined to the hedgehogs and their disciples. At best, it may, like mainstream economics, be accepted by the field and neighboring ones, but not by outsiders. Tetlock has exposed foxes and hedgehogs to foxy situations.

Hedgehogs most often go wrong when they apply theories that work in their own field to others quite different. Consider Paul Ehrlich again: his certainty that he has to be right, regardless of what the evidence shows, perhaps reflects the process of reasoning that led him to his conclusions in the first place. He saw what happens to butterfly populations and applied that model to human behavior (thus his reference to people "breed-

26. Tetlock, p. 23.
27. Tetlock, p. 23.

ing"). After all, he seems to have thought, a scientific approach does not stop at the border of humanity any more than the laws of physics respect international boundaries. Ehrlich considered his opponents as people who want to "'build exemptions ... from the laws of nature.' They did not understand the basic laws of thermodynamics concerning entropy and the conservation of energy. Nor did they understand the simple mathematics of exponential growth."[28]

Ehrlich was dealing with economic problems but dismissed the insights of economists. If the economists did not grasp the laws of nature and mathematics, they could not be right. Simon pointed out that standard economic theory held that people, unlike butterflies, would substitute one resource for another when prices went up. They would also develop new technologies, as butterflies could not. The "ultimate resource," he argued, was not any metal or grain but human ingenuity. In much the same spirit, economist William Nordhaus complained that the model on which Ehrlich relied allowed for "no technological progress, no new discovery of resources, no way of inventing substitute materials, no price system to induce the system to substitute plentiful resources for scarce resources."[29] Moreover, Lawrence Summers contended that the computer models to which Ehrlich and his allies appealed simply reflected back the assumptions by which they were constructed. The objection that computer models can confer a specious authority on dubious assumptions is one that foxes frequently make.

The irony, of course, is that economists themselves have often been accused of field imperialism, as if economic models had to be correct wherever they were applied. We will see examples of such thinking in subsequent chapters.

Perhaps hedgehog theories seem convincing to so many because they appeal to our desire to have at last mastered an important domain. If astronomy was found to follow a few

---

28. As quoted in Sabin, p. 205.
29. As quoted in Sabin, p. 90.

basic laws, why not economics, politics, or history? Elie Halévy famously called this line of thinking "moral Newtonianism."[30] Surely nothing is immune to the laws of nature! Only the inheritance of religion could lead people to imagine that they were exempt from laws governing everything else.

Hedgehog theories also appeal to vanity, to the pleasure of knowing what less enlightened folks do not. And hedgehog theories win out in the contest for public attention and resources.[31] It is easier to get the press, and granting agencies, excited by a revolutionary breakthrough on the order of Newton's laws than by a possible insight tentatively applying to a particular set of local problems. Hedgehogs write best sellers; foxes respond with book reviews.

Perhaps that is the reason why, over time, even the greatest foxes become hedgehogized. No one was foxier than Darwin, but if one reads common accounts of him, he appears to be a hedgehog. And, as we pointed out earlier, the same may be said of Adam Smith in the hands of his followers. Disciples often take one key idea, admittedly very important, for the whole, and the thinker is posthumously characterized as if he had applied that idea, and that idea alone, to all problems. Textbooks, read in place of original sources, aid this process.

Berlin's essay sets up the dichotomy of hedgehogs and foxes in order to characterize Tolstoy as a natural fox who wanted to be a hedgehog, and so every time he arrived at some comprehensive system, his own foxy skepticism eventually discredited it. The authors of this book see ourselves in a similar light: although we are by inclination foxes, we tend to discover a good deal of insight in hedgehog theories. In the pages to follow, we consider a number of both types of thinkers, and our approach to the hedgehogs is, we hope, generous. To be sure,

30. Elie Halévy, *The Growth of Philosophic Radicalism*, trans. Mary Morris (Beacon, 1955), p. 6.
31. See Gardner's chapter "Everyone Loves a Hedgehog" in *Future Babble*, pp. 144–194.

it is important to point out where their logic falls short. But it would be too easy to stop there. Though not universally applicable, the ideas we consider are highly productive. Even when they do not work far beyond the domain that inspired them, it might still pay to ask whether they might shed light.

Literature by its very nature is foxy. Any literary work that could be paraphrased as a systematic theory would be a poor literary work. One turns to Shakespeare or to Tolstoy, rather than to Bentham or Marx, when a sense of the complexity of things is needed. In creating a dialogue between economics and the humanities—with literature seen as the core of the humanities—we are proposing to temper the hedgehogism of traditional economics with the foxiness of the great novelists. We hope to show the value of both and the still greater value of a dialogue between them.

We conclude this chapter with some final words about prediction. Almost forty years ago, Schapiro studied econometric forecasting with Lawrence Klein, who won the 1980 Nobel Prize for creating models predicting economic trends. One day in class Professor Klein joked that the secret to successful forecasting is either to go very short, simply assuming that tomorrow will look very much like today, or to go very long, far enough in the future that when your bad predictions come to roost, you are but a distant memory.

We offer some additional advice in this chapter. Be a fox, even if economics tends to breed hedgehogs. The empirical evidence suggests that foxes do a better job in predictive accuracy. It might be comforting to stick to a single unifying vision of the world that ignores all else, but that isn't going to help you predict the future. Be open to learning from other disciplines, be ready to question the validity of your underlying assumptions, and most of all, be humble. Like the forty-handicap golfer, if you swing enough, one of your shots (or predictions) might inadvertently go straight (or turn out to be right). But that certainly doesn't mean you figured it all out!

Chapter 3

The Power and Limits
of the Economic Approach

Case Study 1—How to Improve
American Higher Education

Higher education in the United States is a very big business—with almost 5,000 "firms" (that is, public and private colleges and universities, four-year and two-year, for-profit and not-for-profit) and 21 million "customers" (undergraduates, graduate students, and professional school students). With total revenues of around $500 billion, it comprises almost 3 percent of US gross domestic product.

But it is more than just a business. It reflects—or should reflect—the loftiest ideals of the nation. When university presidents or prominent professors comment on public affairs, they speak as both the intelligence and moral compass of the country.

Universities are not just another industry. It is important to keep that in mind when applying economic analysis to higher education policies and institutional actions.

We consider several issues, many of them unappreciated by more than a small segment of the public.[1] Few outside the

---

1. Some of these topics are discussed briefly in Michael McPherson and Morton Owen Schapiro, "Moral Reasoning and Higher Education Policy," *Forum Futures 2010*, Forum for the Future of Higher Education, pp. 39–45. For an earlier version, see Michael S. McPherson and Morton Owen Schapiro, "Moral Reasoning and Higher Education Policy," *Chronicle Review*, September 7, 2007, pp. B10–B11.

field of education are aware of all of them, and even within the field, many remain opaque. We begin with the subject of enrollment management, that is, using financial aid discounts to meet a school's enrollment aims. Then we move on to the increasing role of nontenure line faculty in undergraduate education. Next we consider a little known but important problem because it affects all others: "proper" data reporting. After that we consider examples of government policy dilemmas, such as the distribution by states of operating subsidies to their public colleges and universities. This distribution affects the fulfillment of the federal government's desire to increase both college enrollment and completion rates while properly matching students with appropriate schools. Each of these questions can be considered economically but, as we shall try to show, can be considered more effectively using both an economic and a humanistic approach. Our intention in this chapter is to show that while economics has much to say about a wide range of higher education issues, economics alone leads to unsolvable dilemmas and poor policy. Or to put the point differently, even by the criterion of economics itself—arriving at an optimal solution—economics in isolation often fails. Even the question, "Optimal for what?" may not be decided wholly on economic grounds. One also needs good judgment and the sort of wisdom the humanities can instill.

Enrollment Management

Oh, reason not the need! —Shakespeare, *King Lear*

It wasn't that long ago that admissions personnel and those in the financial aid office had little to do with each other. Indeed, colleges used to boast about their separation, the way newspapers bragged about separating reporting from advertising. Admissions staff selected their best class; aid discounts were offered based on affordability. For better or worse, those days are long over for colleges and universities.

Government officials, trustees, and the public at large have implored colleges and universities to "act more like businesses," presumably in an attempt to become more "efficient."[2] But "efficient at what?" is a question they do not ask, as if it were unproblematic. If the goal of a university is to instill a love of learning for its own sake, to ignite curiosity, to appreciate diverse points of view, or to understand the sensibility of different people, that would suggest criteria of efficiency that differ from what we would expect if the goal were to maximize earnings after graduation, provide for the common defense, or create social justice (however defined). For some goals, such as graduating the largest number of students per dollar of expenditure, small classes are inefficient. For others, they are much more efficient than large classes. You can't effectively teach violin playing or foreign languages through large lectures. While large lectures can inspire the love of a subject, they can't provide practice in effective argumentation or unrehearsed public speaking. In short, it makes no sense to speak of efficiency without defining "being efficient" at achieving something in particular.

Of course, these objections could be made insincerely, to defend the sheer waste of resources by any reasonable standard, but that does not make the questions, properly posed and answered, any less pressing.

So what are the efficiency and ethical issues raised by enrollment management? We first note that, surprisingly, only a small number of institutions—roughly 350—are even modestly selective in admissions.[3] The rest take virtually anyone who applies. Some point to higher education as a place that

---

2. For a recent spirited critique of this trend, see David L. Kirp, "It's All About the Money," *American Prospect*, Spring 2015, pp. 119–121.

3. And only around 150 of the 350 are considered to be "national" colleges or universities, that is, schools that draw students from across the country rather than from a particular locale or region.

differs fundamentally from other goods and services since, in those other cases, if a consumer has the money, he or she is typically allowed to purchase the product. In selective admissions, by definition, most people who want to buy in are not permitted to do so; that is what makes a college or university selective in the first place. The rarity of selective schools implies that US higher education is more similar to other industries than most imagine.

Institutions that are selective have been increasingly awarding price discounts to serve their admissions goals. The most heavily endowed of all schools, led, of course, by the Big Four—Harvard, Yale, Princeton, and Stanford—have redefined "need" to provide financial aid well in excess of that awarded by other selective schools with considerable endowments. Hence, it appears that "need" depends on available funds—in particular, on the amount of endowment that is restricted for financial aid.[4] This is one reason why statements about "meeting student need" can be misleading.

Highly selective schools other than those four generally rely on their own common formula to determine a family's ability to pay, with some, in addition, unabashedly offering merit aid that reduces the price below what that formula says a family can afford.

How would an economist suggest that a school provide price discounts to meet its enrollment goals (which include filling beds, promoting academic excellence, enrolling a diverse student body, and keeping alumni and donors happy)? The key to what economists call "price discrimination" is to figure out what a consumer is willing to pay. If someone drives into a BMW car dealership in a BMW and tells the salesman

---

4. When a school has endowment proceeds restricted to undergraduate student aid that exceed the total neediness of its students as defined by a traditional formula, why not change that formula to make students "needier"? That is one way to stay in compliance with the deeds of the gifts.

that he would never drive anything else, you can imagine how any potential discount off the sticker price would disappear. On the other hand, driving into that BMW dealership in a Mercedes, and telling the salesman that she had little interest in switching brands but just wanted to see if she could get a great price, might end up in a large discount. Businesses would love potential buyers to tip their hands.

In higher education, they often do. But while people usually know this when buying cars, they don't when choosing a college.

It isn't all that difficult for selective colleges and universities to predict the willingness of an applicant to accept an offer of admission and then to price accordingly. In fact, applicants and their families, like the BMW driver, gladly, if unwittingly, offer up the information that could be used to charge them more.

We use one study (coauthored by Schapiro) as an example: an econometric analysis of the matriculation decisions made by students accepted to Williams College, one of the nation's most highly selective colleges and universities.[5] The analysis used data from the Williams classes of 2008 through 2012 to estimate a yield model—one that assigned a probability of enrollment for each individual admitted applicant.

The joy for schools is that they don't have to dig for information that helps them predict yield. Applicants provide it for free on their applications, in their financial aid forms, and in

5. Peter Nurnberg, Morton Schapiro, and David Zimmerman, "Students Choosing Colleges: Understanding the Matriculation Decision at a Highly Selective Private Institution," *Economics of Education Review*, February 2012, pp. 1–8. This is not the first time Schapiro has contributed to the enrollment management literature. In fact, he and his longtime coauthor, Michael McPherson, were early contributors to the development of the subject matter. See, especially, "Student Aid as a Competitive Weapon," chapter 9 in Michael S. McPherson and Morton Owen Schapiro, *The Student Aid Game: Meeting Need and Rewarding Talent in American Higher Education* (Princeton University Press, 1998). Not surprisingly, given the discussion that follows, we have mixed feelings about our role in helping create the field.

their behavior. Perhaps the predictive accuracy of the model might be enhanced by collecting other information, but it works quite well based solely on information available to the school at the time of the admissions decision.

These data cover a wide range of subjects, such as academic performance, race, gender, geographic origin, high school quality and type (religious/secular, private/public), extracurricular activities and interests, athlete status, family and other connections to the institution, and academic interests. Many selective schools, including Williams, also compute an overall academic rating for each applicant based on that student's SAT, ACT, and AP scores, high school grades and class rank, essays, the rigor of the high school academic program, and teacher recommendations; along with an overall nonacademic rating, a composite score based on the quality of extracurricular activities. Finally, schools record contact between the applicant and the school (whether the applicant visited campus, signed up at the admissions office before a campus tour, met with an admissions officer at the student's high school, etc.), financial aid status, and in some cases subjective variables designed to capture desirable applicant qualities that appear in recommendation letters or essays but are not sufficiently measured by traditional applicant characteristics. Firms in other industries must surely be envious of how colleges and universities are privy to such a range and depth of information providing unusual insight into consumer interests and behavior.

What did we find? It turns out that the chances a student would accept an offer to enroll depended negatively on her academic rating—that is, the better her standardized test scores and high school GPA, the lower the probability of accepting an offer of admission. This is as to be expected given that the stronger a student's academic profile, the larger the choice set of good alternatives open to that student. In addition, also to be expected, the higher the net price the student faces (the sticker price minus institutional and other financial aid), the lower that student's predicted yield. Again, a downward sloping demand curve is a mainstay of economics—the higher the price, the lower the amount demanded—although in this case it turns out that the price responsiveness is quite small compared with the magnitudes of the other estimated coefficients, perhaps due to the fact that the range of net prices within a tier of schools is rather limited.

The yield prediction, not surprisingly, is also dependent on the applicant's race (with members of underrepresented groups having greater opportunities at other top schools and thereby being less likely, all things equal, to attend any one school) and geographic origin (students generally prefer schools that are closer to their homes), plus the student's artistic, athletic, and academic interests. Finally, one of the most important yield predictors turned out to be whether a student went on a campus tour: if you go on the tour and are subsequently offered a spot in the entering class, you are much more likely to accept. We have no idea whether this is causal. Perhaps visitors are so taken with the attractiveness of the campus (or the tour guide, for that matter) that the probability of accepting an admission offer goes up significantly; or perhaps the fact that a student bothers to visit a school merely indicates her underlying interest in attending there. For the purposes of this analysis, it doesn't matter. We want to know who will accept an offer of admission, and going on a tour is a good indicator. As long as a prospective student signs his name in the admissions office, this is valuable information for a school to know.

Collectively, this combination of variables turned out to be a strong predictor of whether or not the student would matriculate at Williams, and a similar analysis can be (and we assume in many cases is being) applied at other schools. Here are two examples using the prediction equation: Applicant one is an African American male living in a city far from campus, with a very high academic rating, who never visited the school. He has a predicted yield of only 6 percent. Applicant two is a Caucasian female who attends a traditional feeder high school not far from campus, has a high academic rating but not as high as in case one, has a parent who is an alumnus, and went on a campus tour. She has a predicted yield of 98 percent.

There are several reasons why a school might do such an analysis, and some raise no particular ethical problems. Even if it is one of those rare schools that is need-blind (that is, admits students regardless of financial need) and meets the full need of all its admitted students, such a formula would allow a school to anticipate its upcoming revenue picture by forecasting its net tuition revenues. For purposes of budgeting, this is both important and easy to do: simply compute an estimated probability of matriculation for each applicant in the pool of admitted students and add them up. One student may have a 75 percent predicted chance of accepting an admission offer, another 20 percent, and a third only 5 percent. Together, you can expect one student from the three offers. By tying these probabilities to financial need, a school can get a good idea of the size of the freshman class and what share of the sticker price a typical student would pay.

Both are valuable to know. To underenroll is a disaster for many schools that are heavily tuition dependent, and so is enrolling students who are so needy that the financial aid budget exceeds the budgetary plan. What about the most selective, heavily endowed institutions? They have long wait lists to draw upon, so underenrolling is no great fear. Overenrolling, on the other hand, can be a nightmare, as single rooms are turned into doubles and doubles into triples—not exactly the best way to greet new students (and their parents).

But our focus here is on the allocation of price discounts. If a student is very likely to attend, what does this mean for an institution's optimal allocation of need-based and merit offers? Here is where economics might easily collide with ethics.

Why not use a yield formula such as the one described above to "leverage" a school's aid dollars?[6] That is, use the knowledge of how much aid it would take to get a student to enroll, and then offer the smallest price discount required. It could then take the money it saves and invest it in improving its educational programs through shrinking average class size, providing support for needy students to accept unpaid internships that would enhance future job prospects, or paying its faculty and staff more, among many worthy expenditure possibilities. Hence, the money saved is not just lining someone's pocket; it is doing good in a variety of ways. So provide a generous aid package for applicant one, with the 6 percent enrollment prediction, and charge the sticker price to applicant two, with the 98 percent chance of attending, even if the two are in a financially identical position.

If we are talking about allocating merit aid, one might find this approach to be reasonable. By definition, merit discounts are aimed at enrolling students by cutting the price below what their families "could afford." The idea is that the school would then get "better" students than it would otherwise, as

---

6. Or perhaps find an even simpler indicator of a particular student's interest in your school. See, for example, Michael Stratford, "Education Department Will Stop Giving Colleges Information about Students' Choices," *Inside Higher Education*, August 14, 2015. This article reports that some schools have used information provided on an applicant's federal student aid form for unintended purposes. Specifically, the US Department of Education has been providing colleges the entire list of institutions that a student submits when filling out the FAFSA form. Schools have realized that the order in which students place those colleges on the form indicates the students' relative interest in enrolling. The higher the placement, the greater the interest in that college, and the stingier the aid package the school provides. As a department spokeswoman put it, "Some use the information to determine if and how much institutional aid to provide— why spend money if the student would likely come to my school anyway?" As a result, the department announced that, beginning in 2015–16, the entire list of institutions will no longer be provided to any one school. But don't think that Big Data analysts won't figure out other ways for schools to anticipate student behavior. See, for example, Eric Hoover, "Getting Inside the Mind of an Applicant: Data Mining Puts a High-Tech Spin on the Age-Old Competition for Students," *Chronicle of Higher Education*, September 28, 2015.

students (and their parents) select the school over a more "prestigious" one due to the lower net price. Applicant two is almost definitely coming anyway if admitted, so if she happens to be from an affluent family, why charge her an amount that is less than she is willing to pay and less than what her family has the wherewithal to provide?

But, on second thought, this reasoning raises several moral questions. If the aid is called "merit" aid, shouldn't it go to the most meritorious of applicants rather than to those who are less accomplished but otherwise unlikely to accept an admission offer? Don't we assume that merit scholarships should be proportional to merit? We tell students to study harder; we don't tell them to stay away from the tour guest book in order to appear that they are less likely to come and thereby more "deserving" of merit aid.

And doesn't transparency—or its lack—matter in determining what is right? It is one thing to do something openly and another to do the same things while letting people think one is doing something else. Let outsiders think one uses merit aid as the term implies, to reward merit; but then use it to buy good students as cheaply as possible. In everyday life, that is called hypocrisy and, given university pretensions to speak as a moral conscience, suggests numerous pious hypocrites in literature.

Here is a useful thought experiment: What if it were publicly known that an especially talented student was charged more because, among other factors, her dad attended the college and she was naive enough to go on the tour? One could only imagine the outrage among alumni and the unemployment rate among tour guides.

And the humanist would want to ask, If one can't do something openly, should one be doing it at all? That question is particularly pressing if one speaks from a position of moral authority. It is one thing to use surreptitiously gathered information to sell cars—people expect that, and car salesmen do not presume to speak for public morality. Nor do they get tax breaks for serving the public good! But not-for-profit colleges and universities do, and their customers expect them to act accordingly.

In the case of merit aid, the unspoken assumption is that it will be used so that a given sum of dollars allotted to merit-based discounts will be distributed to maximize the merit it rewards. There may be various ways of doing that and the public may not have thought through all the possibilities. But this assumption implies that one type of efficiency is sought—maximize merit per dollar spent. In actual practice, universities are employing a different criterion of efficiency: minimize the cost of admitting a class of a given quality, even if that means rewarding the same merit unequally and deceiving people along the way. Again, the apparently economic criterion of efficiency turns out to raise moral questions the moment we ask, Efficient at what? And can the way we try to reach one kind of efficiency compromise another, arguably more important kind?

Much of the information gathered on financial aid forms or admission applications is solicited for the express purpose of deciding who is the most worthy or the most needy. People supply that information under that assumption. Isn't there an ethical problem in using it for a quite different, and concealed, purpose? A purpose that frustrates the very goals people presume when they volunteer the information?

Of course, as mentioned above, one reply would be that engaging in this sort of misleading behavior allows the school to spend more money on worthy purposes—say, on its career center that helps graduates get good jobs. Might this justify the school's actions? Perhaps it would be immoral *not* to use all available information in order to minimize merit discounts for students who were coming anyway!

The ethical questions here do not have obvious answers, and that is our point. What from an economic standpoint does not raise difficult questions, from an ethical perspective, more natural to the humanist, certainly does.[7]

To take the point one step further, return to our thought experiment and imagine the indignation if this type of economic analysis were applied to the allocation of need-based aid. It would be understandably greater. Need-based aid is presumed to be determined by what parents can afford. If applicant two were from a low-income family, to charge her more based on her demonstrated interest strikes us as a position that is impossible to defend. Sure, to do so would mean that colleges and universities would have additional money to spend for other good purposes, but only because students such as this one are forced to take out more debt than our aid formulas suggest is prudent. And yet, a university trying to build its enrollment of low-income and minority students might be tempted to use such a technique for what it regards as its moral goals.

In short, using this type of information to allocate merit and need-based aid poses ethical challenges. With need-based aid, the ethical objections seem all the stronger. Why should that be so? In both cases, part of the moral objection lies in our reaction to hypocrisy. But when one claims to use need-based aid, one assumes the moral high ground even more than when one offers merit aid. Ethically speaking, it seems a greater virtue to help the poor than to further reward the meritorious. That would not have to be the case, of course, and perhaps such

7. For an excellent example of an economist who has examined the link between ethics (understood philosophically) and economic issues, see the work of Nobel laureate Amartya Sen, for instance, *The Idea of Justice* (Penguin, 2010), *On Ethics and Economics* (Basil Blackwell, 1987), *Resources, Values, and Development* (Harvard University Press, 1984), and *Poverty and Famines: An Essay on Entitlement and Deprivation* (Oxford University Press, 1982). If the extraordinary popular success of Thomas Piketty's monumental volume, *Capital in the Twenty-First Century* (Harvard University Press, 2013) is any indication, the general public seems to have a great deal of interest in the ethical implications of economic realities. See also Michael J. Sandel, *What Money Can't Buy: The Moral Limits of Markets* (Farrar, Strauss, and Giroux, 2012), which we discuss later.

an ethical sensibility reflects the heritage of religious traditions even among institutions that have been secular for many
years. But those very traditions also suggest the danger of self-
deceiving sanctimoniousness. The more one assumes the moral
high ground, the more objectionable is the hypocrisy of doing
something else. It is one thing if a white-collar worker steals
supplies, quite another if a parson robs the poor box.

It is hard to tell how often economic techniques are actually used in this fashion as a tool of enrollment management.
But if you are looking for a case where the application of basic
economic principles may not be appropriate in the real world,
this could be it. A seller increasing revenue when refusing to
discount a price for a naive car buyer is very different from
a college or university increasing the price charged a worthy
student who can't afford it. Ignoring that context isn't really
good economics—it is a misuse of its theoretical and empirical power. Or maybe it is good economics proper; but to make
good decisions, even about economic matters, we sometimes
need more than economics.

We have to believe that stories would help here. If enrollment management gurus actually spoke with some of those
talented, earnest students who were desperate to attend the
institution, would they be as likely to exploit that interest in
an effort to minimize their price discounts? If they followed
students saddled with extraordinary loan burdens, would they
be so proud of how they cleverly replaced grants with loans
in the aid package? Perhaps they would adopt the viewpoint
of the "businesses" they serve, bracketing their other selves.
But even if that were the case, would other interested parties—
faculty, staff, alumni, administrators—sleep so well at night?
We doubt it.

Self-bracketing, so that one's ethical qualms are somehow
held offstage, may actually be a useful technique. On some
occasions, it may even be an ethical one. If the only way a sur-
geon could save a life would be to stop thinking of her patient

as a specific person while surgery was in process—so that she could make calm decisions—self-bracketing would be a necessary skill to develop. But it is also one that can be abused so that ethical questions are disregarded when they should not be. That form of amoralism, justified by ostensibly professional scruples, can easily become a habit. Novelists love to examine how such questionable self-bracketing takes place.[8]

Or tell a different story. What if one of those gurus had a child applying to college? Would he feel comfortable counseling her in gaming the system? If so, doesn't the system encourage a moral miseducation? If not, why create an advantage for what one would regard as wrong if one were in the applicant's position? Or ask the question this way: Would he feel comfortable telling his child of the clever deceit he was practicing? Does moral miseducation of this sort run counter to the very purpose, or at least an important purpose, of education itself?

Finally, there is a related application of this type of analysis that is also morally fraught. Many schools work very hard to minimize their admit rates—that is, the percentage of all applicants that are admitted—acting on the premise that, to the outside world, increased selectivity equates with higher quality. One might think that a published admit rate below 20 percent or even 10 percent might scare away potential applicants, but the opposite seems to be the case. Students are typically attracted to schools that are the most difficult to get into—perhaps thinking about the quality of their potential peers, or maybe the prestige of the bumper stickers on their (or their parents') cars, or the perception of that prestige by future potential employers.

---

8. Dickens made this sort of habitualization, in which a profession loses sight of its real purpose, a common theme. In *Bleak House*, it is the basis of his satire on the courts of law. In *Great Expectations*, Wemmick, while at work in the law office, adopts a thoroughly amoral professional persona, which Pip assumes is his real self. But, as Pip learns to his delight, Wemmick drops this persona entirely outside the office and becomes the warmest of human beings, reversing his professional advice.

Using this kind of formula provides a great way to minimize a school's admit rate. Focus on admitting those students
with high predicted yields (for example, the student with a
98 percent chance of accepting an offer) and, for those with
low probabilities (the student with a 6 percent chance), either
reject them or place them on the wait list. When you limit
admission offers to those who are likely to attend, you don't
have to admit very many in order to fill your class.

This type of yield-protecting activity raises serious moral
issues. Aren't schools "supposed" to admit based on merit?
How do you justify taking an inferior student whom you
know will attend over a stronger student who probably will
not? Once again, we can picture the outrage should such practice become public. And there is another ethical problem here:
When you manipulate statistics such as your admit rate, you
mislead those who rely on that information. And that means
you are being dishonest.[9]

Yet, over the past few decades, it seems to have become
increasingly commonplace that schools reject (or place on the
wait list) students who are "too good" for the place—in other
words, "too good" to come if admitted. Before the enrollment
management gurus took over, the concept of a safety school
was a simple one: just as you apply to a "reach" school (a school
that is unlikely to admit you), find others that are very likely
to take you. Not today. Should you play it too safe, the school
is unlikely to admit you regardless of your qualifications, simply because their yield analysis indicates a low probability you
would come.

So an applicant who is straightforward in presenting his
admission portfolio encounters some schools that are anything but. Applicants may be left without a school to attend,
but even if they aren't, they have been misled.

---

9. If you think this is misleading, just wait till you get to the section on providing data
to *US News*.

If schools were open about what they were doing, at least the charge of deception would disappear. However, other ethical problems would remain. To secure acceptance by the most desirable schools, students would do best to learn not more math and history but more about the techniques schools use in manipulating a complex system of selective admissions. Is that the kind of extracurricular activity we want them to engage in?

One of us (Schapiro) became familiar with this new reality around fifteen years ago. The younger sister of a Williams student was interested in that school, along with some similarly highly selective colleges and universities. Her college counselor recommended a number of backup schools that had substantially lower student characteristics. She was surprised to be either wait-listed or rejected by most of those—her very strong test scores and high school grades, along with the fact that her sister was at Williams, and therefore she might be disposed to attending there as well, surely worked against her at those institutions. It didn't much matter since she was admitted not only to Williams but to MIT, where she eventually enrolled. But what if she had not been? Now, when we teach our Northwestern class and discuss enrollment management, we ask our students whether any of them had not been admitted to at least one of their "safety schools." Many hands go up. Higher education allegedly rewards merit: work hard, do well, and your educational options will increase. But not for some students whose naiveté versus sophisticated practitioners of economic theory and empirical techniques leaves them with a reduced set of choices and higher tuition bills. The lesson would seem to be: pretend to work hard but learn how the system really works and game it.

The moral here is that when the use of economic tools leads you into ethical hot water, you need to think carefully about employing them. Stories can help make that point—but that isn't the limit of their usefulness. Stories can also have a direct influence on how those tools can be reformulated. Recall the example of the applicant with a predicted 98 percent chance of enrolling versus the one with a 6 percent chance. Not all students with very high yield projections actually come, while some students with very low yield projections surprise us by showing up on campus.

In many disciplines, it would be natural to interview the students in question in order to help inform the basic model. But in economics that is rarely done. Why not track down and write to every student who did not enroll despite having a 90+ percent yield prediction? Perhaps we could get a sense of what the model missed. Was there exceptionally poor weather on the tour? A boring school representative at the college fair? Or maybe there were key variables that could be easily quantified and included in the yield analysis. And why not interview students on campus who had a 10 percent or lower yield prediction? You don't even have to track them down; they are in the dorms. Why did they come? What did we ignore? Listening to their stories is a commonsense way to improve the specification of the model, even if it means getting to know your data by name, something that the field of economics usually scorns.

Who Teaches Undergraduates?

The role of tenure in American higher education has been reduced dramatically in recent decades.[10] In 1975, 57 percent of all faculty (excluding graduate students) were in the tenure system; by 2011 that figure had been cut almost in half to 29 percent. Some observers predict that the share of tenure track/tenured faculty will bottom out at between 15 and 20 percent, with tenure being largely limited to the flagship public and private research universities and the wealthiest of the

10. This section draws upon David N. Figlio, Morton O. Schapiro, and Kevin B. Soter, "Are Tenure Track Professors Better Teachers?" *Review of Economics and Statistics*, October 2015, pp. 715–724.

liberal arts colleges. We think they are overly optimistic, with the decline bottoming out around 10 percent.[11]

There is evidence that this trend accelerated after January 1, 1994, when mandatory retirement for faculty was abolished by federal law. This, of course, was not surprising, as the uncapping of the retirement age made tenure much more expensive for colleges and universities while also reducing the number of available slots. Ehrenberg reports that, between 1995 and 2007, the share of part-time faculty rose at almost all institutional types while, among full-time faculty, the movement away from the tenure system has quickened.[12] Especially notable is the rise of full-time, contingent faculty members at PhD granting universities. Their representation within the entire group of full-time faculty went from 24 percent to 35 percent at public doctoral institutions and from 18 percent to 46 percent at private nonprofit doctoral institutions.

This trend has led some to lament the potential blow to academic freedom dealt by the decline of tenure, and to focus on the often challenging employment conditions under which many contingent faculty work. Further, McPherson and Schapiro point to efficiency gains from tenure, as faculty in a long-term relationship with an institution are more likely to take a long-term view of its general well-being and to work toward that goal.[13]

In short, tenure has a number of potential advantages. First, it guarantees academic freedom, that is, it allows professors to espouse what many would consider objectionable political views. Second, it allows faculty to explore potentially

---

11. Gary Saul Morson and Morton Schapiro, "The Future of Higher Education in the United States (and the World)," chapter 10 in our edited volume, *The Fabulous Future?*

12. Ronald G. Ehrenberg, "American Higher Education in Transition," *Journal of Economic Perspectives* 26, no. 1, Winter 2012, pp. 647–659.

13. Michael S. McPherson and Morton Owen Schapiro, "Tenure Issues in Higher Education," *Journal of Economic Perspectives* 13, no. 1, Winter 1999, pp. 85–98.

risky areas of research that may not pay off in publications and grants, by reducing the cost if they do not. Third, it creates the sort of loyalty that makes professors willing to act in ways necessary for the ongoing functioning of the institution, even if they are not directly paid for doing so. Finally, it might just improve the quality of teaching.

While all those considerations certainly have relevance in evaluating the impact of the accelerating demise of the tenure system, here we focus on the final one. There is an educational outcome that may be measured directly: Do undergraduates taught by contingent faculty members learn as much as those taught by tenure track/tenured faculty?

The limited existing evidence on the relative performance of tenure track/tenured professors versus faculty outside the tenure system makes it difficult for college and university deci-sion makers to determine the optimal staffing of their class-rooms. This is particularly relevant for research universities, which face a multitasking problem of maximizing an objective function (a set of goals) that includes both the production of cutting-edge research and the provision of outstanding under-graduate teaching.

A study coauthored by Schapiro provides the first evidence within the research university setting regarding the under-graduate learning effects from different types of faculty.[14] Specifically, we examine the initial classes taken by first-term freshmen in eight cohorts of undergraduates at Northwestern. Contingent faculty members at Northwestern tend to have stable, long-term relationships with the university, and a substantial majority are full-time. This allows us to study the effects of contingent faculty at a major research university where experienced faculty members function as designated teachers (both full-time and part-time).

---

14. Figlio, Schapiro, and Soter (2015) analyzes data on all Northwestern University freshmen who entered between fall 2001 and fall 2008, a total of 15,662 students.

Our empirical strategy involves observing whether students during their first term at Northwestern taking introductory economics, for example, with a tenure line faculty member and, say, introductory political science with a contingent faculty member are (1) relatively more likely to take a second political science class than another economics class and (2) conditional on taking more classes in both subjects, more likely to perform unexpectedly well in the political science class than in the economics class. The answer to both questions is a resounding yes.

The results are quite striking: both full-time and part-time contingent faculty members outperform tenure line professors in the first-term classroom. The estimated effect of full-time contingent faculty is modestly higher than that for part-time contingent faculty, but the differences between these two groups are not statistically different from zero. It is important to note that the overwhelming majority of part-time contingent faculty at Northwestern still have long-term relationships with the university, so we do not equate part-time faculty at Northwestern with "one-off" adjunct instructors—that is, faculty who combine jobs at multiple colleges and have no stable relationship with any of them. Rather, a large fraction of part-time contingent faculty members teach a course or two at Northwestern in addition to their regular professional careers, while adjuncts hired to fill temporary vacancies may not have the same sense of commitment to an institution and its students.[15]

The strong and significant effect of contingent faculty on our measure of learning held for all subjects, regardless of grading

15. This is an important qualification of the study. Schools with large numbers of nontenure line faculty who teach an occasional class there, along with their teaching at other institutions, may have a very different level of teaching effectiveness. When Schapiro worked at the University of Southern California, we used to call those adjunct faculty "freeway fliers," given that they would commute to several schools in a given day. Their rarity at Northwestern makes it impossible to evaluate their impact on student learning in a broader educational context.

standards or the qualifications of the students the subjects attracted. The apparent benefits of taking classes from contingent faculty were particularly strong for tougher-grading subjects and those that attracted the most qualified students, and the benefits were enjoyed more by the less academically qualified students than by the more academically qualified students—the biggest gains to taking courses from contingent faculty were for relatively weak students taking courses in the toughest-grading subjects.

So what do you do with the results of this study? Perhaps there are important policy implications in play.

How about treating contingent faculty better? A rule of thumb is that full-time contingent faculty teach at least twice the load for tenure line faculty: at many research universities that means eight to nine classes versus three to four. The justification for this, of course, is that tenured faculty are typically paid to do research in addition to their teaching, while contingent faculty are not. In addition, contingent faculty are rarely able to avail themselves of many of the perquisites open to their tenured and tenure track colleagues, such as sabbaticals, travel funds, and the like. And perhaps the greatest source of contention is the fact that full-time tenure line faculty are paid more than double that of nonline faculty with similar years of service.

A narrow economic answer would be this arrangement seems to work, so why change it? Contingent faculty not only volunteer to teach; gaining a full-time position is a great accomplishment, beating the employment odds. And students are often blissfully unaware of whether their favorite faculty are in the tenure system or not. (They also seem largely oblivious to differences in academic rank. Everyone is simply "Prof.")

But if the current system is so good, why don't colleges and universities extoll the virtues of its professional teachers in its admissions viewbooks and on its campus tours? As was the case with enrollment management in the preceding section, we have an issue of transparency. Colleges tout their faculty-to-student ratio, but where on a college website does it mention the percentage of undergraduate courses that are taught by nontenure line faculty? Our empirical analysis shows that nontenure line faculty are often the almost invisible providers of some of the best teaching around.

How about hearing the stories of contingent faculty and of the students who adore them? Would department chairs, deans, provosts, and presidents remain so content with the status quo if they learned more about how such valuable members of their learning communities were treated?

The bottom line is that despite a labor situation that seems to work for all involved, we might still choose to adjust salaries, job titles, and working conditions. An economist might think first of tangible rewards, but often "psychodollars" matter as well. Rather than lecturer, adjunct, or visiting professor, how about a title such as "professor of instruction," which better conveys the long-term relationship with the school?[16] There might be a concomitant increase in salary but also eligibility for travel funds to attend professional meetings. Support to attend professional conferences has a symbolic value far beyond the dollars. Since tenure track faculty are hired to do research as well as teaching, contingent faculty, hired only to teach, are usually not given travel money to aid research. Therefore, such funds signal prestige, create a sense of being valued, reflect that the faculty member's future career matters to the institution, and reduce the feeling of being a second-class citizen. That's a lot to get for a few dollars. Also, we are reminded of the following old adage: "Research is to teaching as sin is to confession. If you aren't actively engaged in the former, you eventually run out

16. If an administrator talked with a "visiting professor" who has been teaching full-time at the school for over a decade, he might not like what he hears about this title.

of things to say in the latter." If this is true, attending a professional meeting to hear the latest in research findings could improve teaching effectiveness, even for those with limited personal research engagement. Once again, when fairness is at odds with the pursuit of efficiency, the pure economic approach may not lead to the "best" outcome.[17]

An outsider—say, a state legislator concerned with tuition expense—might ask the following: If contingent faculty teach as well or better that those on the tenure line, why hire anyone else? To this we can provide a two-fold answer. The most obvious is that universities contribute to society through research as well as teaching, and this is what tenure track faculty usually are for.[18] The less obvious answer is that at the advanced level of undergraduate teaching, and of course at the graduate level, tenure track/tenured faculty might very well be more desirable than those outside of the tenure system.[19] If that hypothesis were confirmed, it could be because tenure line faculty know more and are more familiar with cutting-edge research, or maybe for a reason that the humanities would stress—teaching is a species of performance. It is not just a conveying of information but a modeling of how to think. One demonstrates in process how an expert considers evidence, wrestles with new issues, seeks out important new questions. Perhaps seasoned tenured professors

17. We are pleased to report that Northwestern has taken several steps in recognizing and rewarding long-term contingent faculty members for their excellent service. As indicated in Colleen Flaherty, "Northwestern U's Arts and Sciences College Updates Titles for Teaching Faculty and Offers Path to Promotion," *Inside Higher Education*, August 12, 2015, various ranks of lecturer have been replaced by professors of instruction at the assistant, associate, and full levels, and longer-term contracts for teaching-track faculty have been offered. While the article reports that there were no pay raises immediately associated with the new ranks, in fact, this increased recognition has already included financial rewards for a number of nontenure line faculty.

18. One might still ask why it is that universities need to offer tenure in order to attract a first-rate research faculty. We suspect this question will in fact be increasingly raised in the future.

19. Testing that presumption would be a most worthy empirical exercise.

have something special to offer here. Or perhaps the two of us, with our full professor status, just want to think so.

Data Reporting

US News and World Report, the annual ranking all schools purport to hate, looms large within the higher education landscape. Everyone seems to know it, students applying to college consult it, and the public at large accepts it as a significant ranking of educational excellence. Hence, it isn't all that surprising that seemingly every year a school or two gets busted for providing them with fictitious data. How tempting, for example, when asked to provide average SAT/ACT scores for the entering class, to send instead the average SAT/ACT scores of the admitted class? That is, to send the data for all students accepted, not just the ones who are coming. Honest mistake in sending the wrong file? How convenient, given the fact that the academic characteristics of the students whom you admit are always considerably stronger than those you enroll. When merchants miscalculate in your favor, you have no trouble accepting that as an honest error. When mistakes always tend to the merchant's favor, they are not really mistakes. But while outright lies place schools in the media spotlight, there are so many quiet ways to manipulate the data that the resulting numbers border on the meaningless.[20] Who knows how ubiquitous these practices are? Without an authority that verifies the accuracy of the data schools provide, we have no way to tell.

20. The list of schools that have found themselves in that embarrassing spotlight is long and growing. And their actions aren't limited to misrepresenting undergraduate data. A recent example involves the graduate engineering program at the University of Wisconsin–Madison. While they reported to *US News* an admit rate of only 8.9 percent (833 admitted students out of 9,338 applicants), they later acknowledged that the actual admit rate was 18.7 percent (with 1,154 admits out of 6,172 applicants). See Scott Jaschik, "U of Wisconsin Submitted False Data," *Inside Higher Education,* March 31, 2016.

So here is the question: If a rival school is clearly being "creative" with the numbers included on their data form, should you, the administrator of another school, hold yourself to a higher ethical standard?

We begin with a quick lesson on data creativity. We discussed previously the most important measure of a school's selectivity: its admit rate. Seems simple enough—you divide the number of students you admit by the number who applied. But let's start with the denominator. How many did in fact apply? That depends on what you define as an application. A number of schools have what they call a two-part application. While the second part includes essays, recommendations, and the like, the first part is little more than a postcard or an email expressing interest. In fact, many high school seniors are bombarded with so-called fast apps that already have their names and addresses filled in. All they have to do to "apply" is send it back—no application fee, no information on high school performance. Why would schools do this? Could it be so that they can count anyone who sends in a postcard or an email as an applicant?

In fact, there is little doubt that some schools count those who only submitted part one applications among their total number of applicants. Who knows if that is really why they have a two-part application in the first place—so they can misrepresent the size of their applicant pools? Perhaps not, since those schools often say that an initial expression of interest allows them to follow up and get students to fully apply. And yet, one could do that without calling the expression of interest an "application" for statistical purposes.

The Russian philosopher Mikhail Bakhtin insists that utterances, as actions for which we can be held morally responsible, consist not of words on a page but of an exchange between speaker and listener, writer and reader. The words are the material from which utterances are constructed, but they consist of more than words. Utterances are dialogic, and they live "on the boundaries of two consciousnesses, two subjects."[21] That is, their expected response is an essential part of them, and so we must be, in the moral sense as well, responsible when we make them.

It would seem to follow that to determine honesty one does not look for some technical correspondence between the words on the page and the reality they report. One looks at the dialogue: "This is the aspect of it that pertains to honesty, truth, goodness, beauty, history."[22] The question is, do the words deceive and are they meant to deceive?

Consider the question of plagiarism. People who think in terms of words on a page (or "texts") typically ask how much one person's text must resemble another's to call it plagiarized. 50 percent? 90 percent? But a moment's reflection shows there is something wrong with this approach. Parodies can copy a text word for word but are not plagiarisms. If one scholar copies another's work perfectly, but puts it in quotation marks and indicates it is the other person's words, one might accuse him of unoriginality, or if the passage is long enough, of infringement of copyright, but not of plagiarism. Plagiarism involves the intent to deceive.

This obvious point is often missed because of the orthodoxy in literary theoretical circles for the past three-quarters of a

21. M. M. Bakhtin, "The Problem of the Text in Linguistics, Philology, and the Human Sciences: An Experiment in Philosophical Analysis," *Speech Genres and Other Late Essays*, trans. Vern W. McGee, ed. Caryl Emerson and Michael Holquist (University of Texas Press, 1987), p. 106. The idea of language not as sentences in a text but as utterances among people in dialogue is discussed at length in Mikhail Bakhtin, *Problems of Dostoevsky Poetics*, ed. and trans. Caryl Emerson (University of Minnesota Press, 1984), pp. 181–269; and in M. M. Bakhtin, "Discourse in the Novel," *The Dialogic Imagination: Four Essays*, ed. Michael Holquist, trans. Caryl Emerson and Michael Holquist (University of Texas Press, 1981), pp. 259–422. For a summary of this approach to language, see chapter 4 of Gary Saul Morson and Caryl Emerson, *Mikhail Bakhtin: Creation of a Prosaics* (Stanford University Press, 1990), pp. 123–171.

22. M. M. Bakhtin, "The Problem of the Text in Linguistics, Philology, and the Human Sciences: An Experiment in Philosophical Analysis," p. 105.

century that authorial intention does not matter and we must instead speak of texts. Originally, this tenet reflected the desire to make a hard science of literary studies by focusing on something objective like texts, not something vague like meanings. More recent attempts at "literary science," like "digital humanities," often fall into the same trap for the same reason. But the question of honesty shows the problems with such an approach. Honesty involves a relationship among people, not correspondence of words with other words. It is not a matter of counting.

When university administrators defend themselves from charges of lying by saying that they are literally accurate in their reporting of application numbers because they have called a postcard part of an application—so the postcard by itself is still an incomplete application but an application nonetheless—the reply ought to be that such a defense is meant to deceive. Technically accurate or not, it is a form of lying. People who hear the word "application" think of essays, test scores, reported grades, and recommendations, not postcards. And if the administrators have called the postcard part of the application, they have constructed a situation bound to mislead, that is, their dishonesty has been premeditated.

So counting incomplete applications in the denominator of an admit rate calculation is nothing short of lying. It is easy to joke that the number of "rejected" students in this country is considerably greater than the number of students who actually applied to colleges, but that joke is lost on those who rely on *US News* and other media (and even college websites) to report admit rates that accurately represent the chance of getting into a particular school.

And what about the numerator? Surely the number of students admitted is easy to count. Not so fast. Some schools have delayed admissions—rather than invite an applicant to enter in the fall with the majority of other freshmen, he or she is admitted to the spring semester or even to the following year. Can you in good faith define "admitted students" as those who are allowed to come during the regular fall move-in days, counting other students who receive letters of admission as rejects because they technically weren't invited to a school's opening convocation? Why not? some schools say. We rejected them for the fall, and that is all that matters.

Finally, what about those selective schools, desperate to minimize their admit rates, who go to their wait lists shortly after they send out their admission notices and well before the national response date of May 1? Wait a second, isn't the wait list supposed to be used if a school underyields? This game is simple—recall the temptation described earlier to protect your yield by refusing to admit applicants whom your enrollment management guru tells you are unlikely to come. If you place those students on the wait list, the chances you will ever hear from them again are very slim, especially after they are admitted to a number of other good schools. But you never know what might happen if you call one of them in early April or whenever the other admission notices go out, and tell her over the phone that there is a spot for her *if* she promises right then and there to come. If she hems and haws, tell her that you will get back to her (don't mention when hell freezes over). But should she surprise you by saying yes, she is in. No wonder the yield off the wait list is so high. Unless a student agrees to come, she was never admitted. But this is to mislead by allowing people who use the statistics to believe that the wait list is one thing when it is, at least in part, something else. And this is the practice at many fine schools, even at the majority of colleges and universities that wait till May or June to make those phone calls.

In short, when you go to the wait list *after* determining how many students accept your initial offers of admission, it doesn't seem nearly so bad, despite the pressure tactics that may be in play. But doing so in early April, when you have no idea what your overall yield will be, is a thinly veiled gimmick with one purpose—to lower your admit rate in order to trick people into thinking you are more selective than you actually are.

Admit rates receive a great deal of popular attention; so do test scores. Schools readily offer up information on their standardized test scores (either their mean scores or perhaps their 25th/75th percentiles). Consumers use this information to gauge both admissions possibilities and the quality of potential peers. But are all the undergraduates represented in the data set that schools use to compute these numbers? Some schools ignore international students, especially those who were educated in a language other than English. Seems fair, we guess, except when they only leave out their verbal and writing scores from the school's overall calculation, not their math scores. Somehow the 580 verbal score is forgotten but not the 780 math score. How convenient. And what about "special" admits, such as athletes, legacies, and development cases?[23] Or students admitted off the wait list or through delayed admissions? If the public wants to know how strong the total class is, you surely must include everyone. But schools looking to inflate their average test scores do not. It is as if a city touting its low crime rate did not count crimes when the victim was from out of town, or the perpetrator didn't actually fire his gun, or stole property under $100.

Lastly, if you still think that published test scores say all that much about the actual quality of the class, try this one: many schools that are test-optional proudly compute their average test scores, and *US News* is just as proud to print them and include them in its ranking formula. Obviously, if a student has the option of whether or not to send in her test scores, she would be much more likely to do so if she did well, as opposed to having done poorly. When Schapiro was president of Williams College, he was asked at an alumni function why Williams had average SATs of "only" 1450 (out of 1600), while a rival school was at

---

23. Of course there are important economic and ethical questions relating to the general topic of special admits. We leave those to our postretirement book!

1475. The answer given was that the 1450 included every single student in the freshman class, while the test-optional rival might just have had two students represented, one with a 1450 and the other with a 1500. The rest of their freshman class, who knows? But the very fact that someone asked the question showed that the misrepresentation could be effective.

Reputational rankings loom large in the calculation of a school's ranking according to *US News* and elsewhere, with considerable weight in the overall formula. How are such rankings arrived at? The usual way is to ask institutions about each other. The question schools are asked is straightforward—a school's president, chief academic officer (usually the provost or the dean of the faculty), and undergraduate admissions dean are supposed to evaluate the quality of the undergraduate program at each school in their institution's category. Despite an attempt among the liberal arts presidents to boycott this ranking form, many submit these evaluations each year. As you might guess, it is tempting to manipulate those votes to help your school rise in the rankings. Coordinate among your three voters, and perhaps some of your buddies, to give your school the highest ranking and, of course, your rivals the lowest. One college president proudly proclaimed that this is exactly what he does—saying that he uses these rankings to reward his friends and punish his enemies. Not exactly what the public has in mind when considering the legitimacy of reputational rankings.[24]

An outsider might think that colluding with others violates some equivalent to the Sherman Antitrust Act. It certainly involves deceiving those who would accept the rankings as

---

24. The manipulation of reputational ratings isn't limited to *US News* and colleges and universities in the United States. A recent report described the attempt of Ireland's Trinity College Dublin (the highest-ranked institution in Ireland) to influence one of the best-known international higher education rankings. A vice president there sent a letter to academics and others encouraging them to register to vote in the reputational survey, violating the rules set out by the ranking agency. See Scott Jaschik, "Trinity College Dublin's Letters about Rankings Raise Eyebrows," *Inside Higher Education*, March 21, 2016.

honest statements of what universities think of each other, as these rankings purport to be. Businesses that misrepresent their products might be accused of one or another legal infraction, and universities again take advantage of their position as moral beacons, as somehow not mere businesses. That would imply higher standards than mere businesses. An outsider would therefore presume that they do not engage in the sort of tricks one might expect of less than honest businesspeople. But it turns out that this very presumption is what allows them to lie all the more effectively.

Consider that boastful university president. Shouldn't the trustees of the institution realize that such a pronouncement impugns the very justification of the university's existence? What would we expect if a hospital administrator boasted that, although lots of patients died from preventable mistakes, he manipulated the figures to make that seem rare and colluded with neighboring hospitals to make the resulting figures more plausible?

Next up is the school's graduation rate. Again, while it seems pretty clear, it is anything but. The numerator is the number of students who graduate, and that isn't in much dispute. However, the denominator is the size of the "initial" student cohort, and that is a matter for easy manipulation.[25] Is the

---

25. One such attempt recently attracted a good deal of media attention. Scott Jaschik, "Furor at Mount St. Mary's over President's Alleged Plan to Cull Students," *Inside Higher Education*, January 20, 2016, asks "Is a valid strategy to improve a college's retention rate to encourage students at risk of dropping out to do so in the first few weeks, so they won't be counted in the total numbers reported to the US Education Department and others?" The article goes on to say that while the (now former) president of Mount St. Mary's University in Maryland said he was trying to implement a plan for early intervention with students who are having difficulties, members of the faculty said that the actual goal was to have several dozen students leave the school by the end of September, eliminating them from the initial student cohort in order to increase the school's published retention rate. According to one account (Susan Svrluga, "University President Allegedly Says Struggling Freshmen Are Bunnies That Should Be Drowned," *Washington Post*, January 19, 2016), the president told some faculty that "this is hard for you because you think of the students as cuddly bunnies, but you can't. You have to drown the bunnies … put a Glock to their heads."

entering class the number of students who show up on move-in day? The number who last at least one week in college? The number who make it through drop/add during the first semester? The number that complete the first semester? Obviously, the later you define the cohort, the higher the graduation rate. How about limiting the denominator to those students who make it past their finals in their senior year? Wow, a graduation rate of 100 percent! Once again, members of the public look at published graduation rates and believe those numbers represent the truth, but they shouldn't necessarily be so sure.

Finally, what about alumni giving? Schools are so proud to trumpet the fact that a sizable proportion of their living undergraduate alumni give every year because a high rate suggests a happy experience at the school. But what does "give" actually mean? And who gets counted as undergraduate alumni? The numerator is supposed to be the number of individual donors, but what if you get a single check from a regional alumni association? Say an alumni club puts on a golf tournament that results in a check to the school of $20,000. Assume for the sake of convenience that 20,000 undergraduate alumni reside in that region. You guessed it, the temptation is to record 20,000 $1 gifts. What a "clever" way to inflate your alumni giving percentage! And it just might be true for all you know. Too bad it is so misleading.

But is lying the same as stating something you know to be false, or does it also include a falsehood you don't verify when you easily could? Tolstoy's Stiva Oblonsky, Anna Karenina's brother, conveniently assumes that if he is not consciously telling a falsehood, then he is being truthful. He thinks he is "a truthful man," but in fact he is, from Tolstoy's perspective, dishonest. The author's point is that if someone could readily know whether what one says is true—say, by checking an easily available source or bothering to check one's own memories—but fails to verify it, that failure doesn't shield one from a charge of falsehood. Indeed, it is itself a form of dishonesty, because it represents a deliberate policy to avoid knowing inconvenient facts. Of course, it might be true that there are 20,000 $1 gifts, but surely that is highly unlikely, and the simple failure to ascertain what is the case does not entitle one to claim whatever is most convenient.

It gets worse. One school even allegedly experimented with sending $10 bills to its alumni, with a letter from the president asking "donors" to return at least that amount in an addressed and stamped envelope that was included in the mailing. The hope, of course, was that alumni would send back more than the $10, but nonetheless it is hard not to be cynical about the intention here, which was to increase the alumni giving rate, even if it only meant returning money that the school had provided.

Speaking of cynical, our favorite example of this type of manipulation took place at one of the most prestigious schools in the country. One year its published alumni giving rate was below its peers; the next year it was well ahead. What happened? Did they figure out an effective way to engage the alumni body, leading to a much larger percentage of them sending checks? No. Allegedly, they went through their alumni giving records, identified thousands of graduates who hadn't given in more than a decade, and purged them from the denominator, as if they no longer existed. Now they might have wanted those folks dead, but declaring them as such is a separate matter.

We could go on, but you get the picture. What the public treats as certified facts is nothing of the sort. There is no "data sheriff" out there, no Federal Trade Commission or other agency certifying the accuracy of statistics so many believe as the truth.[26] The shocking thing about schools that get busted

---

26. While the College Scorecard (the White House's ballyhooed attempt to provide students and their parents a good way to compare colleges) is far from perfect, it provides some previously unavailable data on a school's student debt, loan repayment, and the earnings of its graduates. See Andy Thomason, "5 College Rankings Based on the White House's New College Scorecard Data," *Chronicle of Higher Education*, September 14, 2015. Thomason writes that "the White House has essentially given the college-rankings industry federally verified data on which to base future best-of lists." Perhaps this is a start in verifying all the data a college produces.

for "making up" their numbers is that they didn't need to do it. All they needed to do was to be "clever" with how they manipulated their data.

But wait: If these data are reported by US News, shouldn't they be checking their accuracy? They lay out rules on how to calculate each number but then accept most anything a school provides as fact. It is not as if these tricks are not known to them and other rating entities. The two of us actually asked the person who runs the US News rankings this very question. The answer we got was that since the listings are a commercial success, what is the incentive to change them? Perhaps a better answer would be that colleges and universities should feel bound to hold themselves to a high standard. If they don't, that is their problem. In any case, don't expect US News (and other publications) to act as a data police force. As we heard, they are profit-making entities. If they provide a genuine service of informing the public with accurate information, fine, but if not, they can laugh all the way to the bank.

But to market figures one knows to be unreliable as if they were reliable, especially when people are shaping their lives and spending considerable money based on them, is more than ethically questionable. And that is true of any rating agency. We do not allow credit rating agencies to make what they know to be mistakes or to knowingly allow false information to affect people's credit rating, and they are expected to correct errors when they become known. Why isn't that the case with college rankings? One might imagine that honesty would be a simple matter for universities: Whatever the consequences, don't lie. Report the figures honestly. But it is not as simple as that.

If everyone else exaggerates their numbers but you do not, are you being honest? After all, the main point of these data is comparative. That means if you report a lower alumni giving rate than other colleges with which you are compared, when in fact your giving rate is higher, is that not also misleading? It appears there is more than one way you can be

misleading: by how you present the figures, which is entirely
your own decision, and how you allow yourself to look compared to others, which is not. But this reasoning can itself be
a dishonest conscience saver. Anyone who knows the great
realist novels—Tolstoy's *Anna Karenina*, Dickens's *Great
Expectations*, Trollope's *Can You Forgive Her?*, George Eliot's
Romola—becomes suspicious of any justification of lying. If
there is one psychological fact on which realist novelists seem
to agree, it is that people have a remarkable ability to find
moral justifications for what suits their self-interest. If a process of reasoning just happens to save one's conscience, one
should be especially suspicious of it.

It is remarkably easy to justify a certain amount of data
"exaggeration"—too little and you misrepresent the truth; too
much and you do the same. Why not just lie the "optimal"
amount? Let us repeat: As great literature teaches us, an ethical question is not one in which one has to decide whether
to behave ethically. It is one in which it is not clear what the
ethical way to behave is. In situations in which dishonesty is
the norm, one's most ethical course of action is not easy to
determine. And what happened, you might ask, to the notion
of colleges and universities acting to promote the public good,
exemplifying the finest of a nation's values?

Good question.

The Allocation of State Operating Subsidies

Recent years have been tough ones for public higher education.[27] Leaders of the most prestigious public universities talk
about their schools having been privatized—as they receive a
smaller and smaller portion of their operating budgets from
the state. But at least they have hope of filling this gap with
donations, endowment payouts, research support from the

---

27. Once again, for more detail, see chapter 10 in *The Fabulous Future?*

federal government, tuition from out-of-state students, and so on. On the other hand, state colleges and universities with regional or local (rather than national) reputations have little other than state money and limited tuition revenue on which to rely.

The situation is likely to get worse. Whereas public higher education used to attract a stable share of state expenditures— once 7 percent or so—that figure has declined to around 5 percent. Those two lost percentage points amount to around $30 billion per year, more than a third of current state appropriations to higher education. Where has the money gone, and might it come back? Almost all of those dollars have gone to health care, specifically to Medicaid. Our best hope is that the situation in the 1990s repeats itself, with state budgets rising faster than the higher education share of the pie declines. But that would take robust economic growth along with reining in not just health expenditures but also state pension obligations. Good luck with that.

The question considered here is, how might states best make those increasingly tough decisions on which of their public colleges and universities deserve the most support? The fundamental principles of economics, after all, concern the allocation of scarce resources. But what if economic criteria alone are, while helpful, insufficient to make choices?

Many state higher education systems are divided into tiers. There are the "flagship" institutions: major research universities that sometimes have international reputations, such as the University of California's Berkeley and UCLA, the University of Michigan, Ann Arbor, the University of Wisconsin–Madison, and the University of North Carolina at Chapel Hill. At the other end of the spectrum there are community colleges offering associate degrees and catering quite often to the least affluent and typically the least academically prepared students. In the middle are regional four-year colleges and universities, such as Central Michigan University and the University of

Wisconsin–Whitewater. So when resources are cut, the question is, which group of schools bears most of the burden?

One way to think of it is to provide money to maximize college enrollment. With that outcome measure defining efficiency, the decision is simple: support most generously community colleges, since that is where students who are most sensitive to higher tuition are found. If state funding cutbacks make the net price (the sticker price less aid discounts) at the state flagship university rise, most of those students will still find a way to pay the price, or perhaps go elsewhere to a less expensive educational option. But raise the price at a community college, and many of those students leave higher education for good.[28]

We can certainly rely on countless economic studies that have established the following: the price responsiveness to increases in net tuition is quite high for students from low-income backgrounds; those students can be disproportionately found at the less selective parts of the public higher education system. But that doesn't necessarily imply the optimal policy.

But again we can ask, what are we trying to be efficient at? Educational institutions have more than one goal. Enrollment matters, but so does educational excellence. A state that continually starves its flagship university in order to distribute its funds more broadly will end up having its "best" university losing much of its luster, perhaps irreparably.

Each state, by definition, has at least one flagship university—it is simply the head of its system. But only 34 public universities in the United States are members of the Association of American Universities (AAU), the collection of universities (which includes 2 Canadian public universities and 26 US

---

28. The data indicate that some of those students would have been destined for failure had they in fact enrolled at community colleges, in which case the public policy problem is less significant than it at first might appear. But many others would succeed if given the opportunity, and having them priced out of the market is extremely troubling from both an equity and an efficiency point of view.

private universities) that defines research excellence. Some states have more than one representative (Michigan, for example, has both the University of Michigan at Ann Arbor and Michigan State; California has a whopping six public members—Berkeley, UCLA, UC-Davis, UC-Irvine, UC-Santa Barbara, and UC-San Diego), while many have none.

Does that matter in terms of allocating state higher education subsidies? We suggest it might. A flagship that is not merely the most prestigious in its home state but also among the "best" in the country, given its AAU membership (and, given the stature of US higher education, among the most illustrious in the entire world), is not a school to be taken lightly. Its research improves the human condition; its teaching inspires leaders; its reputation attracts undergraduates, graduate and professional students, and postdoctoral students from throughout the world. Does anyone want to give that up?

Let us offer an analogy. In 1990, Yale University announced it would be closing its flagship literary journal, the *Yale Review*. When shepherding its resources to deal with deferred maintenance and other issues, it seemed that money could be much better spent elsewhere rather than on a journal reaching a relatively small audience at a very high cost per reader.[29] Yale president Benno Schmidt observed that the humanities might be better served by "a position for an additional poet or novelist in residence."[30] Schmidt also cited a concern on the part of the faculty that "the *Review* does not serve effectively as a vehicle for the writing of the Yale faculty"—a concern that

---

29. Circulation had been steadily declining, and advertising revenue was scarce, so the university subsidy had been steadily increasing. See Alex S. Jones, "Yale's President Orders the Closing of Its *Review*," *New York Times*, June 29, 1990, http://www.nytimes.com/1990/06/29/arts/yale-s-president-orders-the-closing-of-its-review.html; and Alex S. Jones, "The *Yale Review* Wins a Reprieve: A New Life," *New York Times*, August 5, 1991, http://www.nytimes.com/1991/08/05/arts/the-yale-review-wins-a-reprieve-a-new-life.html.

30. Jones, 1990.

suggests a division regarding its very purpose: to publish the best writing or to help Yale faculty publish. These two conflicting goals have also led to difficulties at university presses. If we are talking about the efficient allocation of scarce resources, the question again turns on what goals one hopes to be efficient at achieving.

A committee formed to save the *Review* argued that an interesting temporal asymmetry obtains here. It is easy to close an old journal, but one cannot create an old journal. One can always bring in a poet in residence for a semester, but if in the future Yale wanted to have a literary magazine, it could not re-create what it had: all it could do was start a new magazine, which would necessarily lack the tradition and ethos of the one closed. The *Yale Review*, the oldest literary quarterly in the United States, traces its roots to 1819 and was founded in its current form in 1911. It has published a variety of famous writers, including Henry Adams, Thomas Mann, H. G. Wells, Leon Trotsky, Virginia Woolf, H. L. Mencken, Wallace Stevens, William Butler Yeats, Robert Frost, and Eudora Welty. Closing it entails losing that history. Wouldn't it be better to cut something that could easily be restored? If one demolishes a historical building, one cannot at a future date decide to have it there again.

In Tolstoy's *Anna Karenina*, an elderly landowner tells Levin how a neighbor offered him sound economic reasons why he should cut down his old lime trees and use the capital more profitably. But the landowner and Levin understand that you can easily cut down old trees but cannot re-create them. Asked why he defies his economic self-interest, the landowner can only say that he "feels a duty to the land," by which he means an ethical obligation to tradition.[31] As this phrasing suggests, the argument has also often been used in environmental con-

---

31. See Leo Tolstoy, *Anna Karenina*, the Garnett translation revised by Leonard J. Kent and Nina Berberova (Modern Library, 1965), pp. 686–687 (part VI, chapter 29).

texts. You can chop down the cherry orchard to build profit-able summer cottages, but you cannot easily restore it or the forms of life it nourished (that is the theme of Chekhov's play, *The Cherry Orchard*). Environmentalism, a respect for tradition, and a concern with reversibility are closely linked. It is hard to find anyone in America who defends an aristocracy of birth, which we have never had. But a traditional argument, favored by Levin in Tolstoy's novel, is precisely that you need someone who does not think in terms of economic efficiency in its usual sense but instead takes a longer view, extending over generations, which a class of capitalists is neither inclined nor equipped to hold.

Something similar happens with the best flagship universities. If a world-class chemistry department is destroyed, it is almost impossible to re-create it, and if the university at large is seriously degraded, the culture nurturing its great departments goes too. As anyone who has tried to change or create a deep-set culture knows, it is almost impossible to do so, for good or ill. If this reasoning is accepted, then our logic must go beyond the calculation of efficiency. The flagship university, if it is good enough, has an additional claim.

So what's a governor and state legislature to do?[32] An economist might be stymied. The less prestigious the school, the more likely it is to be populated with students who are vulnerable to price increases resulting from a reduction in state funding. But the more prestigious the school, the more it has to lose in terms of reputed excellence. Perhaps the enrollment

32. For an illustrative discussion of what happens to a regional university when it experiences a dramatic decrease in state funding, see Kellie Woodhouse, "University of Wisconsin–Eau Claire Responds to Massive Cuts in State Support," *Inside Higher Education*, July 29, 2015. The article reports that, as a result of a two-year $250 million cut in the overall state allocation to Wisconsin's public higher education system, along with a tuition freeze, the Eau Claire campus ended up with a total of $22.1 million in state support (out of its $82.2 million operating budget) for the 2015–16 academic year, as opposed to $29.8 million in state support the year before. In order to decrease its expenditures, it has announced a plan to cut at least 11 percent of its faculty and staff.

consideration matters more if the flagship school isn't operating on the world stage—that is, it is not an AAU member.
But if it is, there is much more reason to keep it flourishing,
regardless of the fact that its students are virtually certain to be
substantially more affluent relative to others attending public
colleges and universities in that state.

And so we have more than one imperative here. This is a
question that no formula can solve but requires judgment.
If one is thinking of keeping as many students in college as
possible, one supports the community colleges. Likewise, if
helping the poor is one's highest goal, that leads to the same
conclusion, unless research discoveries from well-supported
flagship universities play a major role in fighting poverty. But
it may be that those who would benefit the most from a world-
class university, and who may be somewhat better off economically, should count more than their numbers since one would
be giving them an opportunity that might not otherwise exist.
And society as a whole might benefit more by educating those
who get the most out of it and by sponsoring research not
done at community colleges and regional universities. And as
the example of the *Yale Review* or the landowner's lime trees
suggests, reversibility matters. While a decline in community
college or midtier funding can easily be restored when money
is available, one cannot so easily rebuild a great university.
Economic considerations here are relevant but not enough.
What's more, in different circumstances, hard or impossible
to specify in advance, good judgment might arrive at different
answers.

We conclude this discussion with one more thought. When
states cut back on allocations to flagship universities, many
institutions seek to make up for those losses by increasing
their percentage of out-of-state undergraduates. It makes
sense for the schools—those students usually pay a sticker
price far in excess of charges for state residents. But there is
a problem here: all students are typically subsidized, that is,

even out-of-state full payers contribute less than the full cost of educating them. So the taxpayers in Michigan are subsidizing residents of, say, California when students leave Los Angeles to be educated in Ann Arbor. Not only that, those Californians take seats that would otherwise go to Michigan residents. And some of those displaced Michigan students end up at less prestigious state schools, displacing still other potential college students. Is the state therefore really better off reallocating operating subsidies from the Ann Arbor campus to other tiers, in the name of providing an education to the largest number of residents? Perhaps not.

Again, there is no easy answer here. It would be nice if the great Russian novels solved all our problems! But what one gets from them is not the answers but a deeper appreciation of the questions. We are still left with economic arguments and data, and questions of fairness that take economists far from their comfort zones.

The Federal Interest in Enrollment, Completion, and Matching

It is not surprising that college enrollment and completion loom large on our nation's federal agenda. While the economic return from a college degree is at or near record levels, we are falling further behind other developed countries in college attainment.[33]

As mentioned previously, economists know quite a bit about the enrollment response to changes in net prices—the price elasticity of demand is high for students from low-income backgrounds, but the responsiveness drops precipitously as income rises. This, of course, is not surprising. Even the most talented students from modest backgrounds, despite high potential returns from higher education investments, suffer

33. Both points are discussed in chapter 10 in *The Fabulous Future?*

from the classic problem of imperfections in capital markets. That is, while they would earn a substantial financial return should they obtain a bachelor's degree, they don't have the collateral to borrow money to make the initial investment. Hence, it isn't surprising that economists tend to focus on increasing federal, state, and institutional financial aid, thereby lowering the net price needy students face.

But it is clear that price isn't all that matters. In recent years we have learned about a variety of "noneconomic" factors that play a role in whether students go to college and, if they do, which colleges they choose. And we have learned this not just from the traditional analyses economists perform but from other types of studies as well. As you will see, this is an excellent example of how effective policies can be developed by supplementing an economist's models and empirical techniques with qualitative investigations, and insights suggested by great literature.

As a case study, let's focus on public high school students in Chicago. A superb paper by Melissa Roderick and Jenny Nagaoka is highly instructive in this regard.[34] Roderick and Nagaoka start off with a shocking fact—while 83 percent of Chicago public high school (CPS) graduates report that they aspire to a four-year college degree or higher, simulations by the authors suggest that only 15 percent will eventually obtain one. Even more striking is the case of African American males: 87 percent want a degree; 9 percent get one. There must be more at work here than affordability.

The authors examine high school grades, and some of this puzzle unfolds. Thirty-five percent of CPS graduates leave high school with a grade point average (GPA) below 2.0 in their core courses, and another 24 percent have a GPA between 2.0

34. Melissa Roderick and Jenny Nagaoka, "Increasing College Access and Graduation among Chicago Public High School Graduates," in *College Success: What It Means and How to Make It Happen*, Michael S. McPherson and Morton Owen Schapiro, editors (College Board, 2008), pp. 19–66.

and 2.5. Hence, 59 percent of CPS graduates have such weak high school records that college success is surely a distant dream. In fact, the average unweighted GPA in core classes for all CPS graduates is only 2.33. Returning to the case of African American males, the disconnect between aspirations and reality is even clearer—56 percent graduate with a GPA below 2.0 and an additional 24 percent with a GPA in their core courses between 2.0 and 2.5. The average GPA in core courses for all African American male CPS graduates is 1.97.[35]

Given the strong relationship between standardized test scores, race, and income, the challenges low high school grades present in gaining college admission are, not surprisingly, compounded by low ACT scores. Sixty-five percent of CPS graduates (and 75 percent of African American males) score 18 or below on the ACT (equivalent to 870 out of 1600 on the SAT).[36]

The problem here isn't merely the price many CPS graduates would face in college; it is the fact that many are academically unprepared for further education. Perhaps community colleges remain a viable option (where a good portion of the education is aimed at high school remediation) but certainly not a selective college or university or, in many cases, even a nonselective four-year institution.

But what about the strongest performers among these graduates? Here the story unfolds in a fascinating way. Using standard econometric analysis, the authors find that CPS graduates with a 3.5 to 4.0 GPA in their core courses have an 81 percent chance of going to college. But do they go to a selective or very selective college or university or, in the parlance of higher education policy, do they "undermatch"?

35. And this is among the students who actually graduate high school—beginning with a cohort of African American males in the ninth grade, only around half of them get a high school degree.

36. The authors report that the national average for college-bound students is around 21 (990 out of 1600 on the SAT).

The authors focus on those CPS graduates who have the grade point average, ACT score, and coursework that would allow them to attend either a selective school or a very selective one. Let's focus here on the very selective category. Only 3.6 percent of all CPS graduates are eligible by these criteria (the number falls to just 1 percent for African American males). Surely these few extraordinary students avail themselves of this opportunity, no?

Alas, most do not. Fourteen percent of these elite students didn't attend any college after high school graduation; 31 percent enrolled at a school far below the selectivity for which they were qualified; 22 percent enrolled at a school somewhat below their proper match; and just 33 percent matched at the appropriate level. This deserves greater emphasis: there are relatively few CPS graduates who have the high school performance and standardized test scores to attend virtually any "great" college or university in the country; two-thirds of them throw away that opportunity and undermatch, some going to no college at all.

Perhaps, the authors ask, these students are choosing to be "big fish in a small pond," attending less selective schools where they are sure to thrive. If this is their reasoning, it is unfounded. Roderick and Nagaoka simulate the graduation probabilities these top students would face at different schools, and the results are shocking. Here is one example that strikes very close to home: the simulations suggest that CPS graduates with a 4.0 GPA have a 97 percent chance of graduating within six years from Northwestern University (a very selective institution) versus only a 29 percent chance if they attended Northeastern Illinois University (a nonselective institution). Why does college choice matter so critically? Shouldn't the best prepared students be able to succeed regardless of the college option they select? You might think so, but this illuminating application of empirical techniques shows decisively that you would be wrong. As the authors state: "While it is clear that improving students' preparation for college is an essential step for increasing college access and degree attainment, the gains from these efforts can be rendered meaningless if students are not given the support they need to make good college choices."[37] "And, too many CPS students enroll in colleges that are less selective than they are qualified to attend, suggesting that they actually could have worked less in high school and ended up at the same colleges."[38] In explaining why this is the case, they cite the work of sociologist James Rosenbaum, whose interviews with high school students provide important insights that augment economic analysis in a very helpful way.

Rosenbaum's qualitative studies address a number of the questions Roderick and Nagaoka raise.[39] What is of particular interest here is the undermatching of "the best and the brightest" from CPS. In a series of papers with his various coauthors, Rosenbaum gains critical understanding into what high school students are thinking by actually asking them. While economists might shudder at the idea of engaging with your data in this way, sociologists, here acting like humanists, fortunately think differently!

We focus here on one of these papers.[40] The authors explore why it is that many more students from low socioeconomic status (SES) backgrounds aspire to college than actually go. Are the main barriers poor academic skills and a lack of financial resources, or is there more going on here? And why do high-performing, low-income students often select colleges and universities that enroll students with average academic characteristics far below their own?

37. Roderick and Nagaoka, p. 62.

38. Roderick and Nagaoka, p. 63.

39. See, for example, James Rosenbaum, *Beyond College for All: Career Paths for the Forgotten Half* (Russell Sage Foundation, 2001).

40. James Rosenbaum, Kelly Hallberg, Jennifer Stephan, Lisbeth Goble, and Michelle Naffziger, "Institutional Assumptions in the College Application Process in High- and Low-SES High Schools," Institute for Policy Research, Northwestern University.

Their interviews took place at two high schools in the Chicago area: a large high school located in an affluent suburb and a slightly smaller one located within the city of Chicago. Enrollment at the first school reflects the local community—it is 80 percent Caucasian and few students come from disadvantaged backgrounds. The other school is racially and ethnically diverse (54 percent of its students are Hispanic, 18 percent are Caucasian, 14 percent are African American, and 13 percent are Asian American), and 84 percent of its students come from families poor enough to qualify their children for free or subsidized lunch.

Students were asked about their high school experiences and about their aspirations and practices in terms of applying to college. The authors found that high SES students could barely imagine not going to college. They see college "as the inevitable next step in their personal and academic development."[41] On the other hand, while students from low SES backgrounds express similar hopes for attending and completing college, they are much less confident that they will in fact attend college and view investment in college as a risky proposition.

Importantly, the authors found that low and high SES students see the hierarchy of higher education institutions very differently. Students from more privileged economic backgrounds view even small differences in institutional selectivity as being critical. For them, attending the most selective school possible is an important criterion in choosing a college. However, low SES students see all colleges as being pretty much the same—a college is a college is a college.[42]

---

41. Rosenbaum et al., p. 5.

42. While proclamations such as those from President Obama that "more students should go to college" are laudable, they might just contribute to the confusion about the fact that colleges differ greatly in producing educational outcomes. Colleges are not commodities, that is, not goods or services that are undifferentiated by quality.

High SES students carefully collect information from college guidebooks, guidance counselors, friends, and family members in selecting "reach" and "safety" schools.[43] They use their high school's computer software program to learn where past graduates with similar test scores and grades were admitted, rejected, or placed on the wait list. In other words, they are very sophisticated consumers.

Low SES students are not. There is no talk of "reach" or "safety" schools and little understanding of the degree to which colleges and universities differ in prestige. The authors quote one student as saying, "I don't think that it makes a difference because if you're a good smart student, it doesn't matter which school you go to or which university."[44] Not surprisingly, low SES students not only didn't use any sophisticated computer programs, they had little wise advice from counselors, friends, and family. In one case, a college access program encouraged a student to apply to very selective schools based on his stellar record in high school. He did not. Why? He reported, "I got explained through a relative that it doesn't really matter what college you go to."[45] The authors point out that low SES students are most trusting of their family members, and that many of these relatives had limited college experiences and those who had attended college were less than successful there. Maybe that is why so many low SES students think all colleges are the same—they hear little from trusted sources who ever graduated from a selective school.

There are other considerations in play. While high SES students prefer distant colleges to those that are local, low SES students say they would rather not be separated from family and neighborhood friends. Most of them plan to live at

43. In doing so, they might want to read the section on enrollment management that came earlier in this chapter!

44. Rosenbaum et al., p. 12.

45. Rosenbaum et al., p. 12.

home while attending college, not just to save money but to assist their families. The authors speculate that this strong bias toward local colleges among low SES students might result from their having had limited travel opportunities and little if any chance to live apart from their families during summers and the like. Some, they say, also fear racial discrimination should they leave their local environment.

The authors conclude that programs and reforms aimed at increasing college preparedness for low-income students are very important. But they alone will not solve the problem, especially when it comes to undermatching. Returning to the empirical analysis from Roderick and Nagaoka, no wonder only one of three stellar CPS students enroll at a college that is "appropriate" for them—those highly prestigious schools are typically located outside their neighborhoods, meaning a separation from family and friends. Why would they risk that if all colleges are thought to be the same?

The study by Roderick and Nagaoka laid out a set of perplexing questions; the study by Rosenbaum and colleagues helped point to the answers. Using the results from both, we are much more likely to develop effective policies.

The work of two economists, Caroline Hoxby and Sarah Turner, does exactly that.[46] They have determined that the principal problem with the underenrollment of talented low-income high school students isn't at the admissions or the matriculation stage, it is at the application stage—they would

46. For a summary of their work, see Caroline H. Hoxby and Sarah Turner, "What High-Achieving Low-Income Students Know about College," *American Economic Review: Papers & Proceedings* 2015, 105(5), pp. 514–517. There is a growing literature on undermatching, especially among high-achieving African American and Hispanic students. See, for example, two articles by Sandra E. Black, Kalena E. Cortes, and Jane Arnold Lincove, "Academic Undermatching of High-Achieving Minority Students: Evidence from Race-Neutral and Holistic Admissions Policies," *American Economic Review: Papers & Proceedings* 2015, 105(5), pp. 604–610, and "Apply Yourself: Racial and Ethnic Differences in College Application," National Bureau of Economic Research Working Paper 21368, July 2015.

get into good schools and enroll there if only they applied to them in the first place.

Their Expanding College Opportunities project relies on a randomized controlled trial, the kind of analysis that is more common in medical than economic research. Their interventions are exactly the type suggested by Rosenbaum's work: they provide low-income high achievers with information on applying to colleges, the prices they would face at various schools, and how schools differ in terms of graduation rates and instructional expenditures. Application fees were waived and all materials were customized to meet the circumstances of individual students and their families.

The results were remarkable: 48 percent more students from the treated group applied to college versus the control population; and they were 56 percent more likely to apply to a top school that was appropriate for them based on their excellent high school performance.[47] They also discovered some other important information based on their surveys. These students were underrepresented at liberal arts colleges. Why? They had little understanding of what these schools had to offer. When asked why they didn't apply to a liberal arts college, their responses included the following:[48] "I am not liberal." "I don't like art/art related subjects." "Liberal arts is for people who aren't good at math." What about the fact that so many of them failed to apply to the state's flagship university? Surprisingly, few said that the reason was a reluctance to leave the neighborhood. Instead, they talked about nonacademic characteristics that they found to be off-putting: "Too much party and not enough academics." "I was not interested in attending an institution with such a sports-centered atmosphere." The authors

---

47. Note, however, that their sample is restricted to high-achieving low-income students. What to do with the rest of the low-income cohort is quite another question.

48. These quotes can be found in Hoxby and Turner (2015), pp. 516 and 517.

conclude that individual survey responses are an important way to understand human behavior.

The humanist among us does not view these findings as surprising, and his thought process suggests other policies to adopt. What strikes a humanist most readily is the importance of something economics tends to forget: culture. Economic models—whether mainstream, behavioral, or neuro—typically leave out culture because culture cannot be quantified, specified in a lab experiment, or discovered in neurons.[49] And yet it is essential to what people are. As we argue in chapter 7 when we discuss the work of the philosopher John Rawls, to think of people apart from culture is not to think of people at all. People may belong to different cultures, but they all belong to some culture, just as they all speak some language. We are not just biological organisms.

And so the first question that occurs to a humanist when thinking of poor students applying to colleges is not just income but, more importantly, cultural difference. When F. Scott Fitzgerald remarked that "the rich are different from us," his friend Ernest Hemingway allegedly replied, "Yes, they have more money." But most humanists would regard Fitzgerald as in the right and Hemingway as seduced by the opportunity for a witticism. The entire history of the realist novel suggests that the rich differ in culture as well as income.

Balzac devoted his many novels to exploring the countless social gradations of France: he was concerned to delineate differences in status, region, occupation, and myriad other ever-changing aspects of culture. He showed the immensely various ways people think, the feelings they experience, the temptations they face, and the moral standards they take for granted. Realism, indeed, is about the difference that such differences make. They shape one's experiences of the world, the choices one makes, and the very sense of what life is all about.

49. We celebrate some of the exceptions in chapter 7.

And so a standard plot of a realist novel concerns a young person from the provinces, like Dickens's Pip or Balzac's Rastignac, coming to the capital to make his or her way. Or perhaps a young woman comes from a less-well-placed background and, like Charlotte Brontë's heroines, serves as a governess to a culturally different rich family or a teacher in a school for the well-off. These heroes and heroines must negotiate a different culture. Bewildered and tempted by different values, and perhaps losing their bearings or committing acts they later regret, they grow up, mature, and become wiser in the process. With Henry James, the plot may concern Americans and Europeans, with all of America being a "province." Variants on this plot are used not only by Balzac and James but also by Turgenev, Dostoevsky, and countless others who explore people in terms of their culture and illuminate cultures by having different ones interact.

There is an old saw that the European novel can be summed up in the titles of two of its best-known works, *Great Expectations* and *Lost Illusions*. And since Dickens uses the term "great expectations" ironically, the two titles turn out to mean pretty much the same thing. So when one thinks of a student from a culturally deprived background attending an Ivy League or similar school, one thinks of Pip going to London or Rastignac to Paris; and one understands the reluctance to do so and the difficulties one might encounter.

Here are three real stories of our own. One concerns an African American young man who was valedictorian of his Chicago high school. No one in his family had ever gone to college, and his school had no guidance counselor with experience to help seniors in his situation. He had the record, drive, and personal characteristics that would have earned him a scholarship to attend a highly selective school, but he wound up taking out large loans to attend a private trade school— a good and respected one but not at all commensurate with what he could have attended. He knew that with a degree from that school in a technical field he would get a decent job, and in fact he did. But he did not come close to achieving his academic potential.

A second story concerns a Polish American young woman from a working-class home in Chicago. Exceptionally bright and academically accomplished, she was admitted both to a local nonselective college and to a top Ivy university. She chose the former because, as she explained, at the Ivy, everyone would laugh at her accent and her choice of words. Despite her remarkable command of written formal English and high verbal SAT score, she spoke like other people in her neighborhood and would have thought it a betrayal to speak differently. With relatively conservative social values, she feared that her beliefs would lead to ridicule. She had already seen a friend of deep religious faith mocked at a selective school. Why should she subject herself to that?

A third concerns a young woman from a rural community whose family presumed that with her good grades she would attend a Christian college they knew. The student was aware that her record might have earned her admission and financial aid at a much more prestigious institution, but a visit to that illustrious school's campus, and attentive reading of its materials, convinced her that the school had no place for someone with her mores and beliefs.

Each of these stories would make a good novel. A writer would sketch the counterfactual and imagine the student actually attending the prestigious college and finding himself or herself at sea. The most basic assumptions about what academic life is, how to select courses, and what norms govern life in dorms or social settings, would be foreign. A good novelist might show fellow students or professors, with no ill intent, speaking as if anyone with religious or traditional beliefs must be stupid. For all their professed concern with the underprivileged, they would be unaware that their attitudes reflected institutional practices in which the rich reproduce themselves not only economically but culturally, and include others only insofar as they abandon their previous culture and values. Those who do not suffer constant, if unintended, insults—or as we would say today, microaggressions. Is it any wonder, then, that if these experiences become known, many other students remain "undermatched"?

In different ways, these stories suggest that culture matters. The sort of concerns that would not be caught in an analysis of quantifiable factors but might appear in "thickly described narratives" could give a clue as to what is going on. These narratives might make us uncomfortable in the way equations would not. As every good novelist knows, but most of us usually forget, people tend to assume that other people think the way they do—how else could one think? They are therefore unable to put themselves in the position of those unlike themselves. They imagine poor people to be rich people without money, not the way great novels portray them.[50] They do not imagine what potential applicants to their school may be assuming or not know.

By the same token, people surrounding themselves with others who think as they do have difficulty imagining an intelligent, well-intentioned person who thinks differently. Wittingly or not, they may convey the message that such people are evil or absurd. The narrower the set of values entertained and entertainable by our major educational institutions, the less empathetic they become of the population at large and the more they wind up turning themselves into training grounds for one social group to maintain its preeminence. That is so

---

50. The essential idea of Dostoevsky's first published work of fiction, the novella *Poor People*, is that poverty is not just economic but is also a cultural, and above all, a psychological fact. While the social commentators of his day (and since) have tended to think of poverty in purely economic terms, and think of wholly economic remedies, Dostoevsky enabled his readers to get inside the minds and the souls of the poor and to see what really goes on there.

even among those who imagine that is the last thing they would want to do.

Where does that leave standard economic methods and analyses that are supposed to underpin effective educational policies? We think, needing more.

That gets us back to the Hoxby/Turner paper. Two economists try to develop a set of interventions designed to serve talented, low-income students in a way that no policy has thus far succeeded in doing. And how do they inform and present their work? By quoting from study participants. In an economics journal! Here the power of economics, combined with the approaches of other disciplines, produces government policies that are much more likely to meet their intended aims. What an excellent example of what can happen when we move beyond our disciplinary biases!

Chapter 4

Love Is in the Air ...
or at Least in the Error Term

Case Study 2—What Economists Can and
Cannot Teach Us about the Family

Indeed, I have come to the position that
the economic approach is a comprehensive
one that is applicable to all human behavior.

—Gary Becker[1]

Our guess is that even the staunchest critics of economic "imperialism"—the idea that economics provides *the* model for all social sciences—wouldn't have much trouble with the economics of higher education as discussed in the previous chapter. Sure, they might question some of our conclusions, or argue that other disciplines could contribute even more in determining optimal policy than we suggest. But the application of economic theory and empirical techniques in understanding topics such as how students choose colleges and how governments might better allocate funds to increase

1. Gary S. Becker, *The Economic Approach to Human Behavior* (University of Chicago Press, 1976), p. 8. We also draw on his pathbreaking 1981 book, *A Treatise on the Family*, cited here as Gary S. Becker, *A Treatise on the Family*, enlarged edition, (Harvard University Press, 1991).

enrollment is, for the most part, safely within the sweet spot of the economic discipline.

In this chapter it gets highly personal. Whom do you marry (and divorce)? How many kids should you have? If economics can explain these choices, perhaps it *can* explain everything!

That is exactly the view of one of the most influential economists of all time, Gary Becker. When he received the Nobel Prize in 1992, the Nobel committee cited his "having extended the domain of microeconomic analysis to a wide range of human behaviour and interaction, including nonmarket behaviour." And extend it he did—from his seminal work on racial discrimination to his insights on crime to perhaps his most important contribution, the economics of the family.

We read Becker as the ultimate hedgehog. He seems to be saying that all other social sciences can be better understood in economic terms. They are really economic problems in disguise. As with many hedgehogs, a great deal of his appeal lies in the excitement that such a comprehensive view provides. He is offering a kind of "market Marxism," a key to all disciplines. And so his pronouncements are thrilling. What had previously seemed complex and obscure is now revealed to be simple and clear.

Becker is far from the only social thinker to have advanced such claims. Just as Newton demonstrated that the amazingly complex motion of the planets could be explained by a few simple laws, many have felt that the same must be true of all human behavior. One need only find the equivalent laws. The historian of ideas Élie Halévy therefore referred to such social thinkers as "moral Newtonians." They have a strong tendency to model their theories on physics and use lots of mathematics to express it. Auguste Comte, who coined the term "sociology," originally planned to call his new discipline "social physics." Léon Walras, a founder of modern economics, sought to base the laws of economic equilibrium on those that he supposed ensured the stability of the solar system, and he wrote to the greatest mathematician of the day, Henri Poincaré, to garner his support. The title of his last paper was "Économique et Mécanique."[2] Even cultural anthropology was smitten with moral Newtonianism. Its modern founder, Bronislaw Malinowski, deemed anthropologists capable of discovering social laws that would forever banish the concept of "adventitious and fortuitous happenings" and allow for "prediction of the future."[3] Closer to our time, the French anthropologist Claude Lévi-Strauss enthused about the ability of social scientists, following the structuralist model, to formulate a table of human possibilities "that would be comparable to the table of elements which Mendeleieff introduced into modern chemistry." Looking at such a table, we would "discover the place of languages that have disappeared or are unknown, yet to come, or simply possible."[4]

Social hedgehogs typically use the language of novelty and totality. The discoverer of the new method is an intellectual Columbus. He has found a new, unexpected world. "I named the process *repression*; it was a novelty, and nothing like it had ever before been recognized in mental life," wrote Freud.[5] It is easy enough to find such language in Marx, Bentham, Lenin, and Skinner. Becker finds his place in an important tradition:

> The heart of my argument is that human behavior is not compartmentalized, sometimes based on maximizing, sometimes not, sometimes motivated by stable preferences, sometimes by volatile ones, sometimes resulting in an optimal accumulation of information, sometimes not. Rather, all human behavior can be viewed as involving participants who maximize their

2. See Stephen Toulmin, "The Physics That Never Was," *Return to Reason* (Harvard University Press, 2001), p. 58.

3. Bronislaw Malinowski, *A Scientific Theory of Culture and Other Essays* (University of North Carolina Press, 1944), p. 8.

4. Claude Lévi-Strauss, *Structural Anthropology*, trans. Claire Jacobson and Brooke Grundfest Schoepf (Basic Books, 1963), p. 58.

5. Sigmund Freud, *An Autobiographical Study*, as cited in *The Macmillan Book of Social Science Quotations*, ed. David L. Sills and Robert K. Merton (Macmillan, 1991), p. 70.

utility from a stable set of preferences and accumulate an optimal amount of information and other inputs in a variety of
markets. If this argument is correct, the economic approach
provides a unified framework for understanding behavior that
has long been sought by and eluded Bentham, Comte, Marx,
and others. (*Economic Approach*, p. 14)

In his view, Becker has actually achieved what those giants
claimed to have achieved.

In principle, the economic model can explain everything
in human behavior. To be sure, Becker allows that the economic approach "has not provided equal insight into and
understanding of all kinds of human behavior: for example,
the determinants of war and many other political decisions
have not yet been much illuminated by this approach (or by
any other approach)." But that is only because "the economic
approach has not been systematically applied to war, and its
application to other kinds of political behavior is quite recent"
(*Economic Approach*, p. 9). This is the "young science" argument we mentioned in chapter 1.

Like Malinowski and other moral Newtonians, Becker
reacts with scorn to the very idea that anything is to be attributed to "luck or chance" rather than to our "ignorance of
or inability to measure additional systematic components"
(*Economic Approach*, p. 12). If one cites an apparently chance
event, Becker replies that it simply has not been explained yet.
Of course, such a view makes counterevidence impossible.

Becker is aware that postulating costs or other economic
factors when equations do not account for what is happening
risks making his argument "tautological," but, after all, even in
physics, "postulating the existence of (sometimes unobserved)
uses of energy completes the energy system, and preserves
the law of the conservation of energy" (*Economic Approach*,
p. 7), so he is only following the practice of physicists. The
problem with this reasoning is that the conservation of energy
has already been established as a physical law on quite other

grounds, and while physics has proved its status as a hard predictive science, that is precisely what Becker is trying to prove for economics. He is not entitled to prove scientific status with arguments based on its already having been proven. This sort of tautology is characteristic of hedgehogs. Indeed, however slack the logic, it may often be forgiven when, generally speaking, the light shed by the theory is strong enough.

Becker expresses scorn for "sociology, psychology, or anthropology" when, "with an ingenuity worthy of admiration if put to better use," they account for "almost any conceivable behavior" by resorting to "ignorance and irrationality, values and their frequent unexplained shifts, custom and tradition, the compliance somehow induced by social norms, or the ego and the id" (*Economic Approach*, p. 13). In his view, the frivolous tendency of such disciplines to reach for such ad hoc explanations whenever convenient simply cannot compete with the economic approach that, with a single model, explains everything.

It would therefore seem that culture (custom and tradition), specifically sociological factors (social norms), and individual psychology ("the ego and the id") are no longer needed. In effect, they represent a sort of prescientific phase of understanding human behavior, a phase now superseded. But Becker does allow for other disciplines to play some role. He explains: "Just as many noneconomic variables are necessary for understanding human behavior, so too are the contributions of sociologists, psychologists, sociobiologists, historians, anthropologists, political scientists, lawyers, and others. Although I am arguing that the economic approach provides a useful framework for understanding all human behavior, I am not trying to downgrade the contributions of other social scientists, nor even to suggest that the economist's are more important" (*Economic Approach*, p. 14). This statement, appearing near the end of the essay we have just been citing, would seem to contradict what Becker has already said. Is it a mere throwaway concession?

Not exactly. Becker hastens to clarify what he means by it. "At the same time," he immediately continues, "I do not want to soften the impact of what I am saying in the interest of increasing its acceptability in the short run." The economic approach does indeed "provide a valuable unified framework for understanding *all* human behavior" (*Economic Approach*, p. 14, emphasis in the original). Nevertheless, economic decisions are made in a world where noneconomic factors have set the field in which choices are made. "Obviously, the laws of mathematics, chemistry, physics and biology have a tremendous influence on behavior through their influence on preferences and production possibilities. That the human body ages, that the rate of population growth equals the birth rate plus the migration rate minus the death rate, that children of more intelligent parents tend to be more intelligent than children of less intelligent parents, that people need to breathe to live … or that an assembly line operates according to certain physical laws—all these and more influence choices, the production of people and goods, and the evolution of societies" (*Economic Approach*, p. 13).

As for the other social sciences, Becker allows that they may contribute to determining what people's stable preferences, which the economic approach assumes are in place, might be and how they have come about. "For example, the preferences that are given and stable in the economic approach, and that determine the predictions from this approach, are analyzed by the sociologist, psychologist, and probably most successfully by the sociobiologist" (*Economic Approach*, p. 14). Notice how even when Becker allows for culture and psychology he immediately favors a hard science that bypasses culture and individuals, since sociobiology deals with facts true of humanity as a species, not of Poles or Khmer, Ivan or Rachel. The best other disciplines can do is set from outside the ground within which the economic approach works; but where the two can offer competing explanations, the explanations offered by other social sciences can survive only until a superior economic explanation is formulated.

Nevertheless, it is possible to soften Becker's arguments, or, as Stephen Toulmin describes this approach to hedgehogs, to "escape distortions by 'de-universalizing' them" (Toulmin, p. 60). Such a "soft Becker" position would hold that in every sphere of human action, even apparently noneconomic ones, it would pay to consider an economic approach. That is, the economic approach may or may not add something significant, but it is always worth trying. What look like purely cultural, political, or sociological facts may also be shaped in part by overlooked economic factors, or factors best understood by an economic approach.

This would be a fox's way of appropriating hedgehog insights, and one we tend to favor. It avoids a characteristic hedgehog error, the confusion of *universality* with *totality*. An explanation can be applicable everywhere without being very important anywhere, or in very few places. But when universality applies, it is tempting to leap, let us say, from "everything has a historical dimension" (since everything that happens, by definition, happens in history) to "historians have the key to everything." Or, framed in another context, because everything expressed is in language, and literary scholars best understand language and its uses, literary analysis must dominate all fields (the so-called linguistic turn in many disciplines). The problem is that many other fields may have as much or more to say about everything human, and each may find it tempting to leap to the conclusion that it enjoys priority over the others.

A soft Becker approach allows one to grasp what is valuable in his insights even when his language is off-putting to noneconomists. Our argument is that soft Becker has a lot to offer, but hard Becker is flawed from a variety of viewpoints, especially those best understood by the humanities. That does not change the fact that humanists might still learn something from it.

Do Preferences Change?

Let's examine Becker's argument more closely. While he dramatically expanded the reach of economics, he didn't do it by questioning the basic assumptions underlying economic study—"the economic approach does not take refuge in assertions about irrationality, contentment with wealth already acquired, or convenient ad hoc shifts in values (i.e., preferences)" (*Economic Approach*, p. 7). Perhaps it is the third assumption that humanists, among others, would find the most troubling. Stability in values means that "preferences are assumed not to change substantially over time, nor to be very different between wealthy and poor persons, or even between persons in different societies and cultures" (p. 5). Note again the importance of avoiding culture. But, some might cry out, "I used to love eating a good steak but now I only order fish—isn't that a change in preferences?"

An economist might offer two distinct answers. First, there may not have been a change in preference but rather a change in the relative prices of the two goods or a change in your income. Second, even if relative prices and income have not changed, that is not the sort of preference change the economic approach precludes. The preferences Becker assumes to be stable don't concern market goods and services but instead are preferences over "fundamental aspects of life, such as health, prestige, sensual pleasure, benevolence, or envy" (*Economic Approach*, p. 5). As indicated in the story about declining mortality rates in chapter 1, economists are highly skeptical of explanations that rely on preference shifts. So, as mentioned earlier, to say that a rise in birth rates results from people all of a sudden having a greater inherent appreciation for children is like saying a decline in mortality results from people all of a sudden having a smaller inherent appreciation for dying. Assuming stability in preferences "prevents the analyst from succumbing to the temptation of simply postulating the required shift in preferences to 'explain' all apparent contradictions to his predictions" (p. 5). If we fall into the trap of allowing everything to vary at once—prices, income, and tastes—we end up with "a bundle of empty tautologies" (p. 7).

What Becker has in mind is the lazy attempt to account for failed predictions by simply postulating changed preferences whenever they occur. That would result in "empty tautologies" because no theory could ever be disproven. If its predictions work, then the theory is *proven*; if they fail, the preferences have changed, but the theory is still right. Becker is surely correct to be suspicious of this kind of reasoning. And economists can show numerous examples of economic explanations for what look like shifts in preferences, so his caution is well taken. But a humanist would add that he should be equally suspicious when he makes a similar move for failed *economic* predictions, attributing them to "ignorance of or inability to measure additional systematic components" (*Economic Approach*, p. 12). Is not such thinking an "empty tautology"?

But isn't it possible that even fundamental preferences do change? Isn't that an empirical question, not one to be decided a priori? Becker makes a logical error here, common in many disciplines. Making a certain assumption enables a discipline, so the assumption is made. Then the discipline concludes that it has proven the assumption. In other words, if we do not assume X to be true, the discipline cannot proceed. Therefore, X must be true. Malinowski, for instance, insists that a science of anthropology is possible only if societies work with every part serving a survival function, not existing as a mere vestige from an earlier period. So there can be no such vestiges, or we would not be thinking scientifically.

In like manner, Becker says that unless we assume stable preferences we cannot do significant analysis; therefore, there must be stable preferences. One might as well say (as some people have) that unless one assumes punishment and reward in the afterlife, there will be much less restraint on crime;

therefore, there must be an afterlife. The need for something to be true is no argument that it is true. Otherwise, the Jehovah's Witness who argues that God must exist because you would be happier if you believed in him would have a good argument.

A humanist might continue that it is not necessary to assume preferences are all that stable. Couldn't economic analysis work if fundamental preferences changed slowly, over many years? Because they evidently do change. People mature. For millennia people have described the process of growing up and growing old in terms of shifts in fundamental values. Character changes in response to tragedy, life events, and everyday experience.

That, at any rate, is the fundamental assumption of the real-ist novel. As characters make choices and experience a world different from what they expected, gradually, and bit by tiny bit, their character shifts. Although one cannot identify any single moment as *the* moment of change, by the end of a long realist novel, the change is apparent. Indeed, that is one rea-son the novels of George Eliot and Tolstoy are so long, so that small changes can accumulate.

Becker is tacitly assuming a model of human beings simi-lar to that offered in some other literary genres, such as the adventure story. James Bond and Dick Tracy are always the same. Their fundamental preferences do not change. That is why it is possible to view Bond films or read Dick Tracy sto-ries in any order. In classic adventure novels, going back to the Hellenistic "Greek romances," it would be possible to scramble the order of the adventures without causing any perceivable incongruity. But you could not rearrange incidents in the lives of Jane Austen's Elizabeth Bennett or George Eliot's Dorothea Brooke because these heroines change. They would, at differ-ent stages of their life, react differently to a similar situation.

Becker's confidence in the widespread application of this approach was unwavering, as indicated in the quote that began this chapter. "For whatever its worth in evaluating this conclusion, let me indicate that I did not arrive at it quickly ... I applied the economic approach to fertility, education, the uses of time, crime, marriage, social interactions, and other 'sociological,' 'legal,' and 'political' problems. Only after long reflection on this work and the rapidly growing body of related work by others did I conclude that the economic approach was applicable to all human behavior" (*Economic Approach*, p. 8). And it is important to keep in mind that Becker wrote this line forty years ago, so the growing body of supporting work to which he alluded is much greater now, some of it done by Becker and his many coauthors and students but most by a range of economists using a variety of methodological approaches.

The Economics of the Intimate

But *all* human behavior?

What about deeply personal decisions, such as the selection of a life partner? One might assume that what is intimate is furthest from the marketplace and its logic, but that is why Becker chooses to show the opposite and why his success struck people so strongly. "Participants in marriage markets are assumed to have limited information about the utility they can expect with potential mates, mainly because of limited information about the traits of these mates" (*Treatise*, p. 325). So what do they do? They forecast based on "information on traits that are readily assessed—such as religion, education, family background, race, or appearance" (p. 326). And what if those forecasts turn out to be wrong? "A husband and wife would both consent to a divorce if, and only if, they both expected to be better off divorced" (p. 331). If one of the partners turns out to do better than his or her traits would indicate—earning more money in the marketplace, being a better parent, being healthier or better looking than expected—the other partner would of course be thrilled. But does that mean a more stable marriage? No. That would make the marriage more likely to dissolve since the person who aged and developed surprisingly well is no longer well matched: "the person with the better-than-expected traits should be matched with a 'better' person than his spouse, and she should be matched with a 'worse' person than he turns out to be" (p. 335).

So viewed, marriage and divorce seem so simple. "According to the economic approach, a person decides to marry when the utility expected from marriage exceeds that expected from remaining single or from additional search for a more suitable mate. Similarly, a married person terminates his (or her) marriage when the utility anticipated from becoming single or marrying someone else exceeds the loss in utility from separation" (*Economic Approach*, p. 10). One also has to include the costs in time and money of separation, and so raising or lowering such costs will also affect the divorce rate.

What about children? Ah, you mean "marital-specific capital." For Becker, children feature in the divorce decision in a straightforward way—if you are worried about the future of your marriage, you have fewer children, since "such capital is less valuable after a divorce" (*Treatise*, p. 329). In fact, "Expectations about divorce are partly self-fulfilling because a higher expected probability of divorce reduces investments in specific capital and thereby raises the actual probability" (p. 329). If you are not sure your marriage will last, you may not have children, and without children, the marriage is less likely to last.

Sounds harsh and so highly impersonal, but doesn't it make sense? Isn't marriage a prediction about the future? Doesn't having children make a divorce more traumatic? Here we sense that humanists would find all this much harder to swallow than economists. The language is off-putting, but it's not only the language. Where, they might ask, is love?

Becker doesn't ignore love nor think it is unimportant. Rather, he argues, "Since lasting love is not easily distinguished from momentary infatuations, little confidence would be attached to any direct assessment of love prior to marriage. Indirect assessments of love would be used instead; for example, education and background would be important in part because love is more easily developed and sustained between persons with similar education and backgrounds" (*Treatise*, p. 327).

A humanist might note that Becker's use of the passive voice—"little confidence would be attached"—seems designed to deny individual agency in favor of economic forces. But she might also be amazed at the assertion that because "lasting love is not easily distinguished from momentary infatuations, little confidence would be attached" to any assessment of love before marriage. Perhaps he means "should" rather than "would"? To a humanist, it would seem obvious that people do confuse infatuation with love and do place great weight on it before marriage. All of popular as well as high culture would seem to testify to that. "Where both deliberate, the love is slight:/ Who ever loved, that loved not at first sight?" wrote Marlowe. Shakespeare quotes the last line, and such love happens often in his plays, most obviously in *Romeo and Juliet*, where hero and heroine attach great confidence to their assessment of love. Not only much drama but also the many novels of adultery depend either on mistaking infatuation for love or actually loving that intensely, but in either case placing great confidence in the assessment.

Yes, Becker contends, some people fall hopelessly in love and, all things equal, get married despite a range of indicators that this economic model would suggest might doom the marriage to failure. Others do not marry, despite indicators suggesting the marriage would work well. But such counterexamples do not mean the economic model fails. It just means that the model can't (yet) explain every single individual decision. The model still works in the aggregate and offers good predictions statistically. This is a powerful argument.

Love makes people do all sorts of things; so does its absence. But Becker's point is that certain variables have predictable impacts on marriage and divorce—income and family background, for instance—and that love doesn't affect those variables. In other words, on the long list of items in the error term—things that affect the decisions you make over your lifetime but aren't easily measured (such as your relationship with your mother and whether you were popular in high school)— love is simply one more factor influencing behavior, but not in a measurable way.

An economist, as well as a humanist, might notice a problem in the explanation of "love is in the error term." The idea is that love does not affect the impact of the various independent variables, even if it explains why those variables don't account for every single case of why one person marries and another does not. But what if the error term is *most* of what is going on? What if, contrary to the way Becker analyzes the situation, the variables he mentions are a relatively minor factor?

It might just be true that the error term is enormous, in which case, sure, people marry based on a number of identifiable traits—family background, appearance, and the like. But if those variables explain only a small amount of the variation in marriage activities (who gets married and who doesn't), we aren't learning very much about human behavior. If so, Becker could be right about how his variables operate, all things being equal, and yet his analysis would hardly shape our picture of what is going on since no one denies those factors have *some* effect.

Whether Becker's variables play a large or a small role, a humanist, who is honest with herself, would need to concede the basic point here. One can hardly deny the existence of a "marriage market" and a "dating market," as the very coinage and use of the term "marriage market" would seem to indicate. And it is obvious that whole industries exist to increase one's value on that market, from cosmetics and plastic surgery to lingerie, trendy men's and women's clothing, weight loss and muscle building salons, Botox, and countless other ways to market oneself more effectively. Dating sites certainly seem to work like a market. And does anyone doubt that attractiveness and high income make one better able to choose a desirable partner? Not only is this point true but it is commonly accepted, even without Becker. What Becker has added to this common insight is, first, the rigorous use of it by applying several economic tools not familiar in everyday life and, second, the extension of the idea to aspects of married life to which it is not usually applied, such as children.

If we are dealing with "soft Becker," there isn't much to object to, assuming the specific applications are right; and since they are offered statistically, they can be tested empirically. All other things being equal, a given factor (say, income above a certain amount) changes incentives and outcomes by so much. Of course, those other things that are held equal may be most of the story.

A humanist might ask, what about the role of culture (discussed in detail in chapter 7)? Sociologists and anthropologists would be apoplectic about simply assuming culture away. Why people marry and why they have children surely depends importantly on the social context of their lives, and even if certain traits matter in general, they must matter differently across groups in a given society and across societies. For Becker, a well-educated heterosexual woman might seek a similarly educated man in the marriage market and (as explained later), given the opportunity cost of her time out of the labor force, might engage in a more goods-intensive rather than time-intensive production of the commodity that directly turns children into a source of satisfaction. That is, she might have fewer children, but invest more in each child. Perhaps that is true in the US context, but is it equally true in all societies?

A humanist would caution that if the same empirical test could be run in other cultures, or could have been run at earlier periods in Western culture, the result might have been quite different. The effect, say, of income or attractiveness might vary considerably. And the role of factors Becker cites might prove more or less important. Becker seems not to be aware that "marriage" and children are not understood the same way in different periods and cultures. In some, love does not matter at all. What's more, his market model presumes two parties who consent to be married, but in the early Middle Ages consent was not required. As George Duby has shown in his celebrated study of medieval marriage, the church fought a long battle for the principle that both parties had to agree to the marriage—a man could not just abduct a bride.[6] The agency of the partners, the value and meaning of the marriage, and the responsibility of fathers (in some cultures it is uncles) for children do not have to fit the American scene. And, of course, this country has always had a sizable portion of its population that has only recently come here after being raised in a culture with different norms. But Becker cannot take such variables into account, except to the extent that one can allow for varying preferences, because he has to rule culture out of court. As in many social sciences that try to universalize, what purports to be acultural is really the social scientist's culture presented as the human condition.

And yet even with that objection accepted, a good deal is left to Becker's model. If not the marrying parties, there must be *some* agents involved. And it is possible that some very different sort of market, but a market all the same, operates with them. And for soft Becker to be useful, that is all that's needed.

Importantly for Becker, and any social scientist, this analysis has numerous implications about behavior. Without the potential for falsification, the model is otherwise meaningless. Do people tend to select partners with similar traits as their own? Does the presence of children, all else equal, really lower the probability of divorce? And are marriages in fact more likely to dissolve not only when earnings and health fall short

6. George Duby, *Medieval Marriage: Two Models from Twelfth-Century France*, trans. Elborg Forster (Johns Hopkins University Press, 1991).

of expectations but also when they exceed them? All yes, or rather, yes in our culture as it works today.

But we find the most impressive support of the economic model (even if we remain somewhat skeptical) to be the following: If preferences change—people "grow apart" or long for the excitement of new romance—one would expect that marriages that end in divorce would do so after decades, rather than after a few years. In fact, most failed marriages end rather quickly, as predicted by Becker, whose analysis relies on the cost and use of information as a critical variable. Becker argues that it doesn't take very long for people to realize that the highly imperfect information on which they based their marriage decision was a poor predictor of marital satisfaction. Such factors as personality conflict and sexual incompatibility surface quickly, and so does the end of these marriages.

To be sure, a humanist might caution that the cost of information could be key, but one does not need to resort to anything beyond common sense. It does not take an economic model to predict that in a culture like ours, where love is often based on infatuation and marriage is based on love, there are going to be a lot of early disappointments when infatuation wears off. And in a culture that does not especially frown on divorce and makes it relatively easy, there are going to be a lot of early divorces. Becker writes as if the only alternative to an economic model would be an ad hoc resort to changing preferences, but that is not so.

One school of thought has argued that the key factor here is the culturally specific idea of "romantic love," as opposed to love based on everyday intimacy. The former is not compatible with marriage and leads to serial adultery, as the realist novels of adultery show. That, at any rate, is the argument of Denis de Rougement's renowned study of romance, *Love in the Western World*.[7] And it is also the central argument of *Anna Karenina*. If

---

7. Denis de Rougement, *Love in the Western World*, revised edition, trans. Montgomery Belgion (Harper and Row, 1974).

so, the problem may not lie in information, or not in information alone, but in culturally shaped values and expectations.

In some religious traditions, marriage is seen not as a contract but as a sacrament. Some of that thinking survives even among the nonreligious in our culture when they recognize that for a marriage to work they must truly commit themselves to it and, as it were, bind themselves to it, as in the story of Odysseus and the Sirens. If the marriage doesn't work, they keep trying to work it out. By contrast, if they enter the marriage with the idea that they will leave it under the conditions Becker indicates—when the minuses outweigh the pluses—then they are not really understanding marriage at all.

It would seem to follow that to think like Becker when entering into a marriage is to affect what the marriage will be like. To imagine marriage as no different from any other economic transaction—to dismiss that there is something sacred in it—can itself be a factor in making divorce more likely. A sort of uncertainty principle works here: the analysis of the phenomenon changes it. As Michael Sandel has argued, "Economists often assume that markets are inert, that they do not affect the goods they exchange. But this is untrue. Markets leave their mark."[8]

That mark may have moral implications. Viewing some activities as transactions may change them. Social norms may be corrupted when "market values crowd out nonmarket values worth caring about" (Sandel, p. 9). A society where people generally, not just economists, come to accept Becker's analysis might expect its divorce rate to go up and its social cohesion to decline. What would be the effect on children who learned they were a consumption good like any other?

As it happens, such considerations—that the analysis itself can change what is being analyzed—led to concepts like "self-

---

8. Michael J. Sandel, *What Money Can't Buy: The Moral Limits of Markets* (Farrar, Strauss and Giroux, 2012), p. 9. For Sandel on Becker's approach, see pp. 47–51 and the critique that follows.

fulfilling prophecy" developed by one of the sociological greats, Robert K. Merton. Not only are there self-fulfilling prophecies, Merton explains, there is also such a thing as a "self-defeating prophecy." Sometimes, "activities oriented toward certain values release processes which so react as to change the very scale of values that precipitated them.... Public predictions of future social developments are frequently not sustained precisely because the prediction has become a new element in the concrete situation.... Other things will not be equal just because the scientists have introduced a new 'other thing'—their predictions."[9] Models based on physics—Merton's example is predicting the return of Halley's Comet—do not have to take into account the possibility that comets will learn the theory and change their behavior accordingly. It may well be that this possibility makes a hard social science ultimately impossible, which may also explain why Becker does not attend to it.

Such self-referential ideas figure prominently in the realist novel, particularly when authors examine a key psychological fact, self-consciousness. How do I look to others, how should I regard myself, can I understand my own thought processes, do my emotions block emotional understanding? Self-consciousness changes consciousness, and ultimately itself. To take just one example, in *War and Peace*, Princess Marya mistakenly imagines that she cannot be attractive precisely because when she looks in the mirror her face takes on an unattractive strained expression, concealing the enchanting glow her eyes have on occasions when she is not consciously examining how they look.

Anthropologically and psychologically, marriage is not a contract like any other. After all, people enter into this "contract" without even inquiring into its provisions. Who learns the legal conditions of marriage and divorce in their state

9. Robert K. Merton, "The Unanticipated Consequences of Social Action," in Merton, *On Social Structure and Science*, ed. Piotr Sztompka (University of Chicago Press, 1996), pp. 180–181. His classic 1948 essay, "The Self-Fulfilling Prophecy," is on pp. 183–201.

before saying "I do"? Marriage is something above and beyond its legal stipulations, which is why gay couples would not accept civil union with the identical legal provisions as marriage. For reasons entirely unspecified in the contract, a civil union is not the same as a marriage.

Children

If some shudder at the thought of children as "marital-specific capital," what do they think of children being "normal goods"? Here, again, is Becker at his best. His analysis illuminates what might seem like anomalies.

As economists define the term, a normal good is simply one that consumers want more of when income rises. To the contrary, an "inferior good" is one where demand declines when income rises—think Hamburger Helper, or other goods whose demand runs counter to the business cycle (rising in a recession and falling in an expansion). But isn't it the case that couples with higher income tend to have fewer children than those less wealthy? Does that imply children are in fact inferior goods, in this sense of the word "inferior"?

First of all, don't forget the ever important economic caveat of *ceteris paribus*—all things equal—which means that everything but income stays constant, including the opportunity cost of a parent's time. Affluent couples tend to have high levels of education, which implies substantial forgone earnings from dropping out of the labor force, which often happens after a birth. And, in one of Becker's most insightful contributions to the economics literature, he revisited the basic question of what gives people satisfaction.[10]

---

10. Two examples are Becker's classic article, "A Theory of the Allocation of Time," *Economic Journal* 75(299), 1965, pp. 493–517, and his article with H. Gregg Lewis, "On the Interaction between the Quantity and Quality of Children," *Journal of Political Economy* 81(2), 1973, pp. S279–S288.

In brief, it is too simplistic to assume that people get direct satisfaction from consuming goods. A couple might go to the store and buy some fish and some wine, but those items don't give them utility directly. Instead, the couple engages in a production process where the fish and wine are inputs, along with the stove, napkins, lighting, time, and much more. A particular production technology translates these inputs into an output that Becker refers to as a "commodity," in this case a dining experience, and it is the commodity that provides the utility the couple enjoys. Just as a college takes its inputs (students, faculty, staff, physical infrastructure) and through a production process produces something we might call "educational services," there is a household production function that turns inputs into commodities, and it is these commodities that are in a household's utility function.

Think of "child services" as the commodity that provides the utility a couple receives from having a child. The child is merely an input, and when combined with lots of other factors, such as educational and psychological investments and of course time, a couple produces something that gives it, in the best case, joy. Richer couples typically have a higher opportunity cost of their time, so they engage in a more goods-intensive production process to produce "high-quality" children. Private schools, tutors, vacations, and nannies are a sensible and predictable way to produce a small number of goods-intensive children, in light of the fact that having more children (with fewer resources invested in each one) likely means less time the parents may spend in a highly compensated labor market. So even if income goes up and the number of children remains very low, the commodity "child services"—the utility you derive from having at least one child—may be rising.

What unsettles a humanist about this analysis is what it leaves out. It is one thing to say that economic decisions affect how many children people have because of greater investment in each child. It is quite another to say, as Becker seems to, that the reason people have children is that they provide "child services." There is something deeply disturbing about regarding other human beings simply in terms of the utility they provide. So viewed, other people are no different from useful things, except that their use is different. This is not to say people do not provide utility, but that there is something else.

In the *Nichomachean Ethics*, Aristotle devotes two chapters to analyzing "friendship," a topic that philosophers have usually overlooked. For Aristotle, friendship is not just a good like any other but is essential to a meaningful life. "For without friends no one would choose to live," he observes.[11] He quotes the phrase from the *Iliad*, "two going together." And we recall that what motivates Achilles, the hero of the *Iliad*, to give up his sulk is not loyalty to the group—Odysseus, Ajax, and Mentor appeal to these values in vain—but the death of his friend Patroclus. Friendship means more to him than the whole Greek expedition; it even means more to him than his own life.

For Aristotle, a true friendship is something beyond the people who make it up. Becker would treat friendship like marriage, as a contract for mutual benefit. Aristotle allows that this kind of friendship exists, and he calls it friendship for utility: "Those who love for the sake of utility love for the sake of what is good for themselves ... and not insofar as the other is the person loved.... And thus these friendships are only incidental" (Aristotle, p. 1060). No one expects them to be permanent, to define a life. When young people have amorous relationships this way, "they fall in love and quickly fall out of love, changing often within a single day" (Aristotle, p. 1061). But there is also a form of friendship in which the friends wish each other well not for the sake of themselves but for the other. "Now those who wish well to their friends for their sake are

---

11. Aristotle, "Nichomachean Ethics," *The Basic Works of Aristotle*, ed. Richard McKeon (Random House, 1941), p. 1058.

most truly friends" (Aristotle, p. 1061). Such relationships are by nature meant to be both intimate and permanent, even if in fact they do not turn out to be so.

In *War and Peace*, Tolstoy cites a Frenchman whose best friend has died, lamenting that now the theater of his actions is gone. One's actions have significance when and because they are told to a friend (or spouse) and so can seem pointless after his or her death. That is because one's actions have not really been just one's own but have belonged also to the friendship or marriage. The friendship is a thing in itself, and people sacrifice themselves for it, which is not a choice based on personal utility. Those who have studied army units report that soldiers typically sacrifice themselves not for the nation or for a principle but for their buddies in a small group.[12]

In fact, so long as one continues to think of one's actions in this way, death does not necessarily end the friendship. A friendship may last beyond the grave, in the sense that the presence of your friend is felt and cherished, and you hold the same sort of dialogues with her as you did when she was alive but far away. Like a missing limb, one feels the other even beyond the possibility of presence. It does not feel that way when some other contractual partner goes out of business. The loss is different from losing a cherished possession or even a useful human being.

None of that would be encompassed in the notion that friends provide "friendship services." Still less does "child services" capture much of what is involved in having a child. Especially with newborns, parents often feel that they would make any sacrifice for the child. It is not a question of whether the sacrifice would be worth the potential recompense in future joy. One senses that one no longer exists for oneself, but for the child. As a parent, one has exposed oneself to unanticipated pain, for one

---

12. See William H. McNeill, *Keeping Together in Time: Dance and Drill in Human History* (Harvard University Press, 1995).

comes to feel the child's suffering vicariously, sometimes even more than the child does. If all one risked with a child was the total loss of child services, as with other investments, parenting would be a lot easier.

The hero of *Anna Karenina*, Konstantin Levin, is surprised that the sight of his newborn son does not fill him with feelings of joy or triumph but with "pity and disgust." He feels pity because of the intense vulnerability of the infant, which he knows as the child does not; and that vulnerability is his own. He feels disgust because that is how one responds to humanity reduced to sheer fleshiness, which is why those who work in an operating room have to get used to the sight of a body opened for surgery. There is a sense in which the baby is still just a wriggling body. You suffer all the more for that body as a *potential* person, as the person it will be only if you help to make it one. You discover that this feeling never quite leaves you, even after the infant becomes an adult. Francis Bacon famously wrote that when a man has children he gives hostages to fortune.[13]

Think, for instance, of the Biblical story of the binding of Isaac.[14] God has demanded that Abraham sacrifice Isaac, whom he cherishes more than himself. That, indeed, is why God demands the sacrifice, to test whether Abraham truly cherishes God most of all. Abraham journeys three days to the place of sacrifice, and the Bible lets us imagine what he is thinking. With his deep care for the boy, he lets him believe that the sacrifice will be a lamb, and with deep poignancy he keeps dangerous implements from the boy along the way. "So they went both of them together" (Genesis 22:8); at such

13. "He that hath wife and children hath given hostages to fortune." *The Yale Book of Quotations*, ed. Fred R. Shapiro (Yale University Press, 2006), p. 38.

14. Perhaps the most remarkable book in the field of comparative literature offers an unforgettable analysis of this biblical story. See Erich Auerbach, *Mimesis: The Representation of Reality in Western Literature*, trans. Willard R. Trask (Princeton University Press, 1953).

a moment, that sense of being "together"—a parent and child, a unit, felt by both of them, beyond each of them as individuals—shows what Abraham must destroy for God. His loss of a son would be the same if he instead just had the boy killed, but he must do it himself, face to face, when they are "together." Kierkegaard imagined that Abraham both firmly believes and firmly disbelieves that the sacrifice will take place, a state of mind hard to capture in rational choice, or just about any, psychology.[15] God has demanded not just any sacrifice but something of infinite value, something Abraham would save at the cost of his own life, as parents often do.

It is hard to imagine capturing any of this complexity under the covering term "child services," which might seem to a humanist essentially wrong-headed. And the humanist might further reflect that the reduction of all relationships to utility destroys the very foundation of morality, which depends precisely on viewing people not merely in terms of their utility but as ends in themselves. The problem mentioned in chapter 1, the low value an economist would calculate for saving many poor Africans from river blindness contrasted with our intuition of improving so many lives with the gift of sight, comes to the fore here.

To be sure, the humanist would be stymied by problems that economists could resolve and that real life frequently presents. Courts have to assess damages for lost lives, and the humanist notion that lives cannot be measured economically would be of no use here. Neither would the humanist truism that a human life has infinite value, since one cannot assess infinite damages. Or that it is "priceless." One must allocate resources efficiently, and a lot of humanist ideas, taken as if they were all there is, can get in the way, just as economic ideas so regarded can.

---

15. The story occasioned one of the great works of modern philosophy, Søren Kierkegaard, *Fear and Trembling*, trans. Alastair Hannay (Penguin, 1985).

Crime and Punishment

To make our analysis of the strengths and weaknesses of Becker's approach clearer, let's turn for a moment to his work on crime. The famous story is that Becker once had to choose between a legal but inconvenient parking space and an illegal but convenient one. After weighing the cost of a ticket and the likelihood of being ticketed against the added convenience, he rationally chose the crime. And then it occurred to him: What if such calculation, rather than mental illness or social oppression, is the best way to account for crime? What if one approached it not psychologically or sociologically but economically? It then becomes possible to design more effective ways to set punishments and deploy resources. It was an important insight and opened new ways to design policies.

Becker observes: "The approach taken here follows the economists' usual analysis of choice and assumes that a person commits an offense if the expected utility to him exceeds the utility he could get by using his time and other resources at other activities. Some persons become 'criminals,' therefore, not because their basic motivation differs from that of other persons, but because their benefits and costs differ."[16] Becker is fully aware that others will be "repelled" by this approach.[17] As for other approaches, such as "vengeance, deterrence, safety, rehabilitation, and compensation," even these may best be achieved through an economic approach. Fines could be used to compensate victims, for instance, and "since the same could also be demonstrated for vengeance or rehabilitation, the moral should be clear: minimizing the loss in income is actually very general and thus is more useful than these catchy and

16. Gary S. Becker, "Crime and Punishment: An Economic Approach" in *Essays in the Economics of Crime and Punishment*, ed. Gary S. Becker and William M. Landes (National Bureau of Economic Research, 1974), p. 9, http://www.nber.org/chapters/c3625.pdf.

17. Becker, "Crime and Punishment", p. 45.

dramatic but inflexible desiderata."[18] A humanist will immediately notice that among the other approaches Becker does
not list is justice, which is not the same as either deterrence or
vengeance.

If we read this article in the spirit of soft Becker, he seems to
make some important points that other social sciences and the
humanities tend to miss. To see the humanist value of Becker's
approach, recall that if a goal is worth pursuing, it is a moral
thing to pursue it efficiently and not deploy limited resources
in vain. And if Becker's approach would lead to a more effective use of the limited resources for combating crime, it should
be seriously considered.

Once again, the problem comes with the idea that such calculation is all there is to crime and punishment. The title of
Becker's article seems to allude to Dostoevsky's novel *Crime
and Punishment*, perhaps the most famous book ever written
on the topic. As it happens, the novel considers a fairly similar
argument, phrased in the utilitarian terms then current. The
novel's hero, Raskolnikov, argues to himself that on utilitarian grounds he not only may, but positively ought to, murder
a noxious, cruel old pawnbroker woman, and as he contem-
plates this course of action, he happens to overhear two students considering the same possibility:

> But look here: on one side we have a stupid, senseless, worth-
> less, ailing, horrid old woman, not simply useless but doing
> actual harm ... and who will die in a day or two in any
> case.... On the other side, fresh young lives thrown away
> for want of help and by thousands ... a hundred thousand
> good deeds could be done and helped on that old woman's
> money, which will be buried in a monastery ... Kill her, take
> her money and with the help of it devote oneself to the ser-
> vice of humanity and the good of all. What do you think,
> would not one tiny crime be wiped out by thousands of good

18. Becker, "Crime and Punishment", p. 44.

deeds?... One death and a hundred lives in exchange—it's simple arithmetic![19]

The core problem here is the application of utilitarian "simple arithmetic" to a human life. Becker's analysis began, as we have seen, from taking a parking violation as a model for crime. But isn't there a qualitative difference—not just one of degree—between a parking violation and murder? One risks a fine for overstaying the meter, but no one, we think, has ever suffered pangs of guilt for having done so, and no one thinks to attach moral blame to such a person. There is something fundamentally wrong-headed with taking, as a model crime, one that has no moral value. Then it is easy to apply economic calculation and treat that as the end of the matter.

Just as marriage is more than a legal contract, crime is often more than a legal violation. To think otherwise may seem scientific, but it seriously distorts what one examines and so is anything but.

In *The Brothers Karamazov*, Ivan is torn apart by two contradictory beliefs about crime. The way he poses the question is, why not commit crimes? One reason is the one Becker proposes, that if one is caught, one will be punished. It would follow that if one could commit a serious crime with perfect safety and benefit greatly from doing so, one should commit it, much the way Becker calculated he should take the convenient parking space. But there is another reason not to commit crimes, and that is that they are simply morally wrong. Whether one is caught is a separate question. Ivan is torn apart by stories of child abuse, and he wants to say—as many of us would say when thinking about crimes from Ted Bundy's to the Holocaust—that they are simply wrong, the way religion says they are. Ivan is not religious and is well trained in the sciences, so is inclined intel-

---

19. Fyodor Dostoevsky, *Crime and Punishment*, trans. Constance Garnett (Modern Library, 1950), pp. 66–67.

lectually to the "rational" approach, but he is sure in his gut that there is something fundamentally insufficient about it.

Again, we can say: take Becker as arguing that the economic approach is not all there is to crime or any other behavior, but that it may shed important light and can indeed be useful. But there is, again, a strong tendency to stray into hedgehogism and say that is all there is. In much the same way, sociobiologists leap from asserting that certain moral tendencies arose because they served a survival function to asserting that this argument *explains* the moral. The hedgehog has the psychological satisfaction of being mentally superior to all those sentimental sloppy thinkers who are not smart enough or brave enough to accept his theory, and the temptation to such satisfaction often proves irresistible, especially when seconded by like-minded colleagues who assure each other that their fraternity is uniquely correct. Indeed, one might account for hedeghogism in economic terms, as a belief that is rational (in terms of satisfaction) to adopt.

Three Responses to the Economic Model

We have seen that Becker does allow for other fields to have some input. They set the ground in which the economist operates. But within that ground the economist's explanations are supreme. Stephen Toulmin, who traces mainstream economic thought to an ill-founded analogy with the astronomy of the solar system, argues that even within the economic domain, strictly defined, there is room for humanistic insights. He offers examples from the field of development economics (the topic of chapter 5) in which "reliance on pure economic theory was empirically empty without full consideration of the social, cultural, and historical conditions of its application."[20] "Universal

20. Stephen Toulmin, "Economics, or the Physics That Never Was," chapter 4 in *Return to Reason* (Harvard University Press, 2001), p. 64.

economic theories have too often led economists to overlook 'non-economic' factors" (p. 64).

For Toulmin, the core error of development economics is that economists imagine that the way to understand the world is theoretically, and that policy should simply be theory rigorously applied. But in practical affairs, as Aristotle long ago pointed out, one needs a fundamentally different sort of reasoning inasmuch as actual cases have features no theory can anticipate. One needs judgment, wisdom, and experience. In practical reasoning, one begins with a deep understanding of the specific situation and reasons from there. The more experience one has in examining particular situations, the better. Theory is a useful tool to apply when possible or to modify to fit the existing circumstances when appropriate.

Not surprisingly, Toulmin agrees with the great economist Joseph Schumpeter's description of the attempt by economic theorists to apply their work top down to the real world as being "dilettantic." Toulmin asks, "How can Economics best be put to use, in dealing with practical issues of government or business decision-making?" (p. 65). He provides the answer: "All economic problems are in practice cultural and social problems, too, and long-term planning that fails to take this into account is liable to be shortsighted and unproductive" (p. 66). We can imagine that Toulmin would have had a field day with the Becker model.

And you don't need to be a humanist to have problems with Becker's approach. In a review of the impact of Becker's work, economist Robert Pollak both praises and criticizes it.[21] On the one hand, Becker created a new field of inquiry, the economics of the family, and that by itself is a monumental feat. On the other, Pollak reviews his own work that over several decades takes Becker to task, especially for two foun-

21. Robert A. Pollak, "Gary Becker's Contributions to Family and Household Economics," *National Bureau of Economic Research Working Paper 9232*, October 2002.

dational assumptions underlying the economic approach—maximizing behavior and the notion of equilibrium. Note that he doesn't have a problem with another assumption—stable preferences—since, Pollak points out admiringly, Becker's later work "introduces new models of preference formation and change."[22] Pollak's critique is fairly technical, and we leave interested readers to study it on their own. Despite his criticisms, he concludes by saying that regardless of how the economics literature evolves, economists "will surely honor Gary Becker for laying the foundations of the economic approach to the family" (p. 42).

Some other economists, however, have been far less charitable. Barbara Bergmann's paper "Becker's Theory of the Family: Preposterous Conclusions" rejects virtually all of his analysis.[23] She writes, "Economic theory as applied to the family should increase our understanding of the phenomena we are studying, and allow us to implement fruitful interventions in cases where we are not satisfied with what is occurring. Much if not all of the theory of the family fails to achieve these aims" (p. 141). For Bergmann, the naive application of the neoclassical model to family issues means that key personal dynamics are sacrificed in favor of the usual mathematics that allows economists to reach a solution they might consider elegant but most others would consider offensive and absurd. The standard economic model may work, she says, in analyzing markets but certainly not in analyzing the family. The family is different—we are talking about individuals and couples, not abstractions.

22. Pollak, p. 11. That is an important point. The idea that preferences seldom evolve is surely problematic for humanists. But don't forget Becker's quote earlier in the chapter that preferences are not very different between rich and poor or between people in different societies and cultures. How many humanists would agree with that? Very few, we would guess.

23. Barbara R. Bergmann, "Becker's Theory of the Family: Preposterous Conclusions," *Feminist Economics*, Spring 1995, pp. 141–150.

Our aim is certainly not to try to resolve this debate here. We only seek to raise the possibility that taking a more humanistic approach might lend some additional insights.

Irrationality of the Second Order

As always, a key assumption underlying economic models is that people are rational—they identify what makes them happy and make decisions aimed toward that end. But what if people are perverse—that is, they don't seek to maximize their satisfaction in the first place? If so, such systematic behavior doesn't apply.

That is the possibility suggested in Edgar Allan Poe's story "The Imp of the Perverse" and, with much greater sophistication, by the narrator of Dostoevsky's novella *Notes from Underground*. I love someone, for instance, and that is precisely why I will not marry that person, even if the person's traits suggest we would be good partners. Why? I am Dostoevsky's underground man and, as mentioned in our opening chapter, it is my unpredictability that gives me joy. If someone is "able to discover a peculiar sort of enjoyment ... the enjoyment, of course, of despair," then it follows that "one may choose what is contrary to one's own interests."[24]

And why would someone make a choice that leads to harm and despair? Because he finds the essence of humanness in unpredictability, in the capacity to surprise. As the greatest literary critic of this work, Mikhail Bakhtin, puts the point, our humanity, and our individual identity, depend on "surprisingness."[25] Or as the underground man says, "What man needs is simply

---

24. Fyodor Dostoevsky, *Notes from Underground* and *The Grand Inquisitor*, ed. Ralph Matlaw (E. P. Dutton, 1960), pp. 8 and 23.

25. M. M. Bakhtin, "Methodology for the Human Sciences," *Speech Genres and Other Late Essays*, trans. Vern W. McGee, ed. Caryl Emerson and Michael Holquist (University of Texas Press, 1986), p. 167.

independent choice, whatever that independence may cost and wherever it may lead" (Dostoevsky, p. 23).

There is no place for surprisingness in the rational choice approach. For that matter, there is also none possible in behavioral economics (which we discuss in chapter 7) or any other social science that models itself on classical physics. You might as well imagine that Mars could decide, just for the hell of it, to change its orbit.

If utilitarianism is correct, the underground man reasons, his actions are in principle completely predictable. Given a set of preferences, there is one and only one choice he could make in any situation. Much as an election with one candidate is no election at all, a choice among one possible outcome—it is odd even to express the idea—is not really a choice. If someone would "some day ... truly discover a formula for all our desires and caprices" (Dostoevsky, p. 24), there would be no caprices at all. "There will be no more incidents and adventures in the world" (p. 22). As we saw in chapter 1, the need for narrative would disappear because everything could be derived from the formula. Actions could, in principle and perhaps someday in practice, be looked up in advance, as in a railway timetable or "tables of logarithms." Then a person "will at once be transformed from a human being into an organ stop or something of the sort; for what is a man without desire, without free will and without choice, if not a stop in an organ?" (p. 24).

It is to foreclose this possibility that the underground man deliberately acts perversely. The economic model assumes that people exercise choice in making allocative decisions that increase their satisfaction. Not here. The choice being made is to exercise the right to act *against* our interests since that action "preserves for us what is most precious and most important—that is, our personality, our individuality" (Dostoevsky, p. 26). Find out what would be to the greatest advantage and act against it. Indeed, we believe, this actually happens rather often among people: they do not want to be counted on, predicted, thoroughly known from outside so that there is nothing of their own. Perhaps this is one reason why trying to change someone's behavior by showing it runs contrary to his advantage so often backfires.

So people behave in a way we have come to call Dostoevskian. This idea has led to several modern dystopian novels, in which a hero from a world in which all wants are satisfied finds life meaningless for that very reason. There is nothing to work for, nothing to achieve, no possibility of real risk, no way to prove one's devotion to another by sacrifice, no adventure. And so the hero rejects a situation that maximizes his utility and chooses instead to leave the utopian world. He leaves it precisely because it is utopian. That is the plot of Eugene Zamyatin's *We* and Aldous Huxley's *Brave New World*, a plot already suggested by the underground man:

> What can one expect from man since he is a creature endowed with such strange qualities? Shower upon him every earthly blessing, drown him in bliss so that nothing but bubbles would dance on the surface of his bliss, as on a sea; give him such economic prosperity that he would have nothing else to do but sleep, eat cakes and busy himself with ensuring the continuation of world history and even then man ... would play you some loathsome trick. He would even risk his cakes and would deliberately desire the most fatal rubbish, the most uneconomical absurdity, simply to introduce into all this positive rationality his fatal fantastic element ... simply in order to prove to himself ... that men are still men and not piano keys ... because, after all, [in such situations] the whole work of man seems really to consist in nothing but proving to himself continually that he is a man and not an organ stop. (Dostoevsky, pp. 27–28)

But couldn't one regard the desire for independence as another good to be included with all the other advantages? Well, one can't, because this is really second-order irrationality. This is not a desire but a desire about desires, which differs from other desires the way a mathematical set differs from a set of sets. Treated as just another desire, one could incorporate it into a preference function and again maximize utility, but if one did so, the desire for caprice would deliberately violate that maximum, too.

Yes, it is tempting to incorporate this kind of thinking into the standard economic model. Why not just change the signs of the arguments of the utility function so that you maximize utility by minimizing the consumption of what you like best? I love going to the movies, so going to the movies makes me unhappy. I would rather deny myself the pleasures of life than be only as free as an organ stop. But where would that leave us? Nowhere. If someone maximized utility by never consuming the goods that would make her happy, she would be as predictable as someone who maximized utility by always consuming those goods. And it is predictability that the underground man would avoid at any cost. Remember Becker's admonition that ad hoc adjustments of the economic model lead only to tautologies. Whatever adjustment one might try to make, losing the rationality argument is devastating to the economic model. We return to that point in chapter 7.

Selling Kidneys

Finally, let's return to a theme of our volume—that there are important moral issues at stake that economic analyses often ignore. We quoted Becker earlier using preferences and values as synonyms. Humanists would take issue with that. Preferences are what we enjoy; values are something else entirely. What if we enjoy things that hurt other people, today or in the future? I love to play my music very loudly, ignoring my neighbors. Or I love to keep the heat blasting in the winter, with my windows open so I can breathe fresh air. What about the moral issues that values reflect?

This brings us to one of the last things Becker published before his death in May of 2014, a coauthored essay in the *Wall Street Journal*, "Cash for Kidneys: The Case for a Market for Organs."[26] It is vintage Becker—provocative, insightful, and pushing the economic model to its limits (and perhaps beyond).

Becker and Julio Elias argue that the long waiting list for new kidneys implies a large number of needless deaths. Their answer: a market for organs. Since individuals can live a normal life with only one kidney, why not pay donors for their organs and eliminate the gap between supply and demand? The price? They estimate that the market would clear at around $15,000 per kidney (with the variation in their estimate ranging from a high of $25,000 to a low of $5,000).

They cite Iran as one of the few countries in the world that already allows the open purchase and sale of organs, and that at a price of only $4,000 per kidney, there is now a sufficient supply to meet demand.

Perhaps anticipating the moral outrage, the authors go on to propose that individuals willing to give their organs after they die should be allowed to do so for a fee. Individuals would be permitted to sell organs "forward," and their heirs would receive payments after the donor is deceased and the organs are harvested.

They predict that even this proposal would be deemed by many to be immoral, especially given that a disproportionate number of donors would likely be desperately poor. But they suggest that critics weigh those concerns against the fact that thousands of deaths result each year due to the excess demand for organs to be used in transplants. They ask, "How can paying for organs to increase their supply be more immoral than the injustice of the present system?" They acknowledge that "initially, a market in the purchase and sale of organs would

26. Gary S. Becker and Julio J. Elias, "Cash for Kidneys: The Case for a Market for Organs," *Wall Street Journal*, January 18, 2014.

seem strange, and many might continue to consider that market 'repugnant.'" But, they conclude, "Eventually, the advantages of allowing payment for organs would become obvious. At that point, people will wonder why it took so long to adopt such an obvious and sensible solution to the shortage of organs for transplant."

Is this another case of the World Bank/Summers phenomenon? Recall the words of Brazil's secretary of the environment about using economic analyses to develop real-world policies: "Your reasoning is perfectly logical but totally insane." Funny how the application of the classic economic model often seems to strike economists as "obvious and sensible." Perhaps they should pause to consider why so many other smart people feel so strongly to the contrary.[27]

There are several aspects to the essay that we find of particular interest. First of all, kidneys are very different from organs such as hearts and livers—you could donate one and still survive. Second, selling organs after you die is different from doing so while still alive.

Here are three different policy proposals:

1. You be allowed to sell your kidneys, or any organ for that matter, after your death, with your heirs receiving the payment;
2. You be allowed to sell a kidney while you are alive, receiving the payment yourself, assuming your

---

27. It may be relevant to report here on a recent study by three economists who surveyed U.S. residents about their attitudes on payments for organs. See Julio J. Elias, Nicola Lacetera, and Mario Macis, "Sacred Values? The Effect of Information on Attitudes toward Payments for Human Organs," *American Economic Review: Papers & Proceedings 2015*, May 2015, pp. 361–365. The authors found that support for selling organs increased from 51 percent to 71 percent once documented and verifiable information about its potential benefits were laid out to respondents. They conclude that ethical principles are "evidence based." Apparently, the general public is more easily swayed by economic arguments than we thought. We are not, however, convinced this is necessarily for the good. And what if those surveyed were presented with arguments for the opposing position?

remaining kidney is functional enough to virtually
guarantee your survival;

3. You be allowed to sell any organ you choose, with the
payment going to your heirs since the removal of that
organ will kill you.

The strongest application of the economic model would support all three options, including the third. What if someone
is dying anyway (say, from an inoperative brain tumor)? Why
interfere with her "right" to provide educational funds for her
children if she wanted to sell her healthy heart on the open
market? Once again, this is a case where you probably don't
want to leave it up to economists, who might just come up
with a policy that is obvious and sensible. To them.

For a humanist, the possibility of selling organs raises real
ethical questions, by which we mean not that it is necessarily
wrong but that the moral issues are complicated. It is possible
that the economic solution will turn out to be the correct one.
Even so, the issue is not nearly so simple as Becker, or the economic model taken alone, would allow.

On the one hand, if kidneys were sold, lives would be saved.
If one considers how many people suffer and die waiting for
a kidney when others are willing to make them available and
would live healthy lives on one kidney, it seems callous to say
that the transaction cannot take place. It is all very well to say
that donations, or organs from people who die and have signed
organ donation cards, should be used, but it is clear that these
do not suffice. The appeal of the Becker-Elias model is not that
it enables a new industry and raises the gross domestic product,
while giving people the chance to make money they might use
for good purposes. It is that people dying for want of a kidney
would live. Any argument against a kidney market (or a market
for other organs) would have to outweigh this one for it.

It is by no means certain that the counterarguments do outweigh it, but they are surely strong. The one Becker anticipates

concerns income: we have a natural reluctance to bless a situation in which poor people are likely to be the sellers and rich people the buyers. Of course, the arrangement could be set up so as not to favor the rich getting the kidneys. And in any case, saving lives, even the lives of rich people, is better than just letting them die, as now happens when kidneys are lacking. And to say that poor people cannot sell a kidney may be to deprive them of their only way to accomplish some important purpose, say, paying for a child's education, a spouse's medical needs, or a parent's care. From this perspective, it may be cruel not to allow the transaction. Such arguments are often made in favor of legalized prostitution. In any case, we do not stop poor people from selling their hair, and we often allow them to sell their blood, so why not a kidney if they can live just as well without it? Whatever its merits, this argument does not seem sufficient, given the advantages in lives saved with a market solution.

But a humanist might also consider a very different sort of argument. As Michael Sandel contends, while some objections to market solutions rely on an argument based on inequality (is a transaction in organs really free and uncoerced for the poor?), there is also a quite different argument based on what he calls bribery or corruption. "The bribery objection is different," he explains. "It is not about the conditions under which the deal is made but about the nature of the good being bought and sold" (Sandel, p. 45). A judge selling a verdict may be an uncoerced transaction, but it corrupts the judicial process itself; and we do not allow people to sell their votes. "We corrupt a good, an activity, or a social practice whenever we treat it according to a lower norm than is appropriate to it" (p. 46). In particular, selling the use of our bodies, whether for surrogate parenting, prostitution, or some other purpose, may entail "self-degradation" (p. 46).

Such transactions, if allowed, may easily cheapen a society's sense of what it is to be a human being. Why is it that we feel a natural aversion to the idea of selling kidneys? Why does the very phrase "a market for organs" seem repugnant? Becker puts the word "repugnant" in scare quotes, as if that were a word and concept fit only for old-fashioned, ignorant, or dim religious folk. But couldn't our repugnance testify to a moral sensibility—at times appropriate—that we have even if we cannot articulate it? Most of us could not give reasons that would stand up in the court of philosophers for why certain crimes are just plain wrong, but we are pretty sure they are wrong anyway. Thinking that every moral question, even the most fundamental ones, must be settled by an argument validated by academics surely favors the power of the academics. It is "natural and agreeable," as Tolstoy would say, that academics would favor such a standard, which puts them in the superior position. But no one has shown that academics, for all their dialectical skill, act more morally than anyone else. Indeed, it is easy enough to show that they have a strong tendency to arrive at obviously immoral positions because professional rewards do not go to the endorsers of common sense.

Repugnance is not itself an argument, as Leon Kass observed in a well-known article in the *New Republic* about the possibility of cloning human beings. Nevertheless, he makes this point as well:

> In crucial cases, however, repugnance is the emotional expression of deep wisdom, beyond reason's power fully to articulate it. Can anyone really give an argument fully adequate to the horror which is father-daughter incest (even with consent) ... or mutilating a corpse, or eating human flesh, or even (just!) raping or murdering another human being?... On the contrary, we are suspicious of those who think they can rationalize away our horror, say, by trying to explain the enormity of incest with arguments only about the genetic risks of inbreeding.[28]

28. Leon Kass, "The Wisdom of Repugnance," *New Republic*, June 2, 1997, p. 20.

And yet, arguments can be given. They concern turning the human body into a market good. One does not own one's body in the way one owns a car or a hammer. A car or a hammer is something I acquired and something I am free to dispose of, without altering who I am. But my body is not something I own but is *me*, or at least, inseparable from me.

We are repelled by the treatment of the body as a collection of spare parts for much the same reason that we are repelled by cannibalism, even if, let us say, one voluntarily sells one's arm to be devoured by gourmets.[29] Ethics, and not just for a Kantian, entails treating human beings as ends. If people are not ends, why is their well-being something to value at all? One could easily imagine maximizing something else, say, the GDP of a society.

Unless we renounce any form of materialism, the self must reside in some organ or organs. If we accept the argument that a person should be allowed to engage in selling his own organs, he could sell himself. We might be inclined to think of the brain as somehow different, but that would be hard to justify from a materialist perspective. There is a Roman Polanski film in which the hero asks if he would still be himself if he lost an arm, and answers he would be. What about both arms? What about everything but his head, if it could be kept alive? If so, he reflects, "What right has my head to call itself me?"

To put the point in economic language, commerce in organs entails a negative externality, a moral coarsening of society. It accustoms us to think of the body as property like any other and people as collections of parts with an economic value. Sooner rather than later, that is bound to shape our view of all moral questions. Do we really cherish the whole human being if it is treated in terms of its marketable parts?

---

29. See Leon T. Kass, "Organs for Sale? Propriety, Property and the Price of Progress," *Life, Liberty and the Defense of Dignity: The Challenge for Bioethics* (Encounter, 2002), pp. 177–198.

It doesn't take an economist to predict that if a market for organs exists, and the price of organs is high enough, some people or governments will find unpleasant ways to procure them. Apparently, China already does. In an article in the *New Yorker*, Jiayang Fan writes:

> Until 2007, nine-tenths of the country's organ supply came from its tens of thousands of death-row inmates, whose executions have sometimes been expedited for the purpose of harvesting organs. For many years, Chinese authorities refused to acknowledge this practice, though a 2006 investigation conducted by two Canadians—David Kilgour, a member of parliament, and David Matas, a human-rights lawyer—concluded that the selling of prisoners' organs without their consent was a "billion-dollar business in China." According to the report, vital organs were regularly harvested from executed prisoners and distributed by shadowy intermediaries.[30]

One Chinese doctor testified before Congress that he had removed skin for transplant from a living person. And if executions have been "expedited" because of incentives to do so, then presumably the same incentives work when deciding whether a person should be condemned to death in the first place. Members of Falun Gong apparently became the next source.[31]

To be sure, here it is an authoritarian regime—one that rejects Western notions of human rights—engaged in treating human beings as sources for organs. Like some used cars,

---

30. Jiayang Fan, "Can China Stop Organ Trafficking?" *New Yorker*, January 10, 2014, http://www.newyorker.com/news/news-desk/can-china-stop-organ-trafficking.

31. See David Matas, "Ending Abuse of Organ Transplantation in China," http://www .david-kilgour.com/2010/Aug_19_2010_01.php; and David Matas, Esq., and Hon. David Kilgour, Esq., "Bloody Harvest; Revised Report into Allegations of Organ Harvesting of Falun Gong Practitioners in China," http://organharvestinvestigation .net/.

these people's parts are worth more than they are intact. But if rejection of human rights favors a market in human parts, then a market in human parts makes it that much more likely we will come to reject human rights. Already the notion of the "sanctity" of human life has come to seem a bit stodgy.

If an American hospital needed money (and they usually do), would there be an incentive not to prolong the life of someone whose organs are worth a lot more than she is? In the United Kingdom, the National Health Service since 2013 has been using "pounds per QALY" as a way of deciding how to allot resources for medical treatment. A QALY, or quality adjusted life year, represents one year of life adjusted for the state of one's health so that, for instance, people suffering from moderate depression would be less worthy of medical treatment at a given price than someone who is "not anxious or depressed."[32] The life of a handicapped person is worth less than that of a perfectly healthy person of the same age. It is even possible for people to have a score below zero, with zero as death. How great a step would it be to decide that a person with a low (or negative) score should be euthanized, and if euthanized, why waste his organs?

These are not the only logical extensions of the arguments for organ markets. Why stop a person from selling herself into indentured servitude, as was once done as a way to pay one's passage to the New World?

It is important to recognize this: people do not *own* themselves, they *are* themselves. What's more, they are custodians of the humanity residing within them. Immanuel Kant observed: "To dispose of oneself as a mere means to some end and of one's own liking is to degrade the humanity in one's person (*homo noumenon*), which, after all, was entrusted to

---

32. Ceri Phillips, "What Is a QALY?," http://www.medicine.ox.ac.uk/bandolier/painres/download/whatis/qaly.pdf.

man (*homo phenomenon*) to preserve."[33] If I am custodian of the humanity within me, then there is more to me than me.

A person's relation to his own body is something like an aristocrat's relation to his inherited land, at least as Tolstoy's Konstantin Levin describes it: he is its steward, not free to dispose of it at will but entrusted with its care. Still more, a person's humanness belongs not just to herself but to something larger. This is the insight that religions express by saying that "man is made in the image of God" and has led some churches to regard suicide as the gravest of sins. But one does not have to be religious to find some other way to express the thought.

The advantages of a market in organs lie in the many lives saved right away; the disadvantages lie in the degrading of humanness and the horrific consequences to which that would lead, some of which are already visible. Where that leaves us is hard to say. But the humanist would conclude that, whatever the answer, one needs more than just economics to arrive at it.

A Foxy Approach to Economic Demography

We realize that we've been pretty tough on the economic approach to understanding the family. But we conclude this chapter by discussing an application that is so foxy that even Toulmin might approve. Pollak cited an authority none other than Paul Samuelson, who was awarded the 1970 Nobel Prize for having "done more than any other contemporary economist to raise the level of scientific analysis in economic theory," for praising the economist Richard Easterlin for his contribution to the field of economic demography. Easterlin incorporates the insights from other disciplines in explaining fluctuations in the demand for children in a way that Samuelson found to be more compelling than the Becker model. Samuelson wrote:

---

33. Immanuel Kant, *The Metaphysical Principles of Virtue*, trans. James Ellington (Bobbs-Merrill, 1964), p. 84, as cited in Kass, "Organs for Sale," p. 185.

"The Easterlin theory is all the more valuable for its scarcity among economic theories, standing out in welcome relief from the rather sterile verbalizations by which economists have tended to describe fertility decisions in terms of the jargon of indifference curves, thereby tending to intimidate non-economists who have not misspent their youth in mastering the intricacies of modern utility theory."[34] Very strong words from the person who contributed more to the development of the modern economic paradigm than anyone.

But we turn now not to that specific work but to Easterlin's contribution to the much more general topic of demographic transition. Country after country has moved from a high fertility/high mortality regime to a low fertility/low mortality one. Most of these countries first experienced a decline in mortality before embarking on a reduction in birth rates. Many demographers have studied this transition; Easterlin, around the time that Becker was first producing his work on the economics of the family, provided a framework that incorporated the insights not only from economists but from sociologists, biologists, historians, and anthropologists as well.[35]

For Easterlin, there are three relevant factors at work here: the demand for children, the natural supply of children, and the cost of fertility regulation.

In the early stages of economic development, it is likely that there is an excess demand for surviving children—that

34. Pollak cites the Samuelson quote on p. 6. The original is from Paul A. Samuelson, "An Economist's Non-Linear Model of Self-Generated Fertility Waves," *Population Studies*, July 1976, pp. 243–247.

35. See, for example, Richard A. Easterlin, "The Economics and Sociology of Fertility: A Synthesis," in *Historical Studies of Changing Fertility*, ed. Charles Tilly (Princeton University Press, 1978), pp. 57–134, and Richard A. Easterlin, "An Economic Framework for Fertility Analysis," *Studies in Family Planning*, March 1975, pp. 54–63. For a review of this work and an application from the economic/demographic history of the United States, see Morton Owen Schapiro, *Filling Up America: An Economic-Demographic Model of Population Growth and Distribution in the Nineteenth-Century United States* (JAI Press, 1986).

is, couples want more children than they are able to have.[36] Why is this the case? The demand for children is high because they are inexpensive relative to market goods as a result both of low direct and indirect (opportunity) costs. Direct costs such as food and housing tend to be inexpensive in a rural setting, and opportunity costs are low (since forgone labor market earnings for the principal caregiver are modest, especially net of the child's contribution to family income, which may be relatively high in an agrarian setting). Moreover, "tastes" for children are often quite pronounced, given social norms regarding large family sizes. So a couple might aspire to have seven surviving children. But what about the supply?

By natural supply of children, we mean the number of surviving children in the absence of a conscious effort to restrict fertility. Here it gets a bit tricky. What if people engage in practices that restrict fertility, regardless of their intention to do so? A good example is prolonged breast-feeding, which gives rise to lactational amenorrhea, the temporary postnatal infertility span preceding the resumption of menstruation.[37] What

36. Note that surviving children are the object of interest rather than births, since it is children that are presumed to provide utility.

37. The issue of lactational amenorrhea is a good illustration of what might be called the endogeneity of "culture," a topic referred to elsewhere in the book. A well-known example deals with the Alaskan Inupiat Eskimos. Their birthrate rose to very high levels during the 1950s (peaking at more than seven births per woman, twice the baby boom birthrate in the continental United States). Did this result from a change of tastes? It turns out that these Native Alaskans had gone from migratory lifestyles, during which breast-feeding was the predominant source of nutrition for infants, to a more settled experience where formula feeding became a popular alternative. Traditional three- to four-year periods of breast-feeding were quickly shortened or eliminated. The result: much reduced birth intervals and a rapid rise in fertility. Larry Blackwood, "Alaska Native Fertility Trends, 1950–1978," Demography, May 1981, pp. 173–179, and Summer Cutting and Mary Beth Flanders-Stepans, "Breastfeeding Prevalence among an Alaskan Inupiat Eskimo Population," Journal of Perinatal Education, Winter 2001, pp. 21–30, document these changes. So while some social scientists might be quick to turn to cultural explanations for the Eskimo baby boom, it appears that the change in social norms resulted from an alteration in economic circumstances and was thereby endogenous rather than exogenous.

might last, in the absence of breast-feeding, only a few months from giving birth to the onset of menses becomes much longer (on average) with breast-feeding. If lactation is intentionally aimed at spacing children (a form of "natural" family planning), then, in this approach, it results from both the demand and supply of surviving children rather than merely reflecting the natural supply. But at early stages of economic development, breast-feeding typically is done for reasons other than fertility reduction.

So the natural supply of children is limited by prolonged lactation, along with high infant and child mortality rates and low levels of fecundity as a result of disease and poor nutrition. Let's say the natural supply averages five surviving children. What would couples do? If they want seven children and can only have five, they certainly wouldn't seek to restrict their fertility.

But over the course of economic development, the demand for children falls and the natural supply rises. On the demand side, both the direct and indirect costs of children rise; on the supply side, lactation practices change, infant and child mortality rates fall, and fecundity improves. At first, couples continue to make no conscious effort to affect their fertility, but eventually this changes. Unregulated fertility means that the natural supply of children, now up to, say, eight, exceeds the demand, now down to three, and the presence of five unwanted children induces families to intentionally use fertility reduction techniques or contraceptives. In economic terms, the disutility associated with unregulated fertility now exceeds the costs (both monetary and psychic) of fertility regulation.

This framework has important policy implications. For one, providing free contraceptives when there is actually an excess demand for children is a total waste of time and money. A much more effective use of resources is to raise the price of children by increasing female education along with female labor force participation rates. There is a reason why so many development experts say that the best contraceptive in the world is a woman's schooling. Some might interpret that as implying that education changes tastes; but Easterlin (and, of course, Becker) would first point out how an increase in forgone earnings raises the price of a child, thereby lowering the demand.

Of course, we can't do justice to all the nuances of the Easterlin approach in such a brief summary. But we hope we have made our point: this framework is interdisciplinary in the finest sense of that term. It doesn't expropriate other disciplines; it integrates them. We doubt that anyone would think of this as an example of economic imperialism or that anyone would call it "dilettantic." While it reflects an economist's usual focus on how changes in income and relative prices affect demand, it also ventures into the realm of biology with the importance of fecundity, infant and child mortality, and lactational amenorrhea, and into sociology and anthropology with regard to social norms concerning family size, age at first marriage, the percentage ever married, the acceptability of out-of-wedlock births, and breast-feeding practices. In a word, it is foxy.[38]

As we discussed in chapter 2, foxes typically don't have an army of zealots as their followers; they usually don't become known for revolutionizing their fields; they seldom win Nobel Prizes. But, we submit, their work nonetheless might serve as wonderful examples for others to follow.

---

38. Still, as one reader pointed out, being a "foxy" economist doesn't necessarily mean that humanists would automatically embrace Easterlin's ideas. Writing about "the number of unwanted children" or the "disutility associated with unregulated fertility" isn't likely to endear him to many humanities professors any more than if he used terms such as "child services" or "marital-specific capital" found in Becker's work.

Chapter 5

The Ultimate Question

Case Study 3—Why Do Some Countries Develop Faster Than Others? Economics, Culture, and Institutions

Economists examine a wide range of important topics. But are there any more critical than why some countries experience rapid (or at least respectable) levels of economic growth while others lag far behind?

We might begin with the South Korea-Ghana puzzle. Back in the mid-1960s, these two countries had very similar levels of per capita income. But Ghana had rich reserves of natural resources (especially oil) and precious metals (namely, gold); South Korea did not. Who would have guessed that fifty years later citizens of South Korea would be almost twenty times richer than those in Ghana?[1]

In this chapter, we turn first to another hedgehog for an answer, a noneconomist who offers to explain differential economic development in terms of a single factor. Why the focus on someone outside economics? This hedgehog's insistence that what looks like irreducible complexity actually reduces to a single factor, along with his dismissal of explanations in terms of all other disciplines as either

---

1. And that is after Ghana has experienced impressive growth in recent years, leaving it with twice the per capita income of most other West African countries, and leading it to be classified as a "lower-middle income" country by the World Bank.

pseudoexplanations or derivable from the single factor that
matters, is a style of thought that recalls "hard Becker" and is
characteristic of hedgehogs generally. Our hope here is that
through an examination of how a noneconomist explains
economic facts in noneconomic terms—in other words, seeing economics treated the way Becker treats sociology and
anthropology—economists may come to appreciate how
they often look to others. If the reasoning seems clearly falla-
cious when done by other social scientists, it will be easier to
see the flaws when the same reasoning is employed by economists themselves.

In Jared Diamond's *Guns, Germs, and Steel: The Fates of
Human Societies*, the diversity of apparent causes reduces to
a single one, the way Newton's laws explain a vast diversity
of astronomical and other observations.[2] "The whole modern
world," writes Diamond, "has been shaped by lopsided outcomes. Hence, they must have inexorable explanations, ones
more basic than mere details concerning who happened to
win some battle or develop some invention on one occasion
a few thousand years ago" (p. 24). For Diamond, great results
cannot arise from many factors interacting haphazardly over
a long period of time. In the pursuit of "inexorable explanations" and "ultimate explanations" (p. 24), no contingency is
allowed to have had a significant lasting effect. It follows that
narratives can explain nothing but temporary fluctuations
with no long-term significance. Beyond that, narratives can
only illustrate how the single cause operated over time. We
see here the same impulse that leads economists to avoid narrative explanations in favor of mathematical models and for
the same reason: narrative is needed when there is genuine
contingency, that is, when important facts cannot be derived
from the preferred model.

2. Jared Diamond, *Guns, Germs, and Steel: The Fates of Human Societies* (W. W.
Norton, 1999). Our citations are from the paperback edition published in 1999.

As an alternative, we discuss a thinker who is both an economist and a historian. Joel Mokyr's *The Enlightened Economy: An Economic History of Britain, 1700–1850*, explains the rise of Britain to economic preeminence through a complex plurality of factors irreducible to any one of them.[3] Their combined result could not have been predicted in advance and allows for no strong predictions for the future. For Mokyr, irreducible contingency plays an essential role. One cannot explain it away by some overarching law.

Mokyr's account is rich in what we have called narrativeness: narrative plays an indispensable explanatory role. Of course, his book invites counterargument and might still prove mistaken, but that is the nature of foxy accounts. They do not promise certainty and arrive at no ultimate, let alone inexorable, explanation.

The Hedgehog of Geography

To be sure, at its best a hedgehog account can, for all its shortcomings as an overall explanation, offer surprising and important insights that others have overlooked or understated. And Diamond unquestionably does that. No one to our knowledge had ever pointed to the distribution of potentially useful plants or large domesticatable animals as an important factor in explaining why some countries develop faster than others. It comes as a shock to discover how much later some parts of the world were settled than others and therefore how much less time some cultures had to develop useful innovations. We are accustomed to thinking in terms of vast stretches of evolutionary time next to which human activity seems both short and foreshortened, but if we focus on the much briefer stretch of human existence, significant differences in time spans become visible.

---

3. Joel Mokyr, *The Enlightened Economy: An Economic History of Britain, 1700–1850* (Yale University Press, 2009).

The geographical ease of diffusion turns out to play a long overlooked role. No matter how inventive a culture may be, most inventions come from somewhere else. Cultures located among others from whom they can borrow, therefore, are much more likely to develop than isolated ones. The larger available population and the absence of geographical barriers gave the Eurasian landmass an enormous advantage over Tasmania, New Guinea, or even sub-Saharan Africa. So did the fact that this landmass extends from east to west rather than north to south, making crops, which are typically suited to a given latitude and amount of sunlight, more readily movable across large distances. These and similar observations establish Diamond's book as an important contribution to our understanding of differential development over the very long term. And that is the nature of the best hedgehog approaches, where monomaniacal attention to a single factor can illuminate surprising facts about its operation.

Diamond begins his prologue by raising the question of differential economic development in an intriguing way. While walking on a beach in New Guinea with a local politician named Yali, he was asked, "Why is it that you white people developed so much cargo and brought it to New Guinea, but we black people had little cargo of our own?"[4] In Diamond's rephrase: "Why did human development proceed at such different rates on different continents?" (Diamond, p. 16).

Diamond's answer to this question reduces to a single factor: geography. Although Diamond pays lip service to the possibility of nongeographical explanations, he repeatedly considers them only to describe them as merely "proximate" causes, which are themselves explicable in geographical terms. In the book's epilogue, Diamond proposes as the next step the extension of

4. Diamond, p. 14. "Cargo" referred to material goods. The so-called cargo cults thought that cargo was the source of the wealth and power of the Europeans and that it came from heavenly powers that could be propitiated. Yali is using the term simply in the sense of material wealth and power.

geographical explanation to shorter time spans. The shorter the time span that can be explained by geographical factors, of course, the less role there is for any other explanation, even to account for minor fluctuations from the main line of development. Would the next stage be still shorter time spans?

For example, Diamond offers a geographical explanation for why Europe, rather than China, led the world in technological development, a development that, given his theory, "is initially surprising, because China enjoyed undoubted advantages" (p. 395). Diamond lists five such advantages, any one of which, given his account, should have been sufficient to ensure Chinese supremacy. But Diamond rejects any cause but other geographical factors:

> Why, then, did the Fertile Crescent and China eventually lose their enormous leads of thousands of years to late-starting Europe? One can, of course, point to proximate factors behind Europe's rise; its development of a merchant class, capitalism, and patent protection for inventions, its failure to develop absolute despots and crushing taxation, and its Greco-Judeo-Christian tradition of critical empirical inquiry. Still, for all such proximate causes, one must raise the question of ultimate cause: why did those proximate factors themselves arise in Europe, rather than in China or the Fertile Crescent? (pp. 393–394)

This reasoning allows for no counterevidence. Apparently, if China had wound up on top, it would have been because of the geographical factors previously mentioned as decisive. The theory would have been vindicated. But as it happened, what the theory would have predicted did not turn out to be the case. But that doesn't mean the theory has been falsified, or even that some good counterevidence has been presented. Rather, it means only that some other geographical factor must be at work. And, of course, there are so many possible candidates that you can always find one to do the trick.

After the fact, when one's prediction has proven wrong, one goes back and revises the theory to yield the prediction that one now knows would have been the correct one and then claims the new theory has been vindicated! We wish we could say that this escape of any possible falsification is uncommon, but it is not. It is especially common among hedgehogs, who repeatedly try to prove their theory with the sort of reasoning that could justify nearly any theory. Astrologers whose predictions fail could also go back and find some other stellar sign pointing to what happened. And one can only wonder if, in the next forty years, China should come to dominate the world, will Diamond find a geographical explanation for that, too—one that accounts not only for Chinese domination but for why it did not dominate forty years earlier? If so, why doesn't he predict it now?

Diamond lists fourteen "proximate causes" invoked by historians and economists, including institutional ones like patents and property laws; social ones like individualism, risk-taking behavior, and the tolerance of diverse views; and intellectual ones like skepticism, a scientific outlook, and religions compatible with technological development. In addition to these, which all favor economic development, some have cited factors that, they say, sometimes work one way and sometimes the other, such as war, centralized government, climate, and resource abundance.

Diamond dismisses the last group because, to him, if a cause can work both ways, it does not seem to be much of a cause. For a humanist, that wouldn't count as much of an objection any more than one could dismiss, let us say, envy, acquisitiveness, or just about any other emotion as explanations for crime, because sometimes they lead elsewhere. That is the nature of many things human. But Diamond is trained as a physiologist and has written on ecology and ornithology, which, for all their complexity, do not entail the complex interactions of self-conscious human agents. In this respect, he resembles Paul Ehrlich, who like Diamond, as we discussed in chapter 2, found it natural when explaining economic facts to bypass economics and go straight to ecology.

Predictably enough, Diamond rejects the other "proximate causes" because they are, well, merely proximate. His reasoning is entirely circular. To prove that an explanation must be geographical, he asks for other possibilities and, when he finds them, discounts them because they are not geographical. Needless to say, proponents of other all-encompassing systems—say, Marxist economic ones—also dismiss other explanations as merely proximate, including geographical ones. Just as Diamond can ask why risk taking or property rights could not themselves be accounted for in geographical terms, Marxists can ask why the effectiveness of geographical causes does not itself depend on economics. Whichever factor one chooses, one can, with sufficient ingenuity, resolve all the others into it. Just as the many advocates of a unique religious revelation all refute each other, so do the many forms of hedgehogism.

Diamond is especially keen to eliminate racist explanations of differential development and, of course, he is not unique in this respect. We know of no school of thought, current in American academic circles, that still accounts for European economic superiority in terms of some alleged genetic superiority of Europeans. The odd thing about Diamond is that he refutes one sort of racism with another.

This fascinating book, in our view, gets off to a rocky start. Diamond goes to some length to immediately dispel any race-based answer, pointing out that in Japan, at least, racist explanations for differential growth rates are often offered without apology. While we, of course, agree with Diamond here, the manner in which he tries to illustrate the point is curious. He asserts that, in his experience, not only are industrialized people no smarter than residents of New Guinea and similar places, they are actually less smart. Speaking from the perspective of more than three decades of working in New Guinea, he concludes that New Guineans impress him "as being on the average more intelligent, more alert, more expressive, and more interested in things and people around them than the average European or American is" (p. 20).

Having thus established the genetic superiority of New Guineans (apparently his own impression is proof enough), he proceeds to ask how it might have come about. He arrives at two explanations. First, low infant and child mortality rates in the Western world mean that most infants survive regardless of intelligence and genes. In traditional New Guinea societies, with high levels of mortality, smarter people are more likely than less intelligent ones to survive. One might reply that it is hard to see why the fact that American children do not succumb to diseases preventable by inoculation makes them on average less intelligent. Microbes do not single out the stupid. Moreover, one might as well argue that because so many of the most intelligent people became celibate priests and monks— and surely many did remain celibate—in the millennium of Catholic domination of Europe, Europeans must have become on average dumber than Russians, who allowed priests to marry, and pagans, where no such restrictions existed at all.

While this natural selection argument certainly seems to warrant documentation, the second explanation seems even more fraught. While Western children grow up being passively entertained by television, radio, and movies (of course, today his worry would be about the Internet), children in New Guinea spend their time engaging with others, developing their mental abilities.[5] Diamond concludes this argument by declaring that Yali's question is especially intriguing given

---

5. While Diamond alleges that almost all studies of child development support his hypothesis that passive engagement with technology inhibits mental growth, there are now a number of studies that argue otherwise. For one example, see Kaveri Subrahmanyam, Patricia Greenfield, Robert Kraut, and Elisheva Gross, "The Impact of Computer Use on Children's and Adolescents' Development," *Applied Developmental Psychology*, 22 (2001), pp. 7–30.

what "I believe to be their superior intelligence" (p. 21). But here again, one might as well argue that since Western societies select for verbal and mathematical abilities, and that those are what most people have in mind when they speak of intelligence, Westerners must be smarter. Even if New Guinea favors some aspects of intelligence, they are not the ones that matter.

Diamond does not appear to choose arguments for their cogency and then discover they lead to his desired conclusion. He seems to select any argument that leads to his desired conclusion even if it is easy enough to construct arguments of the same cogency that lead to the opposite conclusion. That is not what respect for the truth entails. But it is where hedgehogism often leads the most intelligent people.

Refuting racist explanations underlying differential growth is laudable. But turning it around and merely asserting superiority among residents of less-developed nations strikes us as overreaching—especially when the same reasoning used to refute racism could with equal plausibility be used to endorse it.

Diamond isn't shy, as indicated in the first sentence of the volume: "This book attempts to provide a short history of everybody for the last 13,000 years" (p. 9). Like Becker, Diamond lays out a clear and provocative account of how differences among peoples' environments explain differences in economic development. And, also like Becker, Diamond's protests that he, of course, recognizes the limitations of his theory feel somewhat hollow. Diamond says that "geography obviously has some effect on history; the open question concerns how much effect, and whether geography can account for history's broad pattern" (p. 25). But there is little doubt left in his conclusion: "In short, Europe's colonization of Africa had nothing to do with differences between European and African peoples themselves, as white racists assume. Rather, it was due to accidents of geography and biogeography—in particular, to the continents' different areas, axes, and suites of wild plant and animal species. That is, the different historical trajectories of Africa and Europe stem ultimately from differences in real estate" (p. 385). Diamond writes as if there were no alternative to racism or other objectionable theories but his own. Not much room for competing ideas there. Pretending that it is either one's own explanation or an obviously unacceptable one is a rhetorical trick more likely to be found among advertisers and political propagandists than in serious academic work.

In his discussion of technology, Diamond asks whether it is possible that the existence of some genius, and the creation of some surprising invention, might have made a difference. As he is aware, the question applies not just to technology but to all aspects of the historical process. If one asks whether Edison, Gutenberg, or some other inventor made a decisive difference, one might ask (as he does) the same question about Napoleon, Alexander the Great, or Julius Caesar. What if each of these men had not crossed his Rubicon?

Diamond allows that Watt, Edison, and the Wright brothers made important improvements and that, without them, resulting inventions might have been "somewhat different." Nevertheless, "the question for our purposes is whether the broad pattern of world history would have been altered significantly if some genius inventor had not been born at a particular place and time. The answer is clear: there has never been any such person" (p. 245). It is obvious that Diamond could not have surveyed every possible case, so his certainty that there can be no contrary one must itself result from applying a theory the argument is designed to prove.

Diamond offers two main explanations for this conclusion. First, inventors must appear in a culture favorable for such inventions. Otherwise, the invention lacks its needed predecessors and cannot be made or, if made, cannot be implemented. Yes, indeed, but that is to answer a different question. Of course, if Edison were born in sixteenth-century Tasmania he would not have invented the light bulb or the phonograph. But suppose not Edison but someone else had taken advantage of American opportunities; could she not have invented something radically different, something that came to suggest yet other inventions we cannot imagine? If you leave someone in a forest with no paths he will find no place to go, but that doesn't mean that, at an intersection of several roads, it does not matter which one is taken. They may lead to very different places. By the same token, it is difficult to imagine what the world would be like if Alexander the Great had not hellenized it or if Napoleon had not spread the ideas of the French Revolution.

Diamond also returns to what might be called the "factor out" (or "average out") argument. The fact that people have suggested so many reasons for innovativeness makes "the historian's task paradoxically easier, by converting societal variation in innovativeness into essentially a random variable. That means that, over a large enough area (such as a whole continent) at any particular time, some proportion of societies is likely to be innovative" (p. 254). By the same token, some proportion of individuals in a society is likely to be innovative. It follows that prediction is possible in history "when the unique features of millions of small-scale brief events become averaged out" (p. 424).

Diamond is not the only hedgehog to get around contingency by statistics, that is, by assuming that things average out. But in many cases they don't. There may be "black swans," rare and unpredictable events that change everything.[6] In chaos theory, some small events can concatenate to have enormous and irreversible effects. Small contingencies that might easily have been different can sometimes lead to one path instead of

6. As Nassim Nicholas Taleb defines the term, a black swan is an event that is highly improbable, but if it does happen, entails massive consequences. See Nassim Nicholas Taleb, *The Black Swan: The Impact of the Highly Improbable* (Random House, 2010).

an alternative that might just as well have been chosen and, in the process, "lock in" a different course of subsequent events. Recent concepts like these—black swans, butterfly effects, path dependency, lock-in and others—seem to testify to our growing recognition that sometimes things do *not* average out.

A contingent event is one that, as Aristotle explained, "may either be or not be; events also therefore may either take place or not take place."[7] Chance, choice, or an unpredictable combination of causes can all create such contingency. When it happens, the future course of events may swerve. To understand it, one must resort to narrative.

Diamond wants to establish human history as a hard and deterministic science.[8] He recognizes that it cannot resemble physics because experiment and precise prediction are not to be had, but he believes (citing his background in ecology and evolutionary biology) that it can resemble acknowledged historical sciences, such as astronomy, geology, ecology, paleontology, and evolutionary biology. Each of these deals with "chains of proximate and ultimate causes" (p. 422) with the former traceable to the latter. As more than one critic of his book has pointed out, Diamond's ambition, like others who have claimed to have discovered "the laws of history," accounts for history by removing everything historical from it.

Thinkers as different as Herbert Butterfield and Leo Tolstoy have observed that if one stands back from the historical process and isolates a few moments (always placing special weight on the present), it is always possible to construct a simple narrative, which in turn can be seen as the effect of a few simple laws. But that simplicity is the result of a sort of historical optical illusion. Tolstoy likens it to a person who views a distant hill where only trees are visible and imagines that the hill con-

7. *The Basic Works of Aristotle*, ed. Richard McKeon (Random House, 1941), p. 47.

8. Diamond refers to the "complexity and unpredictability of historical systems, despite their ultimate determinacy" (p. 407).

tains nothing but trees.[9] Butterfield describes the illusion as one of "general" versus "particular" histories. The closer one looks at a moment, the more vicissitudes, accidents, and incidentals one sees, any one of which might have been different. To factor them out, writes Butterfield, is to factor out the "historical" itself.[10] "The thing which is unhistorical," Butterfield famously concludes, "is to imagine that we can get the essence apart from the accidents."[11]

Diamond imagines that unless one can have a hard historical science, history reduces to one damn thing after another. Once again we are offered a choice between Diamond and absurdity, with no alternative possible. But surely there is *something* between hard historical laws and sheer chance with no pattern. Stephen Jay Gould has in fact placed evolutionary biology itself in that middle ground. If one were to play the tape of historical events over, he argues, history would be likely, at point after point, to take a different path. But that does not mean there are no patterns at all. Rather, there are general regulating principles operating in the background while contingency plays an important role in the foreground. For Gould, the truly Darwinian position is *"laws in the background and contingency in the details,"* with the contingent able to set things on very different paths.[12]

That is pretty much the approach taken by a predecessor of Diamond in exploring the role of disease in history, historian William McNeill's celebrated study *Plagues and Peoples*. McNeill sought to distinguish himself from bacteriologist Hans Zinsser's

9. Leo Tolstoy, "Some Words about the Book *War and Peace,*" in the Norton critical edition of *War and Peace,* ed. George Gibian (Norton, 1966), p. 1367.

10. For a critique of Diamond's book as an end run around the historical, see Gene Callahan, "The Diamond Fallacy," http://mises.org/library/diamond-fallacy.

11. Herbert Butterfield, *The Whig Interpretation of History* (1931; repr. Norton, 1965), p. 69.

12. Stephen Jay Gould, *Wonderful Life: The Burgess Shale and the Nature of History* (Norton, 1989), p. 290.

Rats, Lice, and History, which argued that disease, and the randomness in when and whom it strikes, does play a key role in history.[13] It is easy enough to imagine counterfactual situations in which a disease struck an important leader, or did not strike an army, at a decisive moment. In Zinsser's view, historians have left disease out precisely because it makes explanation of such events in terms of historical processes impossible, so historians were reluctant to recognize it. Nevertheless, he argues, radical chance demonstrably plays a role.

McNeill grants the point about historians. "Heirs as we are to the Enlightenment, which sought to banish the inexplicable, if necessary by neglecting it, historians of the twentieth century have also preferred to overlook such events. Anything else spoiled the web of interpretation and explanation through which their art sought to make human experience intelligible."[14] Nevertheless, McNeill identifies some intriguing broad patterns of the role of disease in history and its kinship with other forms of "parasitism," including humans who exploit resources parasitically from each other. Conquerors act like "macroparasites." Contingency operates within the framework of broader patterns. In McNeill's account, we return to intelligibility without dismissing the effect of radical contingency. If Diamond and Zinsser stand at opposite poles, each of which imagines that the only alternative is the other, McNeill, like Gould, occupies the foxy middle ground.

Foxy and Other Economists

When trying to explain growth rates, economists—like geographers, biologists, and historians—employ approaches ranging from hedgehog to fox and everything in between.

---

13. Hans Zinsser, *Rats, Lice, and History* (Transaction, 2008), originally published in 1935.
14. William H. McNeill, *Plagues and Peoples* (Anchor Press, 1976), p. 222.

Not surprisingly, this subject matter has long captured their interest, resulting in a large literature on which factors contribute to economic growth. Technology is usually at the forefront of these analyses, with the absence of technological change leading to little or no growth in output. Of course, simply saying that technology matters doesn't necessarily suggest a particular growth strategy. What are the factors that give rise to the discovery and adoption of new technologies? Most agree that education plays a critical role, as investments in human capital make workers more productive and speed the pace of innovation. Innovation is at the heart of growth, according to Joseph Schumpeter, as a process of creative destruction makes old technologies and products obsolete.

Much of this work is quite technical, using sophisticated models and empirical techniques. But in some cases it is also unusually eclectic, at least for economists, drawing on a wide range of influences. Studies that focus on physical capital and the natural endowment of resources, for example, may fit easily into economic models. But there is also work that stresses law, climate, geography, politics, religion, and even culture, which usually do not.

We give examples of a hedgehog, an imaginative and influential approach that is hard to characterize, and then a couple of foxes.

Rostow: Modern History as a Whole

Those of a particular age undoubtedly remember Walt Rostow's 1960 analysis of economic growth.[15] His five stages were once well known far beyond economics. Whether Rostow actually meant this model to be exclusive, he was taken to have believed exactly that: if not a hedgehog, he was rapidly hedgehogized. Briefly, an economy goes from traditional society, to

---

15. W.W. Rostow, *The Stages of Economic Growth: A Non-Communist Manifesto*, second edition (Cambridge University Press, 1971).

adopting the preconditions for takeoff, to takeoff itself, to a drive to maturity, to the ultimate stage in economic development: the age of high mass consumption. It is all very neat and predictable. You begin with subsistence agriculture, limited technology, and little economic mobility; move to stage two where the demand for raw materials induces investments in physical infrastructure and the onset of social mobility; the takeoff stage is characterized by increasing urbanization and industrialization; stage four occurs when the industrial base diversifies and the nonprofit sector grows; eventually, stage five means a consumer-driven economy, where income levels are high enough to promote widespread prosperity.

How tempting it is to present a theory of development that allegedly applies everywhere. Once again, the search for universal laws leads a scholar down the road to hedgehogism. Don't countries vary in so many ways—in size, in location, in their colonial legacies, their religions, their customs? Details, details, details. As we wrote in chapter 2, hedgehogs are sure that all that messy complexity hides simple, far-reaching truths, and Rostow was convinced he had found them.

Rostow saw these stages as universal: "I have gradually come to the view that it is possible and, for certain limited purposes, it is useful to break down the story of each national economy—and sometimes the story of regions—according to this set of stages. They constitute, in the end, both a theory about economic growth and a more general, if still highly partial, theory about modern history as a whole." To be sure, Rostow recognizes that there are major differences between "Khrushchev's Russia, Meiji Japan ... Bismarck's Germany and Nasser's Egypt," and insists that his model allows one to see "the uniqueness of each nation's experience" (p. 1). Nevertheless, that uniqueness takes place within the five stages applying universally.

In one form or another, controversy over arguments like Rostow's has dominated Western culture since the late eighteenth century. As Enlightenment thinkers sketched out a single possible line of progress, romantics, beginning at least with Herder, viewed cultural and national differences as significant. For them, different paths of development are possible.[16] Since the single path typically made France the leader, Germans tended to favor a model of multiple paths. As France took itself to be the model of all "civilization," Germany favored a plurality of "cultures." Civilization came to stand for a single path and goal; culture for a plurality of them. In the former case, history had an inherent direction and the details really affected nothing. In the latter, the details made all the difference.[17]

In Russia, this argument played out in the 1840s as a dispute between "Westernizers" and "Slavophiles." The Westernizers thought that the only way to progress was to follow precisely in the footsteps of Western Europe, whereas the Slavophiles thought that, to succeed, modernization had to be adapted to the peculiarities of a specific culture. It is a common mistake to think that the Slavophiles were Luddites. Quite the contrary was true. Rather, they thought that, for modern technology and institutions to "take," they could not just be imposed from above but had to grow out of the culture adapting them.[18] You can't just export the American or British constitution to Russia, Mexico, or Iran and expect it to work.[19] And what is true of institutions is true of technology as well.

16. On Herder's significance for economists, see Bronck, *The Romantic Economist*, pp. 88–90, 120–121, 149–150, and 175–176.

17. See the classic explanation of Norbert Elias, "Sociogenesis of the Difference between *Kultur* and *Zivilisation*, *The Civilizing Process: The History of Manners and State Formation and Civilization*, trans. Edmund Jephcott (Blackwell, 1994). This idea of historical pluralism also shaped Isaiah Berlin's political and methodological pluralism. See Isaiah Berlin, *Vico and Herder: Two Studies in the History of Ideas* (Random House, 1977).

18. See Nicholas Riasanovsky, *Russia and the West in the Teachings of the Slavophiles: A Study of Romantic Ideology* (Peter Smith, 1965); and Andrzej Walicki, *The Slavophile Controversy: History of a Conservative Utopia in Nineteenth-Century Russian Thought* (University of Notre Dame Press, 1989).

19. Thanks to Firuz Kazemzadeh for the comparison with Iran.

In *Anna Karenina*, the hero Konstantin Levin at first tries to increase the productivity of his estate by adopting Western machinery, seed oats, and work patterns, but he finds that somehow the machines that work in England always seem to break, the seed oats gets ruined, and the peasants just don't seem to be able to follow English work norms. It turns out that all the progressive noblemen he meets have the same problem, even if they won't say so lest such complaints endanger their progressive credentials. Levin even finds one such nobleman who has hired a German accountant to calculate the return on his modernizing investments, only to discover that the return is negative.

Levin at last finds a prosperous peasant who has innovated not from the top down but from the bottom up. He has borrowed some Western technology where it fits, adapted other innovations to fit local circumstances, and jury-rigged solutions loosely inspired by the inventions he has read about, while then adjusting the new pattern to operate as a whole. Instead of following a trajectory given in advance, at each stage he assesses how earlier innovations have worked, drops some, and pursues promising lines of development suggested by others. The result could not have been predicted in advance but works quite well. Levin realizes that this is the way to innovate successfully. And the point applies not only to technology narrowly defined but also to what might be called social technology.[20]

One reason that Russian history is so important is that it was the first country to undergo rapid modernization, a process followed by many countries since. Japan, Turkey, and Iran all had their equivalents of Slavophiles and Westernizers, and the comparison of Ataturk and the Shah of Iran to Peter the Great—all autocrats using their power to modernize rapidly—illustrates how the same issues keep arising. Americans have

---

20. See Gary Saul Morson, *"Anna Karenina" in Our Time: Seeing More Wisely* (Yale University Press, 2007), pp. 143–167.

had a tendency to assume that as a country develops economically, it must also adopt Western-style democracy, as South Korea and Taiwan in fact did. But it is not at all clear that other paths are ruled out. Certainly the Chinese Communist Party, which has transformed itself into a Chinese authoritarian state capitalist party, maintains that a different path is possible and perhaps superior. To use the oft-quoted comment of Singapore's long-term leader Lee Kuan Yew, an Asian country can develop according to "Asian values." To have technology, growth, and entrepreneurs, one doesn't need baseball, Coca-Cola, or divided government.[21]

Rostow's many critics disagreed with his analysis in the strongest terms. They said that, at best, this was a model that explained Western development but certainly not economic growth in Asia or Africa. And it was so predetermined: you do this and it leads to that. Growth becomes inevitable, even though it is hard to find such inevitability in the real world.

A controversial (and many would say problematic) economic model at least provokes discussion and stirs others to contribute to the literature. But if its author takes his view into the policy arena, the stakes are heightened. Rostow became a highly influential presidential adviser, serving in a prominent role in both the Kennedy and Johnson administrations. It isn't clear whether his unmistakable anticommunism (note the subtitle of his book) and faith in capitalism came from the confidence he had in his economic growth model or whether those principles influenced the model itself, but in either case

21. In 1965, Singapore ranked with Chile, Argentina, and Mexico; today its GDP is more than four times that of those countries. Its per capita GDP is larger than that of its former colonial master, Great Britain. See Fareed Zakaria, "A Conversation with Lee Kuan Yew," *Foreign Affairs*, March/April 1994, https://www.foreignaffairs.com/articles/asia/1994-03-01/conversation-lee-kuan-yew; and Orville Schell, "Lee Kuan Yew, the Man Who Remade Asia," *Wall Street Journal*, March 27, 2015, http://www.wsj.com/articles/lee-kuan-yew-the-man-who-remade-asia-1427475547. Schell notes that China now accepts and promotes the Singapore model.

he carried those beliefs with him during his government service. In fact, observers point to Rostow's hawkish attitude toward Vietnam as an important contributor to our nation's stance in building toward and then continuing that war. One wonders if Rostow imagined the United States could impose a single path of social and political development on another culture, a tempting but usually dangerous error in judgment. If so, it is a way of thinking still very much with us.

Alternative 1: Acemoglu, Johnson, and Robinson

For an approach that rejects the acultural model of Rostow (as well as the single-path model of Diamond), we turn next to a particularly impressive and influential paper by Acemoglu, Johnson, and Robinson, which draws liberally on a variety of literatures.[22] The authors recognize that countries that invest more in physical and human capital develop faster. No surprise there—even for Rostow. But then they step back and ask, what encourages those investments? Numerous economists have attributed this positive growth environment to the presence of the "right" institutions—a legal system that enforces well-defined property rights, a government that encourages entrepreneurial activity, and so on.[23] Still, they ask, is it the

22. Daron Acemoglu, Simon Johnson, and James A. Robinson, "The Colonial Origins of Comparative Development: An Empirical Investigation," *American Economic Review*, December 2001, pp. 1369–1401. See also their "Institutions as a Fundamental Cause of Economic Growth," in *Handbook of Economic Growth*, ed. Philippe Aghion and Steven Durlauf (Elsevier, 2005), pp. 385–465, and "The Rise of Europe: Atlantic Trade, Institutional Change, and Economic Growth," *American Economic Review*, May 2005, pp. 546–579; Daron Acemoglu and Matthew O. Jackson, "History, Expectations and Leadership in the Evolution of Social Norms," *Review of Economic Studies*, April 2015, pp. 423–456; and Daron Acemoglu and James A. Robinson, "De Facto Political Power and Institutional Persistence," *American Economic Review*, May 2006, pp. 325–330, and *Why Nations Fail: The Origins of Power, Prosperity, and Poverty* (Crown, 2012).

23. Much of this work stems from the pathbreaking contributions of Nobel laureate Douglass North. See, for example, Douglass C. North, *Structure and Change in Economic History* (W. W. Norton, 1981), and *Understanding the Process of Economic Change* (Princeton University Press, 2005).

institutions that give rise to growth or the growth that provides the wealth to afford better institutions?

It turns out that institutions have a large, independent impact on economic performance, not just in Europe and North America but throughout the world. Recall the puzzle of Ghana. This study asks specifically whether the dismal growth history in Africa results from factors such as Diamond's favorite, geography, or from any of a number of noninstitutional causes. Their answer is no. Instead, Africa is poorer than other continents due to its weak institutions. But why, you might ask, did a poor institutional framework develop in the first place? Are some countries randomly blessed with the right institutions and others cursed with the wrong ones? If we want to foster economic development, we'd better know that answer.

Fortunately, the authors tease this out in terms of the colonial experience that different nations faced. Europeans, they argue, used different colonization strategies, which led to different institutions. In the United States, for example, European powers settled in the colonies, setting up institutions that protected property rights and encouraged investment. In much of Africa, however, colonial powers set up extractive states whose main purpose was to transfer resources back home. The institutions that resulted had a long-term negative influence on economic progress. But why did colonialists settle in some places and not others? Where mortality rates were very high, the Europeans stayed away; in others, they could safely settle.

So the authors nest their questions in an intriguing way. Economic growth comes largely from investments in capital; investments in capital tend to come from the presence of the right institutions; the right institutions by and large are developed where colonialists settle; colonialists often settle where mortality rates are low. Hard to believe that factors affecting where Europeans could settle in the distant past would be linked to economic development today, but the authors show that early institutions powerfully impact institutions today and that those institutions have a strong causal link with economic development. What's more, the authors control for a myriad of other factors—latitude, climate, the current disease environment, religion, natural resources, soil quality, ethnolinguistic fragmentation, and current racial composition—and still institutions play a prominent role. Finally, it is not the case that a country that used to have bad institutions is doomed to poverty. Nations that improve their institutions experience significant economic gains. Remember South Korea? It is presented as an example of just such a change.

Of course, one could also point out that the effects of colonialism were not quite so uniform, depending on the specific colonial power and the society's preexisting institutions and history. The English and the Portuguese treated their colonies differently, and even Ethiopia, which was never successfully colonized, did not have much economic success. In general, one wants to avoid the impression that everything about a culture is due to Western influence—that is, to the culture of most of the people doing the analysis—whether for good or ill, a position that seems to take away all agency from others, however different they may be from each other or from the West.

We decided to highlight this paper from a massive literature because we consider it to be a tour de force. So many economic growth studies comfortably situate themselves within the safe confines of traditional economic analysis—examining the impact of investments in infrastructure, research and development, and the like. Important work for sure, but not the type of inquiries we love and that this book highlights. In their extensive bibliography, the authors cite not only economists but legal scholars, historians, demographers, political scientists, biologists, physicians, and more. They have come a long way from a model that explains all of development in simple economic terms.[24]

Still, no one would argue that Yali's question has been definitively answered. Institutions matter, and they surprisingly appear to reflect health conditions (mortality rates) from long ago. But what of all the other possible explanations for why countries develop? Do certain religions foster more growth than others? Why did India develop differently from Pakistan? Do certain kinds of educational investments help? What about "great men" who seem to have an outsize impact on the world? Would Singapore have developed as well without Lee Kuan Yew or China if the Gang of Four had won out instead of Deng Xiaoping? And why is it that in some places entrepreneurs are rewarded and in others they are reviled?

Does this approach claim to explain all differential economic growth? No. But it does offer a fascinating story—one where institutions matter, even if their origin is explained in a way that surely would make some historians and sociologists a bit uncomfortable.

And what about culture? It seems impossible to account for its extraordinary variability in any one model. Perhaps that is why hedgehogs shy away from it. But foxes embrace it.

Alternative 2: Easterlin and Social Capability

We return now to a foxy hero from the previous chapter, Richard Easterlin, and then move on to another highly influential economic historian, Joel Mokyr. They are willing and eager to cross the boundaries set by traditional economic models.

---

24. There are a number of other excellent examples of economists taking noneconomic factors seriously in explaining growth rates. Deirdre McCloskey's monumental trilogy is especially noteworthy: *The Bourgeois Virtues: Ethics for an Age of Commerce* (University of Chicago Press, 2006), *Bourgeois Dignity: Why Economics Can't Explain the Modern World* (University of Chicago Press, 2010), and *Bourgeois Equality: How Ideas, Not Capital or Institutions, Enriched the World* (University of Chicago Press, 2016).

In his book *Growth Triumphant*, Easterlin asks, "Why isn't the whole world developed?"[25] While technology underpins much of economic growth, inducing investments in both physical and human capital and in the mobility of labor and capital, why did the diffusion of technology vary so greatly country by country? His answer: Some had the appropriate institutions and some did not. Without the right institutions, economic growth could not take root.

The "establishment of the rule of law, enforcement of contracts, political stability, and elimination of arbitrary seizure or taxation of property by despots or others was essential" (p. 56). But how did favorable institutional conditions develop? Education is key, fostering modern economic growth by increasing the mobility of the population. But the overriding factor is "social capability," a term associated with a number of other development experts and referring not just to the level of educational and technological competence but also to the presence of a flourishing set of financial institutions, along with political and social characteristics that foster economic activity and reward entrepreneurs both financially and in terms of social esteem.

Easterlin astutely argues that education doesn't always promote economic growth; it depends on its content. Is it of a secular and rationalistic type? If not, its impact will be muted. And what of the government? Does it establish a judicial system that encourages the pursuit of economic opportunity? A helpful government might not assure economic growth, but an unhelpful one sure can hamper it. It is clear that some factors shaping institutions can't be explained in purely economic terms.

Easterlin concludes by reiterating his faith in institutions—economic, social, and political—and calling for research in

---

25. Richard A. Easterlin, chapter 5, "Why Isn't the Whole World Developed? Institutions and the Spread of Economic Growth," in *Growth Triumphant: The Twenty-First Century in Historical Perspective* (University of Michigan Press, 1996).

how they develop and how they can be changed. Obviously, the paper by Acemoglu, Johnson, and Robinson fits nicely into this framework.

One final point regarding Easterlin: He provides an interesting analysis of the question over which Ehrlich and Simon so strongly disagreed—what is the impact of population change on economic growth?[26] He is especially interested in whether the rapid increase in population that resulted from mortality declines in the developed world has impeded their economic development. On the one hand, doomsayers such as Ehrlich follow a long tradition going back to Thomas Malthus, arguing that rapid population growth leads to a range of horrific scenarios. However, Easterlin argues, such scenarios have not come to pass. Perhaps the improvement in health itself promotes economic growth, or an expanding population has a positive impact on the creation and diffusion of knowledge. Or maybe the threat of population pressure induces changes in behavior that are beneficial to economic increases. With theories for and against the negative versus positive impact of population growth, Easterlin looks to the empirical evidence on the link between population increases and economic changes. The result? Variations in population growth rates have no consistent relationship with growth rates in real per capita income. "To sum up, in both within-country comparisons over time and among countries during a given point of time, one finds mixed results on the association between economic growth and population growth—sometimes no association, sometimes positive, sometimes negative" (p. 92).

Not an answer that would give a hedgehog much comfort, but the world is foxy, and perhaps that is why explanations that purport to work in all places and at all times seldom hold up to empirical scrutiny.

---

26. See our chapter 2 for a description of this debate and Easterlin's chapter 7, "Malthus Revisited: The Economic Impact of Rapid Population Growth," in *Growth Triumphant*.

Alternative 3: Mokyr and What People Believe

We conclude this chapter by taking a closer examination of another fox whose work has been attracting widespread attention not only from economists but from a range of other social scientists as well.

In his book *The Enlightened Economy* (cited earlier in this chapter), Joel Mokyr poses what he calls "the big problem" and "the little problem."[27] The "big problem" recalls Yali's question:

> Why did Western Europe succeed in doing something that no society in history had ever done, that is, break through the confining negative feedback barriers that had kept the bulk of people who had ever lived before 1800 at a level of poverty that is by now practically unknown in the West? Despite their formidable scientific and technological achievements in years past, neither the Ottoman world, nor China, nor India, even came close. (p. 10)

The "little problem" is, why was it Britain that took the (temporary) lead in this process? Perhaps unsurprisingly, it turns out that the two problems are closely related. In direct contrast to Diamond, Mokyr contends that "the answers to both questions in the end need to be sought in the realm of knowledge and institutions, not geography" (p. 12).

Mokyr deems some explanations that have been offered, such as climate, race, and religion, "bizarre" (p. 10). Given the importance of Max Weber's classic study *The Protestant Ethic and the Spirit of Capitalism*, it is not entirely clear why religion, even if we conclude it is mistaken, is "bizarre." And the same may be said of climate, if the concept is expanded to include other geographical factors mentioned by Diamond. For Mokyr, other candidates, such as culture, society, empire, and

---

27. See also *The Gifts of Athena* (Princeton University Press, 2002) and his Economic History Association presidential address, "The Intellectual Origins of Modern Economic Growth," *Journal of Economic History*, June 2005, pp. 285–351.

politics, are "plausible-but-hard-to-prove" (p. 10), which may be as good as we are likely to get with historical explanation.

Quite persuasively, Mokyr rejects any single-factor explanation. He cautions against "hindsight bias" and "teleology," that is, assuming that the outcome we know was inevitable and somehow managed to pull earlier events toward it.[28] And he cautions against thinking that the story he singles out is all that was going on in the economy, let alone elsewhere. "A great deal happened in the British economy that was in no way or only tangentially related to the Industrial Revolution. Just because the Industrial Revolution took place does not imply that everything before and during it necessarily 'caused' or even facilitated it or that everything after was caused by it" (p. 4).

There were many stories, each with many causes, interacting in complex and unpredictable ways. Nothing was inevitable, and contingency played a crucial role. Mokyr's way of explaining is rich in narrativeness. There is no way around stories.

In particular, Mokyr rejects the tendency among some economists to derive everything from economic factors. As with their antagonists, the Marxists, mainstream economists tend to attribute beliefs, ideology, and cultural factors to economic causes. The causal efficacy of these apparently noneconomic factors is therefore economic at one remove, just as, with Diamond, the same factors are geographical at one remove. In this perspective, nothing is "exogenous," and everything "endogenous," to economics.

Mokyr insists that, to the contrary, beliefs that cannot be entirely reduced to economic factors played a crucial role. His book begins, "Economic change in all periods depends, more than most economists think, on what people believe" (p. 1),

28. In narratives, this leads to foreshadowing after the fact, or "backshadowing." See Michael Andre Bernstein, *Forgone Conclusions: Against Apocalyptic History* (University of California Press, 1994), and Morson, *Narrative and Freedom: The Shadows of Time* (Yale University Press, 1994), pp. 234–264.

and this was especially true of British economic development between the Glorious Revolution of 1688 and the Crystal Palace Exhibition of 1851. "In addition to standard arguments … the beginnings of modern economic growth depended a great deal on what people knew and believed, and how those beliefs affected their economic behavior" (p. 1). Mokyr above all has in mind the European Enlightenment, and he quotes John Maynard Keynes's famous 1936 passage on the importance of ideas irreducible to economics: "the power of vested interests is vastly exaggerated compared with the gradual encroachment of ideas … soon or late, it is ideas, not vested interests, which are dangerous for good or evil."[29] But note that Mokyr stresses ideas "in addition to," not instead of, other factors. It, too, is one factor in complex interaction with others.

Ideas in turn depend often enough on yet another non-economic, indeed literary, factor for their success or failure: rhetoric— or as Mokyr calls it, *persuasion*—played a crucial role. People did not always act in their own self- or class interest and were sometimes persuaded to act for the good of the nation. There is no simple answer as to why some ideas win out and others do not. The circumstances need to be right, but some ideas will fail even then and others that might have succeeded do not emerge.

A humanist would add that a lot perhaps depends on particular people. And particular people, too, may or may not emerge. Without Columbus someone else would have discovered America, but it defies common sense to assert that without Milton someone else would have written *Paradise Lost*. Ideas are closer to literary masterpieces than undiscovered continents because there are many possible ideas that could arise at any time, each with its own trajectory to other ideas. If after the fact it looks as if the idea was inevitable, that is only

---

29. Cited from *The General Theory of Employment, Interest, and Money* (Harcourt Brace, 1964), pp. 383–384, in Mokyr, p. 1.

because we are the product of it and it is hard to imagine any other possibility. We succumb to what Tolstoy called "the fallacy of retrospection."[30] The same is true of technological ideas; as Henry Petroski has argued, there is no inherent direction to inventions, which can always lead in multiple directions.[31]

Mokyr observes, "Just as in evolutionary biology we can never know precisely why some highly fit species emerged and others, just as fit, did not, there is a baffling indeterminacy in history. Good timing and contingency explain outcomes" (p. 2). Timing—an event happening at one moment when it easily could have happened at another—and contingency—an event happening when it might not have happened at all— both require explanation in terms of narrative rather than overarching laws.

Britain emerged as preeminent, but it may well have been some other country. And although one can give a plausible account of why Europe, rather than China, created the Industrial Revolution, plausibility is not certainty. It derives not from timeless laws but from historical circumstances and human choices, which require narrative to understand.

The Harm That Hedgehogs Do

In recent years, a number of studies, reflecting on the failure of so many well-intentioned development schemes, have demonstrated the destructive effects of hedgehog thinking. The hubristic claim that economists (or experts in some other discipline) have arrived at hard scientific knowledge, capable of successfully guiding development, has led to disaster after disaster. These experts, armed with that putative knowledge, construct master plans of development often put into practice by authoritarian regimes. For obvious reasons, experts have

---

30. Leo Tolstoy, *War and Peace*, trans. Ann Dunnigan (Signet, 1968), p. 854.
31. See Henry Petroski, *The Evolution of Everyday Things* (Vintage, 1992).

aided such regimes when they are willing to put their schemes into practice. The messiness of democratic institutions makes the imposition of a comprehensive scheme almost impossible.

Cataloging the many "huge development fiascos" in Eastern European and third world countries, James C. Scott, in his book *Seeing Like a State: How Certain Schemes to Improve the Human Condition Have Failed*, points to the towering human cost that overconfidence in all-embracing theories has entailed.

> But "fiasco" is too lighthearted a word for the disasters I have in mind. The Great Leap Forward in China, collectivization in Russia, and compulsory villagization in Tanzania, Mozambique, and Ethiopia are among the great human tragedies of the twentieth century, in terms of both lives lost and lives irretrievably disrupted. At a less dramatic but far more common level, the history of Third World development is littered with the debris of huge agricultural schemes and new cities (think of Brasilia and Chandigarh) that have failed their residents.[32]

We readily understand, Scott continues, how lives can be lost in wars launched by aggressive dictators or in genocidal campaigns, but it is much harder to appreciate why as many lives have been lost by schemes beneficently intended to improve the human condition. It would appear that nothing causes greater evil than comprehensive schemes to abolish it.

Time and again, supposed experts, backed by massive force, put into practice development plans that did not take into account the peculiarities of particular belief systems (viewed as mere "superstition"), the importance of local experience with conditions varying in no predictable way, the role of tacit knowledge that no one can specify but that can make all the difference, and, above all, the need to proceed step-by-step to check whether one change has worked before implementing

32. James C. Scott, *Seeing Like a State: How Certain Schemes to Improve the Human Condition Have Failed* (Yale University Press, 1998), p. 3.

the next. By their very nature, hedgehogs lack the humility necessary to prevent mistakes from becoming catastrophes.

In Tanzania, Scott argues, the World Bank and an ideology of planning expertise combined to back Julius Nyerere's *ujamaa* villages campaign. Beginning in 1973, nomads and farmers were taken from their previous abodes and resettled along main roads so that they could easily receive the appropriate public services, and replace traditional practices with scientific agriculture. Torn from the environment with which they were familiar, they lacked all local knowledge. What the planners thought of as "destructive conservatism" could also have been described as the accumulated wisdom of experience. The result was ecological disaster and famine. In Ethiopia, which under Mengistu resettled over four million people in a year, the result was still worse.

More recently, William Easterly, reflecting on the failure of development schemes in which he himself had participated, came to similar conclusions about the hubris of supposed expertise. His study *The Tyranny of Experts: Economists, Dictators, and the Forgotten Rights of the Poor* stresses that expert schemes have a strong tendency to overlook cultural differences.[33] Outlining the views of Gunnar Myrdal, the Nobel Prize–winning economist whose name had long been identified with comprehensive development planning, Easterly cites the criticism by anthropologist Clifford Geertz. Myrdal's picture of India, Geertz observed, was "completely stereotypic ... astonishingly abstract ... unnuanced and unparticularized.... It would seem impossible to write nearly a million words on a country with so rich a history, so profound a culture, and so complex a social system and fail to convey the force of its originality and the vitality of its spirit somewhere; but Professor Myrdal has accomplished it."[34]

---

33. William Easterly, *The Tyranny of Experts: Economists, Dictators, and the Forgotten Rights of the Poor* (Basic Books, 2014).

34. Cited in Easterly, p. 25, from Geertz, "Myrdal's Mythology," *Encounter*, July 1969, p. 31.

But the failure Geertz mentions is not accidental. If one did take account of everything particularized, nuanced, and complex—all the products of a contingent history—it would be impossible to deduce an overarching plan, good for all developing countries, from abstract principles. Instead, the "tyranny of experts" resorts to a "blank slate" approach. There is one sort of thing called "underdevelopment," which is ostensibly the same in countries as different as China, Colombia, and Benin. But decades of expert advice have produced few successes, and a lot more failures. Still worse, it has often proven counterproductive, as it strengthened the authoritarian regimes on which experts rely to implement their plans. They thereby feed the corruption and lawlessness that serve to impede development.

These are mistakes a fox would be less likely to make. Experience seems to show that, in development, generalized economic theory is not enough. One needs as well an understanding of culture, local institutions, and history—in short, everything that entails narrativeness.[35]

35. Dani Rodrik has argued that it is possible to pursue development entirely in terms of neoclassical economics, without taking culture into account, but still craft policies particular to each developing country. Rodrik describes his book as "strictly grounded in neoclassical economic analysis," which he regards as "not just a powerful discipline for organizing our thoughts on economic affairs, but the only sensible way of thinking about them." Nevertheless, the neoclassical economist's toolkit allows for many sets of recommendations. Of the many possible reforms—"protection of property rights, market-based competition, appropriate incentives, sound money, and so on"—some have to be chosen first, and that decision should depend on local circumstances. See Dani Rodrik, *One Economics, Many Recipes: Globalization, Institutions, and Economic Growth* (Princeton University Press, 2007), pp. 3–6. Rodrik's approach is undoubtedly superior to one-size-fits-all thinking, but in not allowing for culture, our view is that it does not go far enough. A country may lack property rights or the rule of law, for instance, for numerous reasons. One country may simply not have been exposed to the appropriate institutions, while another may be well aware of them and have rejected them—as numerous Russian thinkers have for two centuries—as contrary to the national spirit. For many Russians, it almost feels like a form of treason to advocate "legalisms," while acting against what we think of as the rule of law may be felt as a positive virtue.

When economic thinking turns to stories, and so combines with humanistic explanation, we believe a rich account is possible. On the one hand, Diamond turns to history in an attempt to overcome it; on the other, Mokyr embraces history as a way to answer the "big problem" of differential development.

To be sure, we still don't have a definitive answer to Yali's question. Why Korea and not Ghana? No one knows for sure. But should we ever find the answer—or answers—we suspect it will involve *some* factors that are far removed from traditional economic analyses, entering into the realms of political science and history, sociology and law. It will almost certainly involve institutions, and customs, and faith. And it will be much too random and too unpredictable for a hedgehog to force into a universal model.

Isn't it ironic that perhaps the most important question economists are asked—why some countries develop faster than others—requires them to reach further outside their comfort zones than for anything else they might address? If there were ever an area to be a fox, this is it.

Chapter 6

The Best of the Humanities

Beware the man of only one book.
—Latin proverb

There are certain intellectual luxuries that
perhaps we could do without. [Taxpayers should
not be] subsidizing intellectual curiosity.

—California governor Ronald Reagan, 1967

In a volume about infusing the wisdom of the humanities into
mainstream economics—a topic that for us arose from co-
teaching an undergraduate course—it seems natural to turn
to a subject near and dear to our hearts: undergraduate education. Are there implications for how best to teach undergraduates? Let's assume that we, the authors, had the power to
dictate what was taught. What would *we* do?[1] More generally,
we ask which approaches to the humanities and to economics
represent the best of those fields and how they could be made
to reflect one another.

We begin by returning to a principal question from chapter 1,
fleshing it out in much more detail: How should humanities
education be understood? The answer is key to our argument

---

1. Economists love to come up with improbable assumptions in making their arguments—perfect information, no barriers to entry, full employment, among others. The
assumption that a university president and a literature professor could determine the
curriculum is about equally plausible.

that the economic approach would be more powerful if it were augmented by the best of humanistic methods. What is the "best?" Is it what the humanities presently espouse? If it is, why are the humanities allegedly under siege?

For the past decade or so, a flood of books, articles, and op-eds, along with statements by educators, universities, and professional organizations, have described and regretted a decline in the humanities, by which is meant a sharp decrease in the number of students taking humanities courses or majoring in humanistic disciplines.[2] In the late 1960s, nearly 18 percent of bachelor's degrees came from the humanities, but by 2010 this number had shrunk to 8 percent. Optimists respond that the decline has not been even and that most of it had taken place by the early 1980s, but others have been more alarmed.[3] A recent study of Harvard undergraduates shows a continuing decline, as majors in the humanities fell from 36 percent in 1954 to 20 percent in 2012, with the slide continuing. We were struck by the fact that at Stanford about 45 percent of faculty members in the main undergraduate division come from the humanities, while only 15 percent of its students do.

These numbers will surely give pause to economists, who love market tests. If the product is so good, they say, why aren't consumers buying it? And what's worse, since many colleges

2. See, for instance, the reports by the American Academy of Arts and Sciences *The Heart of the Matter* (http://humanitiescommission.org/_pdf/hss_report.pdf) and *The State of the Humanities: Higher Education 2015* (http://www.humanitiesindicators. org/binaries/pdf/HI_HigherEd2015.pdf). Examples from the national media include Jennifer Levitz and Douglas Belkin, "Humanities Fall from Favor," *U.S. News & World Report*, June 6, 2013, and Tamar Lewin, "As Interest Fades in the Humanities, Colleges Worry," *New York Times*, October 30, 2013. See also our co-authored chapter "The Future of Higher Education in the United States (and the World)" in *The Fabulous Future? America and the World in 2040* (Northwestern University Press, 2015).

3. A recent report indicates that the number of bachelor's degrees in core humanities disciplines declined almost 9 percent between 2012 and 2014. See Scott Jaschik, "Study Shows 8.7 Percent Decline in Humanities Bachelor's Degrees in 2 Years," *Inside Higher Education*, March 14, 2016.

and universities have general education requirements that force students to take courses in the humanities in order to graduate, what would the decline be like otherwise? That is a truly scary thought to contemplate.

Beyond the actual numbers, it is easy to detect a sense of growing impatience among students and society at large with the humanistic disciplines. The more expensive college is, the more each part of it demands justification. While there is a consensus about the economic and social value of science, technology, engineering, and mathematics—the so-called STEM fields—what exactly is the value of studying Latin poetry, French drama, or the many kinds of "cultural studies"?

Now that isn't exactly a new question, as then Governor Reagan's quote at the beginning of the chapter makes clear. But these days it is seemingly ubiquitous. A couple of our "favorites"[4]: "If I'm going to take money from a citizen to put into education, then I'm going to take that money to create jobs.... Is it a vital interest of the state to have more anthropologists? I don't think so" (Florida governor Rick Scott, 2011). "If you want to take gender studies, that's fine. Go to a private school and take it. But I don't want to subsidize that if that's not going to get someone a job" (North Carolina governor Pat McCrory, 2013). "Folks can make a lot more, potentially, with skilled manufacturing or the trades than they might with an art-history degree" (President Obama, 2014). And after the president apologized for this remark, "Pathetic Obama apology to art history prof. We do need more degrees that lead to #jobs." (Florida senator Marco Rubio, via Twitter, 2014).

And Senator Rubio wasn't done. During his quest to win over Iowa voters in advance of their 2016 caucus, he made a number of choice comments, including, we can't "keep graduating people with degrees that don't lead to jobs." "So, you can

4. "Politicians Then and Now on Liberal Education," *Chronicle of Higher Education*," January 30, 2015.

decide if it's worth borrowing $50,000 to major in Greek phi-losophy, because after all, the market for Greek philosophers has been very tight for 2,000 years."[5]

How about another would-be president, Wisconsin gov-ernor Scott Walker? The long-standing "Wisconsin Idea," as pronounced in state law, calls for a "search for truth" as a key mission for the University of Wisconsin. Not good enough for the governor, who, before a groundswell of opposition led his staff to claim the change was inadvertent, tried to drop "search for truth" from the university's charge.[6]

And then there is former Florida governor Jeb Bush: "Universities ought to have skin in the game. When a student shows up, they ought to say, 'Hey, that psych major deal, that philosophy major thing, that's great, it's important to have liberal arts … but realize, you're going to be working at Chick-fil-A.'"[7]

Finally, there is another candidate, Texas senator Ted Cruz. Senator Cruz pledged that, if elected president, he would elim-inate the National Endowment for the Arts. It is hard to believe this is about the federal deficit—the entire budget of the NEA is only $146 million; the deficit is $468 billion. Perhaps he is trying to make a statement about our nation's priorities. As the old Sam Cooke classic might be rewritten:

Don't know much about history
Don't care much for philosophy
Just give me a computer programming book
I just care about the STEM courses I took

5. Erin Murphy, "UPDATE: Rubio Calls for Modernized Economy, Higher Education," *Waterloo Cedar Falls Courier*, August 18, 2015. See also "Marco Rubio vs. Aristotle," *Inside Higher Education*, August 20, 2015.

6. See Philip Bump, "Scott Walker Moved to Drop 'Search for Truth' from the University of Wisconsin Mission. His Office Claims It Was an Error," *Washington Post*, February 4, 2015; and John Nichols, "Scott Walker Objects to the 'Search for Truth,'" *Nation*, February 4, 2015.

7. Curt Mills, "Jeb Bush: Psych Majors Work at Chick-fil-A," *Washington Examiner*, October 24, 2015.

Intellectual curiosity, anthropology, gender studies, art history, psychology, philosophy, the search for truth—all luxuries taxpayers apparently can no longer afford. Of course, it is easy enough for academics to laugh at these comments, but if one looks at the issue from outside the academy—if one does not have a vested interest in academic disciplines regardless of their cost-benefit ratio and is nevertheless expected to pay for them—then perhaps Senator Rubio's and Governor Bush's queries deserve not mirth but a serious answer.

Furthermore, is this just a US phenomenon or is the world following our lead? For so long, it has been the United States that has been committed to broad education, with most other countries embracing much more specialized, and often more technical, training. What is the attitude about the humanities, and about intellectual pursuits in general, in the rest of the world?

One recent article discusses a growing suspicion of the humanities in Japan, and perhaps elsewhere.[8] However, some countries are figuring out what some here in the United States want us to ignore—that training in the liberal arts creates an economically and civically viable population. Why did Singapore invite Yale to open a liberal arts college? Why in China and India is the adoption of a liberal arts curriculum very much on the table?[9] How ironic it would be if, in our panic to match those countries in the production of engineers, they pass us by in the education of students with broader, less technical backgrounds!

8. Mitsuru Obe, "Japan Rethinks Higher Education in Skills Push: Liberal Arts Will Be Cut Back in Favor of Business Programs That Emphasize Research or Vocational Training," *Wall Street Journal*, August 2, 2015, http://www.wsj.com/articles/japan-rethinks -higher-education-in-skills-push-1438571119. The article notes, "With the overhaul effort, Japan joins a swelling number of advanced economies, including the U.S., where shortages of skilled workers have prompted debates about the value of traditional academic disciplines."

9. See, for example, Gerald A. Postiglione, "China Weighs the Value of American Liberal Arts," *Chronicle of Higher Education*, August 29, 2013.

But in our view, the value of non-STEM fields depends on the nature of those disciplines. They can't claim to be valuable regardless of what they do, but they can and often do have great value. How are outsiders to distinguish a serious, if obscure, field of study from one offering nothing better than jargon-ridden propaganda? Surely they deserve an answer.

The very coining of the term STEM, along with its now ever-present use, suggests the belief that these fields are different, as well as more valuable, than others. Apparently, the further from the STEM, the less lovely the flower.

Humanist attempts to defend their disciplines have proven less than impressive. One does not have to share many opinions with noted literary theorist Stanley Fish to recognize the justice of his response to a lengthy report issued by the American Academy of Arts & Sciences, *The Heart of the Matter*, which attempts to offer justifications of humanistic education.[10] After quoting some uplifting but vague sentences, Fish observes: "In each of these sentences, and many others that might be instanced, the key words—'framework,' 'context,' 'complex,' 'meaningfully,' 'understanding,' 'diverse,' 'sensitivity,' 'perspectives'—are spectacularly empty; just where specificity is needed, sonorous abstraction blunts the edge of what is being asserted, rendering it unexceptionable (no one's against understanding, complexity and meaningfulness) and without bite."[11]

Sometimes humanists have resorted to disparaging the vulgarity of their opponents—say, Republican legislators or governors—which, as you saw, is a temptation too enticing for us to ignore. It is always comforting when one's opponents show bad taste. But this easy response proves counterproductive

---

10. American Academy of Arts & Sciences, *The Heart of the Matter: The Humanities and Social Sciences for a Vibrant, Competitive, and Secure Nation* (American Academy of Arts & Sciences, 2013).

11. Stanley Fish, "A Case for the Humanities Not Made," *New York Times*, June 24, 2013, http://opinionator.blogs.nytimes.com/2013/06/24/a-case-for-the-humanities-not-made/?_r=0.

when it comes off as dismissing in advance any objection or demand for justification as so much impertinence. It also may imply that if students are not taking the courses humanists offer, the problem is theirs.

And, in fact, that charge is sometimes explicit. Martha Nussbaum's book *Not for Profit: Why Democracy Needs the Humanities* maintains, as its title suggests, that crass students are interested only in money.[12] Others blame students for their twitterized inability to focus on any long work.

An economist might reply that when a business blames its customers for not appreciating what it has to offer, the business is in real trouble. Here is one case where a brief lesson in economics might help the humanists.

Justifying the Humanities

Why have the humanists been so spectacularly inept at making their case? To begin with, they seem to be used to speaking only to themselves, that is, to people who already accept the value of what they do. They forget that getting paid to do something doesn't mean that you should take the value of what you do for granted. A justification must appeal to those who do not have a vested interest in the activity, particularly if they are expected to pay for it.

Humanists often seem to regard the very demand to justify resources expended on them as a reflection of a value hostile to them, namely, economic efficiency. So when confronted with questions stated in economic terms, they all too often react with outrage at the very question and the "neoliberal" thinking they discover in it.[13] Here again we see two cultures. For economists, or those who accept its idea of scarce resources,

12. Martha C. Nussbaum, *Not for Profit: Why Democracy Needs the Humanities* (Princeton University Press, 2010).

13. See, for instance, Frank Donoghue, *The Last Professors: The Corporate University and the Fate of the Humanities* (Fordham University Press, 2008).

each marginal unit of resources should provide at least as much benefit as it would if spent elsewhere. But in the humanities, this very assumption seems to miss the point. If anything, it seems like the sort of thinking students should be guided away from. Nevertheless, taxpayers and rivals for public funding understandably find the refusal to answer the question perplexing.

Humanists also have difficulty in presenting their case because they are used to speaking one way among themselves and another way to outsiders. To the public at large, they still make statements about the value of great books, of the noblest things said by the most brilliant minds, and of the need to know the Western heritage. They seem to echo Matthew Arnold's definition of criticism as "a disinterested endeavor to learn and propagate the best that is known and thought in the world."[14] Such statements would have been offered sincerely a half century ago, but of course anyone who spoke that way to his or her colleagues in many an English or literature department would be regarded as, at best, clueless. Critics speaking to each other can only quote Arnold with heavy irony.

One will not find uplifting views presented to outsiders in the many recent contributions appearing in the highly influential volume referred to in chapter 1, the *Norton Anthology of Theory and Criticism*. We quote again its paraphrase of how the new "cultural studies" approaches literature: "Literary texts, like other artworks, are neither more nor less important than any other cultural artifact or practice. Keeping the emphasis on how cultural meanings are produced, circulated, and consumed, the investigator will focus on art or literature insofar as such works connect with broader social factors, not because they possess some intrinsic interest or special aesthetic values."[15]

---

14. Matthew Arnold, "The Function of Criticism at the Present Time," in Hazard Adams, ed., *Critical Theory since Plato* (Harcourt Brace, 1971), p. 594.

15. Vincent B. Leitch et al., eds. *The Norton Anthology of Theory and Criticism*, end ed. (Norton, 2010), p. 2478.

But if literary and other artworks are no more important than any other cultural artifact, why give them a special place in the curriculum? When speaking to outsiders one treats the concept of "great literature" as unproblematic, but many specialists believe that there is no such thing as intrinsic value, just the ascription of value for purposes of domination. Value is entirely "contingent."[16] Perhaps another reason literary scholars make an unconvincing case to outsiders is that they do not believe it themselves.

When the *Norton Anthology* speaks of "how cultural meanings are produced, circulated, and consumed," the industrial language is designed to show that there is no difference between art and any other consumer good. In that case, then, why are those politicians mistaken or vulgar if they want to price the good like any other?

Stanley Fish suggested a different sort of answer to give to outsiders, one that would *not* be hypocritical. Do not argue that the humanities will make people wiser, democracy more stable, or society better off, but admit that the study of them is entirely useless.[17] Fish boldly declares: "It is not the business of the humanities to save us, no more than it is their business to bring revenue to a state or a university. What then can they do? They don't do anything, if by 'do' is meant bring about effects in the world. And if they don't bring effects in the world they cannot be justified except in relation to the pleasure they give to those who enjoy them."[18] Of course, this justification would apply equally well to any course of study, however use-

16. As pointed out earlier, the use of the term "contingent" in this sense goes back to Barbara Herrnstein Smith's now classic study of literary value, *Contingencies of Value: Alternative Perspectives for Critical Theory* (Harvard University Press, 1988).

17. See Stanley Fish, "The Last Professor," *New York Times*, January 18, 2009, http://opinionator.blogs.nytimes.com/2009/01/18/the-last-professor/.

18. As cited in "Can the Arts and Humanities 'Save Us'?", Stanford Report, *Stanford News*, February 11, 2009, http://news.stanford.edu/news/2009/february11/future-arts -humanities-fish-021109.html.

less, pernicious, anti-intellectual, or otherwise absurd it might be. If the best case for the humanists lies in the pleasure it gives those who study it, the politicians can win the argument by giving the microphone to the other side.

The Humanities as Often Taught

Morson teaches Northwestern's largest humanities course, in which 500 students a year study Russian novels. Probably fewer than 1 percent of these students plan careers as literature professors, while the majority come from fields distant from the humanities. *The Brothers Karamazov* and *Anna Karenina* are long books, and the study of them requires considerable effort, so why do the students take the course?

When asked, most report that they had not previously understood why literature was worth reading at all. That conclusion was a rational response to the way many had been taught. Judging from their accounts, in secondary school and college, one of three methods predominates. None of these shows why literature is worth the effort.

The most common approach is technical: the student is taught to use terms and identify devices. She learns to recognize "the protagonist" or "antagonist," identify foreshadowing, and, above all, discover symbols. But after she has discovered a symbol of vision, or transition, or Christ, then what? Unless something worth knowing comes from the exercise, reading literature becomes a bit like solving crossword puzzles.

Almost as common is judging literature by contemporary standards. This is not a new approach. People seem to have an irresistible temptation to measure the benightedness of predecessors in comparison with themselves. In *War and Peace* Tolstoy describes how, in histories of the post-Napoleonic era, "all the famous people of the period, from [Tsar] Alexander and Napoleon to Madame de Staël, Photius, Schelling, Fichte, Chateaubriand, and the rest, pass before their stern tribunal and are acquitted and condemned according to whether they promoted progress or reaction ... there is no one in present-day Russian literature, from schoolboy essayist to learned historian, who does not cast his little stone at Alexander for the things he did wrong at this time of his reign." These figures advance "progress" when they approach present values, or rather, the values of the historians who judge them. But all that these objections mean, Tolstoy explains, is that Alexander "did not have the same conception of the welfare of humanity fifty years ago as a present-day professor who from his youth has been occupied with learning, that is, with reading books, listening to lectures, and making notes."[19]

The historians imagine that while their predecessors were blinded by their times and interests, contemporary historians are not—as if they exist out of time or as if the present moment were somehow the first to allow unclouded vision. It always seems as if one's colleagues today have at last arrived at the indisputably right values. The historians also assume that while businessmen, aristocrats, and generals are shaped by the parochial interests and the culture of their occupations, somehow academics are not—or if they are, those conditions are the unique ones that entail no distortion.[20] How convenient it is to have such beliefs! Of course, a generation from now, future academics will shake their heads at the historians of today. Tolstoy is calling for some intellectual humility that all experience suggests is in order.

Many teachers of literature instruct students in judging great writers by their proximity to currently approved values, which are not questioned. And so Shakespeare, Dickens, and

19. Leo Tolstoy, *War and Peace*, trans. Ann Dunnigan (Signet, 1968), pp. 1351–1353.

20. The idea that intellectuals are uniquely free of the particular interests that distort the views of others was perhaps most famously formulated in Karl Mannheim, *Ideology and Utopia: An Introduction to the Sociology of Knowledge*, trans. Louis Wirth and Edward Shils (Harcourt Brace, 1936). See especially the sections entitled "The Sociological Problem of the 'Intelligentsia'" and "The Nature of Political Knowledge," pp. 153–171.

Tolstoy are hauled before the "stern tribunal" of associate professors and high school English teachers. If only divorce laws then had been as enlightened as they are now, Anna Karenina's fate would have turned out differently! Shakespeare's views on gender reflected patriarchal values. We are so much smarter than they were. It should be obvious that this approach guarantees that nothing worth knowing could be learned, since our beliefs are presumed correct and everything else is measured according to them. But in that case, why read literature at all?

A third method for teaching literature, old but still very much with us, treats works as mere documents of their times. "Dickens didn't write in a vacuum, you know!"—as if anyone ever assumed otherwise. And so we learn that Dickens shows us the deplorable conditions of workers of his day, as indeed he does; but a factory surveyor's report might do an even better job. It remains unstated why one should care about the conditions of workers in Victorian England rather than, let us say, peasants in eleventh-century Poland, or any other place. After all, one cannot investigate every period of each culture. This method gets things backward: except in rare cases, one becomes interested in nineteenth-century Russian culture by reading Tolstoy and Dostoevsky, not the reverse.

This approach misunderstands the very nature of literature. And one cannot teach others to appreciate what one fundamentally misunderstands. What makes a work literary in the first place is that it is of interest *outside* the context of its origin.[21] Dickens and Tolstoy have important things to say to us even if we don't care about nineteenth-century England and Russia. Gibbons's *Decline and Fall of the Roman Empire* has long been outdated as a source for understanding ancient

---

21. See John M. Ellis, *The Theory of Literary Criticism: A Logical Analysis* (University of California Press, 1974), chapter 2. "Literary texts," writes Ellis, "are defined as those that are used by the society in such a way that *the text is not taken as specifically relevant to the immediate context of its origin*" (p. 44; italics in original).

and medieval history, but it is still read—as literature—for its insights into human nature, its sense of human experience, its sardonic vision of the historical process, and the inimitable style with which that vision is expressed. Herodotus's *Histories* and Boswell's *Life of Johnson*, though originally offered for their factual content, survive as literature for much the same reasons. And although the great novelists do indeed document their times, that is usually not what makes them great novelists. If all one saw in *War and Peace* was an account of the Napoleonic Wars, one would come away without understanding why it is often regarded as the greatest novel ever written.

Each of the common approaches says true things— literature often uses symbols, people of the past understood social questions differently, and great works, like any other, reflect their time—but none of them gives any reason to think that reading great literature is worth the effort to do so. And that effort is considerable: *Paradise Lost* is difficult; *War and Peace* is long. And so the pay-off would have to be large. Students would be fools to think otherwise.

Why Not Just Read *SparkNotes*?

A good sign something has gone astray is that a work is reduced to a simple message. That, alas, is all too common, because simple messages are easy to teach. A student explained to Morson that she didn't see the point of reading *Huckleberry Finn* if all it told her was (as she had been taught) that "slavery is wrong." Surely, she knew that before; and if that is all the book amounted to, she would be right to think it a waste of time.

This approach not only makes it easy for teachers who do not themselves appreciate literature to have something to say, it also flatters both student and teacher for having mastered a well-known book. And so the two enter into a sort of conspiracy about their understanding of the book, while pretending to regard its distressingly obvious message as profound.

The next step for teachers is to choose works that lend themselves to this approach. Either the chosen works actually convey only a simple message or they can readily be represented as such. But only mediocre literature works this way. A good sign of a futile literary curriculum—one that does not demonstrate why literature is worth the effort—is the replacement of great texts with short, mediocre ones, usually written not long ago, that have a simple, approved lesson everyone already knows. We can call these "slavery is wrong" books.[22]

If all the work does is convey a simple message, then why read it at all? What would be wrong with turning to the *SparkNotes* summary instead? Or why bother even with that—instead, just memorize the brief message. Love your neighbor (*A Tale of Two Cities*). Help the unfortunate (*Les Misérables*). Child abuse is wrong (*Jane Eyre* and *David Copperfield*). Do not kill old ladies, even really mean ones (*Crime and Punishment*). First impressions can be misleading (*Pride and Prejudice*). Don't give in to jealousy (*Othello*). Obsessions can be dangerous (*Moby Dick*). Stop moping and do something! (*Hamlet*). There's no fool like an old fool (*King Lear*). If one cannot provide a convincing reason why such summaries will not do, then one has not really taught literature. The student needs to know why the book is worth *reading*, not just knowing about.

Overcoming the Human

In order to show what a summary might miss, teachers often turn to the technical (or "textual") approach. After all, if one quests after symbols or learns to do a deconstructive or other difficult analysis of "the text," it will probably help to read the words on the page. And as the student pays attention to those words, perhaps he will learn to appreciate them. Yes, indeed,

---

22. Most of the selections in Michael Watts's anthology, *The Literary Book of Economics*, discussed in chapter 1, are of this nature.

but not because of what is taught. Knowing that a text has "devices" or can be read according to a method does not make one love literature. How could it? Rather, appreciation, if it takes place at all, becomes a by-product. Students may experience the joy of reading despite what they are taught to look for. We have all met people who love Jane Austen, or some other great writer, for reasons they think they should be ashamed of.

The key problem with the textual approach is that it equates the literary work with the text, that is, with the words on the page. Looking at literature this way dehumanizes works, which makes it all the more distressing to find the approach so common among humanists. As economists aspire to be physicists, and political scientists to be economists, some humanists aspire to be anything but humanists. Economists suffer from "physics envy"; humanists experience "humanities embarrassment." We see repeated attempts to overcome the merely human element and focus on something hard, scientific, digital, evolutionary, or at least objective, like the solidity of objects. The words on the page can be counted, their symbols catalogued, their devices exposed. The hoi polloi may fall in love with Anna Karenina or Mr. Darcy, but the textualists have gone beyond all that.

But you can't study something by removing what makes it what it is. This is a version of the fallacy of abstraction.[23] Literary works are a dialogue between author and readers about human beings; they are not a display of impersonal forces.

Morson once gave a series of lectures in Norway, where the textual approach governed. A Scandinavian scholar responded, "All my career I have been telling students not to do what you have done, that is, treat characters as real people with real problems and real human psychology. Characters in a novel are nothing more than words on a page. It is primi-

23. This idea reappears in the next chapter, in the discussion of behavioral economics.

tive to treat fictional people as real, as primitive as the spectator who rushed on stage to save Jesus from crucifixion." For
her, it was obvious that serious scholars do not imagine literature is about real people, only philistines do. If the authors
themselves thought otherwise, well, it has been orthodoxy for
decades that the author's intentions do not matter.

We may reply: of course literary characters are not real
people. No one doubts that it would be insane to search Russian
archives for Anna Karenina's birth certificate. No one, including philistines, would think otherwise. But neither are literary characters just words on a page. They are not real people,
but they are *possible* people. That is why we can identify with
them. They experience what we have experienced, and we can
learn from their possible experiences as we can from the experiences of real people. Would we identify with, or learn from
the emotional life of, mere words on a page?

What the textual approach overlooks is that the words on
the page are not themselves the designed literary work but the
mere material for it.[24] The work is the *experience* the words
inspire in the reader. No matter how much one may appreciate symbols or other textual features, if one has not had the
experience the author designed—if one has skipped over all
that philistine human stuff and gone straight to the words
and devices—one has not read the work. With a great novel,
one has to identify with the major characters and coexperi-
ence their inner lives. Equating the work with the text is like

24. In much the same way, as Mikhail Bakhtin argues, we do not speak in sentences (a
series of words) but exchange utterances, and sentences are just the material for utterances.
See M. M. Bakhtin, "Discourse in the Novel," *The Dialogic Imagination: Four Essays*, ed.
Michael Holquist, trans. Caryl Emerson and Michael Holquist (University of Texas Press,
1981), pp. 259-422; M. M. Bakhtin, "The Problem of the Text in Linguistics, Philology,
and the Human Sciences: An Experiment in Philosophical Analysis" and "Toward a
Methodology for the Human Sciences," *Speech Genres and Other Late Essays*, ed. Caryl
Emerson and Michael Holquist, trans. Vern McGee (University of Texas Press, 1986),
pp. 103-131 and pp. 159-172; and Gary Saul Morson and Caryl Emerson, *Mikhail Bakhtin:
Creation of Prosaics* (Stanford University Press, 1990), pp. 123-171 and pp. 271-305.

equating music with its score or expecting a blueprint of a house to keep out the rain.

The humanities, especially literature, are about the human. Or at least the "best" of the humanities—the version of the humanities that can instruct economics in a useful way.

Character and Nanocharacter

A good humanistic approach to literature demonstrates four things:

1. Why is it worth the effort to read it? Can it teach us something that matters?
2. Why will a summary of the work not do?
3. What makes a great work great? How does it differ from a mediocre work? One needs the student to be able to see, not just accept on faith, what makes a superb writer better than a good one, and a good one better than a mediocre one. Just what is it about Shakespeare that makes his plays so much better than those of other dramatists? After students have taken a class on Tolstoy, they should have some sense of why so many writers—Matthew Arnold, Virginia Woolf, Isaac Babel, and others—thought of him as towering over other great novelists, in a class by himself. They should come to appreciate how a mediocre writer would have done a Tolstoy scene, how a great one like Dickens would have done it, and how Tolstoy actually did it!
4. Finally, and most importantly, what is it that we can learn from great literature that we can't learn, or learn as well, elsewhere? Let us now address this question, since it is what we have in mind when arguing that the economic discipline should be "humanitized."

Whichever answer one gives to this last question, and there are several, this is the crucial one to pose if one is to justify the time, effort, and money universities spend on teaching literature. Those who would transform the study of literature to a branch of neurobiology or computer science tacitly presume that there is no good answer and that literature can only be saved by becoming material for some other more serious discipline—some sort of zombie humanities, a spoof discipline.

One does not entrust a discipline to those who do not believe in it.

But there are some important things literature teaches better than other disciplines, and at least one thing that other disciplines—including economics—do not teach in any sustained way at all. Other disciplines can and do teach us something about how people think and feel, but, as we have argued previously, there is an obvious proof that the great writers understood people better than the greatest social scientists. If psychologists understood human beings as well as George Eliot or Tolstoy, they would have produced depictions of human beings as convincing as Dorothea Brooke or Anna Karenina; but none have come even close.[25] Next to such characters, the people we find in social science experiments or theoretical formulations seem remarkably thin—nanocharacters at times. Just what is it that the great novelists know that psychologists don't?

Social scientists often presume, as Freud did, that writers intuit truths they cannot make explicit and that those truths become available for intellectual analysis only when the social scientists appropriate them. As Plato argued, the poets don't know what they have shown and cannot explain their own works. It is an odd idea to apply to Dostoevsky,

25. It is interesting that the social scientists who have come closest have also been influenced by the great writers: think of Freud's case studies, or Margaret Mead's early work, so heavily influenced by Melville and other writers about the South Seas. Some of the greatest works of anthropology may themselves qualify as literary classics, such as Malinowski's *Argonauts of the Western Pacific* and Lévi-Strauss's *Tristes Tropiques*.

whose characters offer long and highly articulate arguments about the complexities of guilt, insult, self-assertion, and self-deception. He is so eager to convey these psychological insights that he puts them in the mouth of implausible characters, like the drunken, brawling Dmitri Karamazov. One could more readily fault him for not letting the action speak for itself. George Eliot, Tolstoy, Turgenev, and other novelists allow their narrators to enunciate psychological truths of great subtlety. Those who specialize in the study of these writers are often mystified when behavioral economists and social psychologists formulate theories that are so painfully obvious they hardly seem worth the effort. You mean, you had to prove that?

Ethics and Stories

Great novelists also have much to say about a key concern of this book: ethics. They inherited, and developed with remarkable power, a tradition of ethical thinking that philosophers cast aside. Where philosophers thought in terms of logical deductions from ethical principles, novelists thought in terms of particular cases. As philosophers strove to see the underlying simplicity of things, novelists looked for their hidden complexity.[26]

A little intellectual history is in order. Surveying the carnage caused by the religious wars of the seventeenth century, which took the lives of a significant percentage of the population of central Europe, philosophers sought a rationalist approach to moral questions, one that would belong to no faith or fac-

---

26. For a description of this turn of thought in the seventeenth century, see Stephen Toulmin, *Cosmopolis: The Hidden Agenda of Modernity* (Free Press, 1990). On the case-based approach to ethics, see Albert R. Jonsen and Toulmin, *The Abuse of Casuistry: A History of Moral Reasoning* (University of California Press, 1988); on casuistry and the origin of the novel, see Jonsen and Toulmin, and G. A. Starr, *Defoe and Casuistry* (Princeton University Press, 1971).

tion. Just as geometry is neither Catholic nor Protestant, it was argued, ethics might be the same sort of deductive science. Such a science might produce truths on which both sides could agree. This approach triumphed and is still very much with us. We see it not only in analytic philosophy but more generally. You know that a view has triumphed when it is hard to grasp that there could be any other way to think.

But there was a way, the one that rationalist philosophy displaced. Instead of reasoning down from general principles, it reasoned up from particular cases. The core insight belongs to Aristotle. Using the term "justice" to mean what you get from following moral rules, Aristotle observes that sometimes this process produces an absurd result. "The reason is that all law is universal but about some things it is not possible to make a universal statement which shall be correct." In such instances, the law "takes the usual case, though it is not ignorant of the possibility of error." Inevitably, cases arise with particulars that no one could have anticipated but that make all the difference. They are bound to, because "the matter of practical affairs is of this kind from the start."[27]

For Aristotle, there is a key difference between practical and theoretical reasoning. Practical affairs cannot be reduced to the application of theory. For Aristotle, the realm of "the practical" includes the ethical. Theory—including mathematics and scientific reasoning—can be of some help but proves inadequate before the unchartable complexity of things. "This is the reason that all things are not determined by law, viz. that about some things it is impossible to lay down a law" (Aristotle, p. 1020). What is needed, as we saw in chapter 2, is good *judgment*.

That, at least, is the tacit assumption of great novels (and of much other great literature). The realist novel derived

27. Aristotle, "Nichomachean Ethics," *The Basic Works of Aristotle*, ed. Richard McKeon (Random House, 1941), p. 1020.

from the tradition of ethical thinking explicitly rejected by
the seventeenth-century rationalists, the tradition then called
"casuistry," or reasoning by cases. Or to use the term we have
employed throughout this book, we need *stories*. The very fact
that the word "casuistry" is now pejorative—nobody would
praise someone by calling him "a master casuist"—shows the
success of the rationalists.[28]

Instead of reasoning down from theories, casuistry reasons
up from particulars. Although principles are used, they serve
not as laws but as reminders of other similar cases and of earlier insights to consider. By constantly reflecting on one's earlier
decisions, and where some of them have proven mistaken, one
gradually becomes more sophisticated in moral reasoning. But
one never reaches certainty.

The hero of *Anna Karenina*, Konstantin Levin, opposes
Russian intervention in the Balkans where Turks were mas-
sacring Bulgarians. His intellectual half brother, Sergey
Ivanovich, tries to distill the essence of the situation by asking
Levin to imagine that, not far away in the Balkans but right
here, a Turk was about to kill a Bulgarian baby. Would Levin
still do nothing, even if saving the baby might mean killing the
Turk? Levin replies, as Tolstoy would, that he does not know,
he would have to decide on the spot. For Sergey Ivanovich,
this answer seems like a mere evasion because no principle
to decide the question is given, but for Tolstoy the casuist, it
is the right answer. No abstract principle given in advance
should decide, because important particulars cannot be foreseen and the consequences of a wrong decision, either way, are
too significant. One has to rely on good judgment, the product
of a lifetime of moral observation and reflection. There is no
substitute.

28. The great attack on casuistry, and its abuse by the Jesuits, belongs to Pascal in *The Provincial Letters*.

When rationalism triumphed in philosophy, casuistry found a home in a new literary genre, the realist novel. The author often credited with founding this genre, Daniel Defoe, began writing articles in casuistry for periodicals. A sort of Dear Abby of his day, he would consider ethical problems posed by readers—or perhaps made up himself. These problems intrigued by their complexity and resistance to easy resolution. The particulars made all the difference and cut both ways. Defoe learned to provide more details to puzzle the readers, and as his case studies expanded, they turned into novels like *Moll Flanders*. In that book, the heroine often gives plausible justifications for actions we sense are somehow still wrong, so we need to consider why. Often enough, we turn to facts the book contains that her self-justification has excluded.

From these beginnings, the realist novel developed its ability to present difficult moral questions. Whereas the fundamental impulse of the rationalist or scientist is to abstract the essence of a situation and apply general principles to it, the novel tends to make the exact opposite move. Instead of showing the essential simplicity of things, it shows their complexity and teaches us to reason appropriately. We learn a lot by seeing how simplification distorts, and how *abs*traction becomes *dis*traction.

When realist novels show someone who believes in a simplifying philosophy—say, some form of materialism, utilitarianism, or socialism—that makes scientific claims to cut through to the essence of things, the plot typically demonstrates how mistaken such views are. Sometimes the author shows us that, although the character thinks he believes in his philosophy because of its logical or scientific cogency, he is actually guided by psychological factors he does not appreciate. At other times, the author shows how a theory promising justice leads in practice to disastrous consequences. The simplifying theory meeting the complexity of life: that is the plot of "the novel of ideas," including Turgenev's *Fathers and Children*, Dostoevsky's *Crime and Punishment*, Conrad's *Secret Agent*, James's *The Princess Casamassima*, and other great works.

In real life, we sometimes need the clarity provided by theoretical reasoning about ethical problems. That is one reason we turn to analytic philosophy and can gain insight from the social sciences. Abstraction often pays off. But ethical reasoning is bound to be dangerously impoverished if that is all we have. To the extent that good ethical reasoning is a matter of sensitivity to particularities and a recognition of unforeseeable complexities, we also need good judgment and the literary works that illustrate it.

Experience from Within

If ethics were a matter of deductive reasoning, then feelings could only get in the way and judgment would be unnecessary. In theory, a robot could be programmed with principles and the rules for applying them, and we could leave our ethical decisions to the robot.[29] But almost all of us sense something wrong with this. An ethical decision left to a machine is not an ethical decision at all. We feel intuitively that we must commit ourselves personally, take responsibility for an ethical action, or as the literary philosopher Bakhtin liked to say, we must *sign* it. There is "no alibi" for personal responsibility.[30]

Might it not be that ethical behavior demands one particular feeling, namely, empathy? Might it not be the case that

---

29. This possibility is being seriously discussed. See Jerry Kaplan, "Can We Design an Ethical Robot?," *Wall Street Journal*, July 24, 2015, http://www.wsj.com/articles/can-we-create-an-ethical-robot-1437758519.

30. The phrase "no alibi" and the related word "non-alibi" recurs in M. M. Bakhtin, *Toward a Philosophy of the Act*, trans. Vadim Liapunov, ed. Vadim Liapunov and Michael Holquist (University of Texas Press, 1993).

sometimes an ethical action includes the feeling expressed in the English aphorism, "there but for the grace of God go I"? Without that feeling, we may sense ethical behavior—the external performance that helps others—but not ethical action, which includes the personal commitment to behave ethically.[31]

Many disciplines, including economics, can teach that we ought to empathize with others. But these disciplines do not usually involve actual practice in empathy. But as we have argued in this book, great literature, experienced and taught the right way, does involve practice in empathy.[32]

When we read a great novel, we *identify* with the heroine. We put ourselves in her place, feel her difficulties from within, regret her bad choices. Momentarily, they become our bad choices. Even when we do not like her, we may wince, suffer, put the book down for a while.

When Anna Karenina does the wrong thing, we may see what is wrong and yet recognize that we might well have made the same mistake. And that thought may temper our desire to condemn because most of us find it difficult to condemn another for actions we ourselves might well have taken. Or if we do condemn her anyway, we may then turn an unwelcome spotlight on ourselves. Both reactions develop our moral sense.

Jane Austen's greatest novels—*Pride and Prejudice* and *Emma*—tempt the reader to make the same mistakes in judgment as the heroine and then learn, as she does, just what

31. If social psychologist Jonathan Haidt is correct, empathy is only one feeling serving as a foundation for ethics. But none of the six he mentions lend themselves to computerized or purely deductive logic. See Jonathan Haidt, *The Righteous Mind: Why Good People Are Divided by Politics and Religion* (Pantheon, 2012).

32. For a powerful and influential study of the role of identification and empathy in literature, see Mark Edmundson, *Why Read?* (Bloomsbury, 2004). See also Gary Saul Morson, *Prosaics and Other Provocations: Empathy, Open Time, and the Novel* (Academic Studies Press, 2013); Alina Wyman, *The Gift of Active Empathy: Scheler, Bakhtin, and Dostoevsky* (Northwestern University Press, 2016); and Clara Claiborne Park, *Rejoining the Common Reader: Essays, 1962–1990* (Northwestern University Press, 1991).

habits of mind led to the mistake. It is hard to deny one's sus-
ceptibility to an error one has just been caught in the act of
committing. By identifying with the character, we discover
our own pride and prejudice.

The process of identification, feeling, and examination of
feeling may happen not just once but, in the course of a long
novel, thousands of times. Indeed, that is one of the reasons
some novels are so long: the real action is as much in the soul
of the reader as in the actions of the character, and the essential story is our own. No set of doctrines is as important for
ethical behavior as this constant practice in ethical thought or
that direct sensation, felt over and over again, of being in the
other person's place.

So do we really believe that simply reading great literature
would help economists develop better policies? Would reading *War and Peace* have given pause to those who were so
convinced that removing price subsidies in Egypt was the best
move? Would the World Bank memo have been written if the
author had read *Oliver Twist*? Would economic theorists produce models that better reflect human behavior if they read
Notes from Underground? It should be so simple.

But skeptics take note—there is evidence, of the sort social
scientists appreciate, that great fiction changes people's thinking. As trumpeted on the front page of the *New York Times*,
"For Better Social Skills, Scientists Recommend a Little
Chekhov."[33] The article reported on a study published in the
journal *Science*.[34] The authors of the study discovered that after
reading literary fiction (as opposed to nonfiction or popular
fiction), people did better on tests measuring empathy, social
perception, and emotional intelligence. The authors go on to

33. Pam Belluck, "For Better Social Skills, Scientists Recommend a Little Chekhov,"
New York Times, October 4, 2013.
34. David Comer Kidd and Emanuele Castano, "Reading Literary Fiction Improves
Theory of Mind," *Science*, October 2013.

suggest that these findings be considered in developing high school and college curricula. We agree, and add, in training good economists.[35]

The best of the humanities allows us to see characters empathize as we are expected to do. Early in *Anna Karenina*, Levin comes to propose to Kitty, who expects to refuse him. But when she sees him, she is shaken: "And then for the first time the whole thing presented itself in a new, different aspect; only then did she realize that the question did not affect her only—with whom she would be happy, and whom she loved—but that she would that moment have to wound a man whom she liked. And to wound him cruelly."[36] Kitty empathizes, senses what she would feel in his vulnerable position, tastes the humiliation he is about to feel. This is how we know that, fundamentally, she is a good person and what it would take for us to be one.

---

35. For an intriguing skeptical study of literature and empathy, see Suzanne Keen, *Empathy and the Novel* (Oxford University Press, 2007). Keen offers careful distinctions among terms (empathy is not the same as sympathy or personal distress), provides a comprehensive survey of work done on the relation of empathy to storytelling, discusses recent work in neuroscience on "mirror neurons," considers the upsurge in attention to empathy, and surveys various criticisms of the idea that novel reading promotes empathy, which in turn promotes altruism. Keen argues that "there is no question … that readers feel empathy with (and sympathy for) fictional characters and other aspects of fictional worlds." Nevertheless, "surveying the existing research in the consequences of reading, I find the case for altruism stemming from novel reading inconclusive and nearly always exaggerated in favor of the beneficial effects of novel reading" (p. vii). Despite its erudition and intelligence, the book is often less than convincing because of (1) occasionally equating people with "feeling brains" (p. ix), (2) finding a failure of empathy when, for instance, readers of eighteenth-century fiction identify with characters who mock the unfortunate or embrace values now found to be unacceptable, (3) imagining that current American beliefs about who or what is worthy of empathy are the only possible ones, and (4) arguing as if empathy were not just one source of morality but the only source. In general, one can say that Keen's usually strong argument becomes muddled when she does not do what great fiction allows (but does not compel) one to do: escape from the tendency to regard the beliefs and values of our own culture, social group, and historical moment as the only possible ones and to measure morality of other beliefs by how similar they are to our own.

36. Leo Tolstoy, *Anna Karenina*, the Garnett translation revised by Leonard J. Kent and Nina Berberova (Random House, 1965), p. 52.

In Balzac's *Père Goriot*, the ultimate father sacrifices everything for daughters who care nothing for him. But the young and still naive Rastignac, who imagines he cares only for worldly success, finds himself experiencing deep empathy for the old man, and watches over his sickbed until he dies. Readers in turn wind up empathizing not only with old Goriot but also with Rastignac, as his empathy inspires ours. Addressing his readers directly, the author remarks, "of course, you could, even after having read 'of the hidden sorrows of Père Goriot,' choose to act like the daughters, and read as they live, merely for your own pleasure. 'Sinking back in a soft armchair,' you could dismiss the story as a mere novel," but if you do, the author stands ready to reproach you. "Oh, you may be sure that this drama is no work of fiction, no mere novel! It is all true, so true that everyone may recognize its elements within himself, perhaps in his very heart."[37]

In Chekhov's story "Enemies," we come to empathize even with the failure to empathize. The story deals with a poor doctor, Kirillov, stricken with grief right after his son has died, summoned by the wealthy Abogin to come save his mortally ill wife. We empathize with the doctor, not only for his own sorrow but for the empathy he feels for his wife, whom he is so reluctant to leave alone, even to save another life. But when Kirillov and Abogin at last arrive, they discover that Abogin's wife has only faked a life-threatening illness in order to elope with her lover. As both men are stricken with sadness, we see how each could have empathized with the other but chooses instead to indulge, as people so often do, in self-righteous anger. We empathize with both, even as we regret their choice not to feel for each other. As the author explains, "the ego-

---

37. Honoré de Balzac, "*Père Goriot*" and "*Eugénie Grandet*", trans. E. K. Brown, Dorothea Walter, and John Watkins (Random House, 1950), p. 4. The novel is usually taken to allude to *King Lear*, another work about those who feel for others and those who do not. Our thanks to Thomas Pavel for suggesting this example.

ism of the unhappy was conspicuous in both. The unhappy are egoistic, spiteful, unjust, cruel, and less capable of understanding each other than fools. Unhappiness does not bring people together but draws them apart."[38] That is still more the case when unhappiness makes people feel morally superior.

Economists may appreciate how much the characters' mutual resentment is grounded in wealth and status. The doctor becomes unpleasantly aware of Abogin's wealth, the higher education indicated by his violoncello, and the fashionably progressive views of the elite that he voices, and so his personal pain turns into class resentment. We experience what that resentment feels like as well as what Abogin must experience when Kirillov voices the "cynical, ugly contempt only to be found in the eyes of sorrow and indigence when they are confronted with well-nourished comfort" (Chekhov, p. 33). No treatise on the distribution of wealth, or measurement of Gini coefficients, could capture this sense of how inequality feels.

It is really quite remarkable what happens when reading a great novel: by identifying with a character, one learns from within what it feels like to be someone else. The great realist novelists, from Jane Austen on, developed a technique for letting readers eavesdrop on the very process of a character's thoughts and feelings as they are experienced. The author paraphrases the sequence of his or her thoughts from within, and does so in the character's own voice. We hear how she talks to herself, how she thinks, how she addresses an inner judge as she justifies herself. Or we eavesdrop on how she talks herself into an action she knows is wrong while we witness the sequence of her emotions, not just their result. If we are to understand how people make moral decisions, and how we could make better ones, what knowledge could be more important?

38. Anton Chekhov, *The Schoolmaster and Other Stories*, trans. Constance Garnett (Ecco Press, 1986), p. 32.

Technically speaking, the author uses the third person to paraphrase what is taking place in the first person. On the train ride home, after her intense flirtation with Vronsky, Anna

> suddenly felt that he ought to be ashamed, and that she ought to be ashamed of the same thing. But what had he to be ashamed of? "What have I to be ashamed of?" she asked in injured surprise.... There was nothing. She went over all her Moscow recollections ... there was nothing shameful. And for all that, at the same point in her memories the feeling of shame intensified, as though some inner voice, just at the point when she thought of Vronsky, were saying to her, "Warm, very warm, hot." (*Anna Karenina*, p. 107)

The passage is in the third person ("she asked in injured surprise"), but the sequence of thoughts, the choice of words, the tone of voice, are hers. It is Anna, not the author, who is saying to herself "there was nothing ... there was nothing shameful." We know immediately that the thoughts are hers because the referent of "he" is not identified, since a person speaking to herself does not have to explain her pronouns. We overhear the steps with which she tries to banish a truth she knows but senses it coming back all the more strongly. After the citation above, the passage continues to trace Anna's dialogue of with herself, a dialogue that leaves her both more ashamed and more erotically aroused.

In that case, why not put the whole sequence in the first person, as a quotation from Anna's inner voice, the way the sentence "What have I to be ashamed of?" comes directly from her? For one thing, the author is able to tell us things she would not notice, like her body posture, her tone of injured surprise, the insistence of an unwelcome feeling she wants to pretend isn't there and so wouldn't comment on. For another, we hear not only her voice explicitly but also the narrator's own voice implicitly commenting on her process of self-justification. In short, we hear two voices in incipient dialogue. Sometimes, indeed, we even detect what other characters would say if they could eavesdrop on this character's thoughts.[39]

So here is how one *can* teach a technique. It is not important what it is called. It is important to show what is accomplished. If one shows how passages paraphrasing a character's inner thoughts work—that what is given in the third person may by meaning be in the first person or a combination of the two—and then demonstrates how we thereby gain access to a character from within, students see the point of the technique and why it matters. That is entirely different from symbol hunting. This is the sort of humanities we believe can best instruct economics.

Sensing the Other

Readers watch heroes and heroines in the never-ending process of justifying themselves, deceiving themselves, arguing with themselves. That is something we cannot do in real life, where we see others only from the outside and can do no more than infer inner states from outer behavior. One reason people feel so intensely about fictional characters is that they are on such intimate terms with them, sharing their most private thoughts, and able to remember things about them that they may have long forgotten.

Sometimes in making ethical judgments it matters whether a person, on the one hand, has not realized the harm an action can do or, on the other hand, has realized it but then banished the inconvenient thought. In both cases, the person can sincerely say after the fact that she does not remember ever having considered the possibility of harm. In novels, we can

39. The technique is sometimes called "free indirect discourse"; Mikhail Bakhtin, who sees it as the defining characteristic of the novel, calls it "dialogic discourse." See Dorrit Cohn, *Transparent Minds: Narrative Modes for Presenting Consciousness in Fiction* (Princeton University Press, 1978), and Bakhtin's celebrated 1941 essay, "Discourse in the Novel," *The Dialogic Imagination: Four Essays*, trans. Michael Holquist and Caryl Emerson (University of Texas Press, 1981), pp. 259–422.

directly detect the difference and appreciate the difference it makes. The best lie detector could not do that.

In such circumstances, a person could search her memory, but even then the thought may not be recoverable. She cannot relive those moments. But if we are dealing with a character in a novel, we can reread what she cannot recall. In this way, we may experience and reexperience the character's inner life as she herself cannot. Known so intimately, it is no wonder characters sometimes come to play so large a part in our own inner life.

Endlessly repeated, this experiencing of another person from within teaches us empathy by making it a habit. This is the most important ethical lesson novels teach. It is not a fact to be known but a skill acquired and a habit performed without effort. One cannot get that lesson by reading a summary of "what the author is saying." One also cannot get it if one has just examined a text instead of experienced a work. It is not in the words on the page but in the experience they enable.

As we argued in chapter 1, you learn to feel what it is like to be someone else, what it is like to be a person from a different culture, period, social class, gender, religion, or personality type. And one learns why even those broad categories won't do, because one senses what it is like to be a *particular* other person. No one, after all, is merely the sum of her sociological categories. And that, too, is an important lesson: no one experiences the world in quite the same way as anyone else.

Other disciplines—including economics—sometimes tell us we should empathize, but only literature offers this constant practice in doing so. There is a big difference between inferring that someone else is humiliated or injured and experiencing moment by moment what that feels like, as one does reading Dostoevsky. Once we have the practice of that moment-to-moment feeling, we can infer all the better what real people experience.

A Sentimentality

A cautionary note is in order: it is a sentimentality to assume that empathy must make us more forgiving. Sometimes, if one really understood how another person was thinking or feeling, one might dislike him all the more. If we could get into the inner life of Adolf Eichmann or Ted Bundy, we might expand our sense of horrors we had never imagined. But even then, empathy would have increased understanding.

Empathy, moreover, can be misused. The best con men are empathetic. Morson once held a summer job as a door-to-door salesman and learned how the most successful salesmen used empathy to get people to buy things they did not need. Still more troubling is the link between empathy and sadism. Knowing what others feel makes it easier, and thrilling, to inflict more pain. One does not torture a stone but another person. In Dostoevsky's novel about his experiences in a Siberian prison camp, *The House of the Dead*, he describes torture as empathy used for bad purposes.[40] In one passage, the narrator speculates on the guards who love to beat prisoners:

> I imagine there is something in this sensation [of inflicting pain] which sends a thrill at once sweet and painful.... Anyone who has once experienced this power, this unlimited mastery of the body, blood and soul of a fellow man made of the same clay as himself, a brother in the law of Christ— anyone who has experienced the power and full license to inflict the greatest humiliation upon another creature made in the image of God will unconsciously lose the mastery of his own sensations. Tyranny is a habit ... the mind and the heart are tolerant of the most abnormal things, till at last they come to relish them. (p. 240)

All good things—scientific knowledge, technology, medicine—can be misused. So can literature and the empathy it

40. Fyodor Dostoevsky, *The House of the Dead*, trans. Constance Garnett (Dell, 1959).

teaches. The difference is that, as the example from *The House of the Dead* shows, literature can teach a cautionary lesson even about the abuse of empathy. It may even do so experientially. More than one reader has remarked how Dostoevsky allows us first to feel pleasure in another's suffering and then to reflect on the horror of which we are capable.

Globalization

If one goal of literary study is to learn from within what it is like to belong to another culture, then literary study assumes special importance in an age of globalization. We do not mean that one can learn all there is to know about being Japanese from reading Japanese novels. Still more important is developing a general ability to inhabit different cultures, to switch one's mind-set, to recognize that assumptions we take for granted may not be shared by others, and to look for alternatives we have not imagined. People who learn languages usually find that the more languages they know, the easier it is to acquire a new one; the same is true of cultures. One learns how to learn, how to enter into another culture's way of seeing. Just think how much more successful development economics would be if its practitioners always "inhabited" the minds of those they seek to assist.

When Morson was a student at Oxford, he was struck by the fact that the British students did not presume, as Americans automatically do, that good manners are what makes other people comfortable. What else could be their point? That way of looking at things, it appeared to the British students, was a "Yank" notion, because manners have nothing to do with setting people at ease. Then why act according to them? "One does it," he was told, "because it is done."

Americans find it difficult to believe that other cultures do not share their values. The cultural egoism, even of those who most vociferously reject cultural egoism, is boundless.

We imagine of other cultures that if only it were pointed out to them that what they are doing violates human rights, or is prejudicial, or is the dead weight of tradition, or leads to a cycle of violence, or makes people poorer, surely they would change their ways! Judging from our leading news outlets, it would appear that it never occurs to Americans that in some cultures tradition, religious belief, and national glory trump peace, wealth, and equality as desirable goals; or that in some cultures the idea of all people being equal—including women, gays, and believers in other religions—is not only odd but decidedly immoral.

When Chinese leader Xi Jinping denounces such Western concepts as "constitutional democracy" and the "universal values" of human rights, Americans find it hard to imagine the worldview in which that is an acceptable thing to say.[41] We are much more used to leaders who claim to believe in human rights as a cover for violating them. It is no marvel to see selfishness masquerading as virtue, a form of hypocrisy that tacitly acknowledges the moral standards being violated. As La Rochefoucauld observed, hypocrisy is the tribute that vice pays to virtue. But Xi forthrightly says that values we take to be as self-evident as the axioms of geometry are not shared. "Democracy" and "human rights" are pernicious ideas. By the same token, Americans cannot quite grasp that Russians are more likely to regard individual well-being as less important than the glory of the Russian state. What is the point of the state if not to promote the well-being of its citizens? Can the

---

41. See Chris Buckley, "China Takes Aim at Western Values," *New York Times*, August 19, 2013, http://www.nytimes.com/2013/08/20/world/asia/chinas-new-leadership-takes-hard-line-in-secret-memo.html. The official "Document No. 9" lists seven forbidden Western ideas including "promoting civil society," which is based on the idea that "in the social sphere, individual rights are paramount and ought to be immune to obstruction by the state." Leslie Lenkowsky, "Forbidden Thoughts: Seven Ideas You Can't Hold in Today's China," *Weekly Standard*, June 30, 2014, vol. 19, no. 40, http://www.weeklystandard.com/keyword/Document-9.

state be more important than the citizens comprising it? For many Russians, it would be strange to think otherwise. People come and go, but Russia remains.

Americans who do not understand this point of view are likely to overestimate the effect of economic sanctions, for example. Many Americans were thoroughly mystified that Russia would actually add sanctions by barring imports of food. By the same token, Russians find it difficult to imagine that Americans could think otherwise, so they take President Obama's most sincere professions as obvious lies because no one could actually think that way. Here again we have the phenomenon of "two cultures," as we defined that term in chapter 1. It is not just that the cultures have different beliefs; it is that each cannot believe the other holds the beliefs it does.

If we could more easily put ourselves in the position of others, think from within as they do, put on a set of glasses to see the world in their way, we might very well, when those glasses are off, still not share their beliefs. But we will at least understand them better, negotiate with them more effectively, or guess what measures will more likely have the desired effect.

Just as important, we will have enlarged our sense of what it is to be human. No longer imprisoned in our own culture and moment, taking our local and current values as the only possible ones, we will recognize our beliefs as one of many possibilities—not as something inevitable, but as a choice. And isn't economics ultimately about choice? The humanities, when taught right, help us understand what motivates those choices.

World Literature and the Curriculum

Studying world literature can develop the mental muscles to transcend place and time. With the revolutions in technology and communication, this flattened world demands that we do exactly that. In the past, "world literature" meant the literatures of Western Europe, ancient Greece and Rome, and the sources of the Bible. The classics of those traditions have indeed been sadly neglected in favor of "documents" or second-rate works with a ready message, and it would be good to expose students to the greatest of them. But it would help if we would also add the greatest works of other traditions.

Let us be clear that we do *not* mean engaging in what often passes for studying other traditions under the rubric of "post-colonialism"; that is, reading recent texts (hopefully good ones) from other traditions showing the evils of the West. In that case the focus of attention is still on us. It is no less ego-tistical to make us the source of all evil than to regard us as the source of all virtue: we are still the cynosure. It's like the old joke: "That's enough talking about me, let's talk about you. What do you think about me?"

Why not study the classics of other cultures, works that are not about us at all, often written before any substantial aware-ness that the West even existed? A good world literature pro-gram would offer translation courses on the classic Chinese novels like *The Story of the Stone*, the eleventh-century Japanese classic *The Tale of Genji*, the Indian epic *Mahabarata*, and the Persian *Shahnameh* (Epic of Kings).[42] A curriculum so constructed might also give a prominent place to theatre and performance studies insofar as they encourage students to get out of themselves and think like someone else.

The discipline of religious studies could also emphasize the theological tenets of other religions. What do Buddhists and Daoists believe, what is it like to think that way, what light

---

42. Several of these works are available in new, highly praised translations. A new Library of Arabic Literature is producing reliable English versions of Arabic classics: http://nyuad.nyu.edu/en/research/nyuad-institute/institute-research/library-arabic -literature.html. The first volume is *Classic Arabic Literature: A Library of Arabic Literature Anthology*, ed. and trans. Geert Jan van Gelder, which will contain an "assort-ment of classical Arabic poems and literary prose, from pre-Islamic times until the 18th century, with short introductions to guide non-specialist students and informative end-notes and bibliography for advanced scholars." Why not make this required reading for economists charged with developing policies relating to that area of the world?

does such a worldview shed on the human experience? For that matter, we have been struck that many of our students, including those from nominally Christian households, have been so secularized that they have not so much as heard of the Sermon on the Mount or the story of Abraham's near sacrifice of Isaac. Completely unfamiliar with the Bible, they have also cut themselves off from the countless works that presume a knowledge of it or rely on its language.[43] Instead of recognizing two thousand years of geniuses commenting on the most diverse aspects of human life, they presume that Christian thought is represented by a Bible-thumping ignoramus who thinks the world is five thousand years old and imagines the Good Book was written in English. Although they are usually too polite to say so, students' view of Judaism and Islam is not much different.

In fact, students could study the history of Christian thought as they would any other alien tradition. But to do so, both literature and religion departments would need to present works in the appropriate way, not as mere documents of their time but as sources of wisdom from which we might learn. Instead of learning the sociology of the Reformation, students might also come to understand from within first, the theological debates of the time, and second, why people were willing to die for doctrines that now strike many as trivial, if not entirely opaque. What are analogous arguments in our culture? Sometimes a simple act of conceptual translation can be a good starting point: whereas people today might ask about the nature of the world in which we live, people then posed almost the same question by asking about the God who created it. The theological "problem of evil" is easily rendered in modern terms, and not just by Ivan Karamazov. Erasmus argued with Luther about free will, and we still argue about

43. See Robert Alter, *Pen of Iron: American Prose and the King James Bible* (Princeton University Press, 2010).

how much responsibility an individual bears for his actions and how much is the result of external forces over which he has no control. It is not exactly the same argument, of course, but once the starting point has been used as an entry, the student can appreciate the debate's differences as well.

The history of ideas has long ceased to be a prestigious field of historical studies, having yielded to social history, which seems less elitist and old-fashioned. But for all the light social history can shed, intellectual history also has something important to offer if one places a value on learning what it feels like to think differently. When we discover minds like Augustine, Leibniz, and Burke, who argued in terms very different from ours, it becomes difficult to regard anyone who does not think as we do as mentally or morally deficient.

From this perspective, the curriculum might feature classes not just in the sciences but also on the history of science, by which we mean not just social but also disciplinary histories. Scientists of the past were not stupid. Given the alternatives available at the time, what made phlogiston and ether seem like attractive theories? What was the evidence that led to their rejection? Students often are surprised to find that Darwin did not reject what we call Lamarckian inheritance of acquired characteristics. And why was it that his critics included not only the religious but also physicists, who found the theory contrary to their discipline?[44]

All too often, students accept science as dogma, while rejecting other ways of looking at the world as dogmatic. That is a natural reaction when science is presented to them complete, as a series of propositions in a textbook, or as algebra

---

44. Darwin took quite seriously the objection of Lord Kelvin, the leading physicist of the day, that given what was known about energy, the sun could not have existed long enough for the evolutionary process as Darwin described it. In subsequent editions, Darwin tried to find ways to compress the required time. The discovery of nuclear energy eventually resolved the problem, so physics caught up with biology, even though physics was the discipline with greater prestige.

word problems with the words coming from physics. Science is fundamentally a way of thinking, and to accept its truths as authoritative propositions all equally beyond question is to accept science superstitiously. One might just as well accept alchemy or any other pseudoscience. In John Milton's memorable phrase from his *Areopagitica* (1644), it is possible to be "a heretic in the truth": "A man may be a heretic in the truth, and if he believe things only because his pastor says so, or the assembly so determines, without knowing other reason, though his belief be true, yet the very truth he holds becomes his heresy."[45]

Writing and Argument

The teaching of writing and argument should foreground the appreciation of other points of view. As literature teaches emotional empathy, good argument demands intellectual empathy. You accept your beliefs superstitiously if you do not know the strongest arguments against them.

"There is a class of persons," writes John Stuart Mill in his classic essay *On Liberty*, "who think it enough if a person assents undoubtingly to what they think true, though he has no knowledge whatever of the grounds of his opinion, and could not make a tenable defense of it against the most superficial objections." But that is not how a rational person holds beliefs. "This is not knowing the truth. Truth, thus held, is but one superstition the more, accidentally clinging to the words which enunciate the truth."[46]

If one is genuinely interested in the truth, one *invites* counterarguments. "He who knows only his own side of the case knows little of that ... if he is equally unable to refute the rea-

45. John Milton, *Areopagitica: A Speech to the Parliament of England for the Liberty of Unlicensed Printing* (HardPress Publishing, 2013).

46. John Stuart Mill, *On Liberty* (Prometheus Books, 1986), p. 42.

sons on the opposite side, if he does not so much as know what they are, he has no grounds for preferring either opinion" (Mill, p. 43). It is not enough to know what your own side says the opposing views are. One might as well conduct a trial with only a prosecutor, who, after presenting the case against the defendant, paraphrases what he says is the case for him. We recognize that the opposing argument must be presented by someone committed to it.

The test of whether you have appreciated the opposing position is whether the most intelligent and best-intentioned people on the other side would accept your paraphrase of their views as accurate.

One has to practice empathy with other perspectives. As Mill says, one has to "bring them into real contact with his own mind." But it is all too easy to be one of those people who "have never thrown themselves into the mental position of those who think differently from them, and considered what such persons may have to say; and consequently they do not, in any sense of the word, know the doctrine which they themselves profess" (p. 44).

The great novelists of ideas describe numerous people who think this way.[47] The reader soon begins to ask, can they really believe in the social justice they advocate? After all, the best-intentioned reforms often fail, or even prove counterproductive, so if they really care about justice, they should want to

---

47. See, for instance, George Eliot's *Felix Holt: The Radical* as well as the political arguments and account of the Revolution of 1848 in Gustave Flaubert's *Sentimental Education*. The more personally disillusioned Deslauriers gets, the more radical his political views become, a process suggesting that something other than the pursuit of justice shapes his politics. We frequently detect self-interest or vanity in ostensibly civic-minded views, as when the bad artist Pelerin, at the head of a group of protesters, demands "a Forum of Art, a sort of Stock Exchange handling aesthetic interests: sublime works of art would be produced because all the artists would pool their genius. Soon Paris would be covered with gigantic monuments which he would decorate; he had already started work on a picture of the Republic" (*Sentimental Education*, trans. Robert Baldrick (Penguin, 1988), p. 294).

hear in advance where a proposed reform might go astray. If they do not, if they denounce all opposition as necessarily stupid or venal, then, Tolstoy suggests, they are really interested in feeling good about themselves, in belonging to the circle of people who have the right ideas, not in actually achieving something worthwhile. Tolstoy's character who does care about actually achieving something, Konstantin Levin, is always attending to opposing views. He seeks them out and sometimes modifies the practices he recommends or even his own views (as Tolstoy did).

To these arguments we may add that democracy depends on a strong sense of *opinion*. It depends on the idea that one's opponent just might turn out to be right, that social views are not scientific and cannot be proven with mathematical certainty. With the best intentions, one might turn out to be wrong. Without that sense of the value of opinion, why allow diverse opinions at all? That was precisely the position held in the Soviet Union, in which elections offered a "choice" between one candidate. Of course we have freedom of speech, the Soviets would explain, we just don't allow people to lie! In the USSR, people were arrested for saying that there was no free speech.

The teaching of the humanities, then, can indeed be valuable not only for practice in emotional empathy, and not only for the disinterested pursuit of truth, but also for the preservation of democracy.

Our recommendation is to always remember that in classes requiring a term paper, it is absolutely crucial, as Gerald Graff has eloquently argued, that students first understand and paraphrase the strongest position on the other side. One then offers the best case for one's own position and imagines what the smartest counterarguments would be. "In the civic sphere," Graff observes, "where we often justifiably lament the low quality of public debate and the pervasiveness of knee-jerk polarization and groupthink, much of the problem stems from our refusal to take the first step of ... summarizing the other side clearly and fairly. Teaching students to begin with an opinion they may or may not agree with, forcing them to examine a position far from their own experience, trains them for democratic civics in which ideas, values, and policies are weighed in open forums." Young people who learn to summarize the view of others in a way those others would accept will "be apt to look upon fellow citizens as interlocutors rather than as foes, seeing others as rivals for power and influence, perhaps, but not as enemies." They will learn to "enter the marketplace of ideas, listen to all sides, and make their arguments in ways that are proper to an open society."[48] That sage advice applies as much to students (and professors) writing economics papers as to those in philosophy, history, or literature.

Conclusion

In short, the humanities, if humanists will only believe in them, have a crucial role to play in education. They have access to truths about human beings other disciplines have not attained. And while other disciplines may recommend empathy, the humanities entail actual practice of it. Their cultivation of diverse points of view offers a model for neighboring disciplines, and for liberal arts education generally, to follow.

Properly taught, the humanities offer an escape from the prison house of self and the limitations of time and place. We live on an island in a vast sea of cultures, past and present. The humanities allow us to escape that island and return to it enriched with the wisdom of elsewhere.

---

48. Gerald Graff, "Why Johnie and Joanie Can't Write, Revisited" in *The State of the American Mind*, ed. Mark Bauerlein and Adam Bellow (Templeton Press, 2015), pp. 62–63. See also Jonathan Haidt, *The Righteous Mind: Why Good People Are Divided by Politics and Religion* (Pantheon, 2012).

If economists want to base their recommendations on a grasp of the cultures and peoples they desire to help; if they want to have a deeper sense of how economic questions like inequality actually affect human experience; and if they want to take into account those aspects of experience that require narrative explanation—it may pay to study great literature. Such study may not be based on some inherent testable "truth," like physics, and it surely requires an approach different from the one economists are used to, but that is precisely why it interests us and may help us avoid some common errors.

Along with its models and empirical techniques, economics thrives in particular when its practitioners are most creative. But economists need to remember one of the most important of all virtues—humility. Only then can economics truly learn from the humanities and other disciplines, rather than simply expropriate them. In recent years, narrative psychology has grown in popularity.[49] Narrative economics has a nice ring to it. And *humanomics*, as a dialogue of perspectives, can enrich our sense of economic problems as genuinely human issues.

---

49. See, for example, Sadie F. Dingfelder, "Our Stories, Ourselves: The Tales We Tell Hold Powerful Sway over Our Memories, Behaviors and Even Identities, According to Research from the Burgeoning Field of Narrative Psychology," *Monitor*, American Psychological Association, January 2011. For a provocative volume on what social scientists can learn from particular historical examples, see Robert H. Bates, Avner Greif, Margaret Levi, Jean-Laurent Rosenthal and Barry R. Weingast, *Analytic Narratives* (Princeton University Press, 1998).

Chapter 7

De-hedgehogizing Adam Smith
The Economics That Might Be

If economics learned from literary studies, it would realize more—not less—of Adam Smith's vision. The realist novel, it turns out, *extended* Smith's key ideas, particularly his psychological and ethical thought, in the direction he was already taking it. And that direction, like the realist novel itself, is inherently foxy.

But, as we pointed out in chapter 1, Smith's thought has been hedgehogized—this is another example of a foxy thinker being misrepresented by his disciples. Neither Darwin nor Smith resemble the picture of them presented in textbook accounts, especially those of social scientists.

When social scientists refer to a process as Darwinian, for instance, they usually mean that competition has driven it to optimality because anything less than optimal would not have survived. But Darwin explicitly argues the opposite case: what proves that organisms developed from a historical process rather than a single act of divine creation is that they are imperfectly, not perfectly, designed. Optimality exactly mimics what a perfect divine mind, not a contingent historical process, would do.

In *The Origin of Species*, Darwin mentions a certain kind of mole that lives its entire life underground and yet has eyes. Even if the mole were to go above ground, the eyes would do it no good because they are occluded by a thick membrane.

These eyes consume calories and can become infected, so they are harmful to survival. They are obviously there simply because they were present to the mole's ancestors, who did live above ground. In the same way, Darwin mentions a certain species of upland geese who never go near the water and yet have webbed feet. "In such cases, and many others could be given," Darwin observes, "habits have changed without a corresponding change in structure."[1] Whether social scientists or authors of biology textbooks, the "Darwinists" who have hedgehogized Darwin have de-Darwinized him.[2]

In much the same way, Smith has been de-Smithed. Those who treat him as the founder of the sort of all-encompassing rational choice theory on display in much of neoclassical economics have turned him from a fox into a hedgehog by taking what he presents as one principle of behavior as the only principle. To be sure, Smith did speak of the "invisible hand." But nothing could be further from his foxy way of thinking than to imagine that mathematical modeling could, even in principle, replace all narrative explanations, which Smith frequently resorts to in *The Wealth of Nations*. Textbooks to the contrary, Smith emphatically did not think that we always act—whether rationally or, as the behavioral economists would say, less than rationally—to maximize our utility.

When members of a discipline believe it has achieved scientific status, they typically do not study its history or read its primary sources. Doctoral training in physics or mathematics does not include the history of physics and mathematics. Over the past half century, graduate training in economics has required little reading of primary sources, even those of such importance as the works of Adam Smith. If it did, gradu-

1. Charles Darwin, *On the Origin of Species: A Facsimile of the First Edition* (Harvard University Press, 1964), p. 185.

2. The argument that Darwin was an imperfectionist was made most famously by Stephen Jay Gould. See Gould, *The Panda's Thumb: More Reflections in Natural History* (Norton, 1982), pp. 19–26.

ate students would immediately be struck by an all too often ignored fact we raised in chapter 1, that Smith is the author not only of *The Wealth of Nations* but also of an important treatise on ethics, *The Theory of Moral Sentiments*. This treatise argues explicitly and repeatedly against the idea that we all act entirely to benefit ourselves.

Indeed, the entire point of *The Theory of Moral Sentiments* is precisely the opposite: people sometimes act for the sake of others in a way that cannot be reduced to an indirect form of "self-love." We quote again, as we did in chapter 1, the beginning of his treatise:

> How selfish soever man may be supposed, there are evidently some principles in his nature, which interest him in the fortune of others, and render their happiness necessary to him, though he derives nothing from it except the pleasure of seeing it. Of this kind is pity or compassion, the emotion which we feel for the misery of others, when we either see it, or are made to conceive it in a very lively manner.[3]

The book's first paragraph then describes this sentiment as "an original passion," that is, as irreducible to any other more fundamental one:

> That we often derive sorrow from the sorrow of others, is a matter of fact too obvious to require any instances to prove it; for this sentiment, *like all the other original passions of human nature*, is by no means confined to the virtuous and humane.... The greatest ruffian, the most hardened violator of the laws of society, is not altogether without it. (Smith, p. 9, italics added)

Smith is keenly aware of the counterargument making compassion a form of self-interest, an intellectual move associated

---

3. Adam Smith, *The Theory of Moral Sentiments*, ed. D. D. Raphael and A. L. Macfie (Liberty, 1982), p. 9. Originally published in 1759.

not only with Hobbes but also with La Rochefoucauld, for whom the driving force of human nature is *amour-propre*, or "self-love."[4] Smith repeatedly rejects all attempts to see compassion as nothing but "self-love" or self-interest in another form. In chapter 2, for instance, he observes:

> Those who are fond of deducing all our sentiments from certain refinements of self-love, think themselves at no loss to account, according to their own principles, both for this pleasure and this pain [that is, occasioned when others share, or fail to share, our feelings]. Man, say they, conscious of his own weakness, and of the need which he has for the assistance of others, rejoices whenever he observes that they adopt his own passions, because he is then assured of that assistance; and grieves whenever he observes the contrary, because he is then assured of their opposition. But both the pleasure and the pain are always felt so instantaneously, and often upon such frivolous occasions, that it seems evident that neither of them can be derived from any such self-interested consideration.[5]

What's more, while sympathy with my joy enlivens it and gives me pleasure, sympathy with my grief does not, as one

4. Among the most famous sardonic maxims of François de La Rochefoucauld (1613–1680) are the following: "Whatever discoveries one has made in the realm of self-esteem, many unchartered regions still remain there"; "We all have sufficient fortitude to bear the misfortunes of others"; "In most of mankind gratitude is merely a secret hope for greater favors"; "What men call friendship is just an arrangement for mutual gain and an exchange of favors: in short, a business where self-interest always sets out to obtain something"; "Self-love is the greatest of all flatterers"; and, to sum them up: "Self-love is cleverer than the cleverest man in the world." See *The Maxims of La Rochefoucauld*, trans. Louis Koronenberger (Random House, 1959).

5. Smith, pp. 13–14. The editors of this edition, D. D. Raphael and A. L. Macfie, add a footnote: "Smith presumably has Hobbes and Mandeville as the leading exponents of the view that all sentiments depend on self-love, but in fact neither of them gives this, or any, account of the pleasure and pain felt on observing sympathy and antipathy. Smith may simply be making a reasonable conjecture of what an egoistic theorist would say" (p. 14, n1). Raphael is a philosopher and Macfie a historian; a literary scholar would immediately think of La Rochefoucauld, whose entire oeuvre consists of aphorisms on self-love.

might by this logic expect, enliven my grief and cause further distress. Or, rather, it does enliven grief and cause distress, but that force is outweighed by "another sort of satisfaction," namely, the delight we take in fellow feeling itself. It is this delight from the "original passion" of sympathy, not any calculation of self-interest, that explains why, even if grief is enlivened by sympathy, it is nevertheless alleviated by it.[6] This subtle psychological analysis, designed to show that human nature cannot be reduced to a single principle of rational self-interest, recurs in Smith.

Smith returns to this point at the end of his study. "Sympathy, however, cannot, in any sense be regarded as a selfish principle." Some may say that when I sympathize with your sorrow and indignation, my sympathy derives from self-love inasmuch as it arises from putting myself in your position and so, as Smith says, "conceiving what I should feel in the like circumstances." In that case, it is really about me, not about you. But this argument blurs a key distinction. When I enter into your grief—say, at your loss of a son— Smith states,"I do not consider what I, a person of such a character and profession, should suffer, if I had a son" who died. Rather,

> I not only change circumstances with you, but I change persons and characters. My grief, therefore, is entirely upon your account, and not in the least upon my own.... How can that be regarded as a selfish passion, which does not arise even from my imagination of any thing that has befallen, or that relates to myself, in my own proper person and character, but which is entirely occupied about what relates to you? (Smith, p. 317)

Consider, for instance, that "a man may sympathize with a woman in child-bed" even though he neither does nor

6. Smith, *The Theory of Moral Sentiments*, p. 14.

could imagine himself suffering her pains in his own person. In short, "that whole account of human nature ... which
deduces all sentiments and affections from self-love, which
has made so much noise in the world ... seems to me to have
arisen from some confused misapprehension of the system of
sympathy"(Smith, p. 317). If Gary Becker attended to this passage, would he simply dismiss Smith as unable to understand
his own theories?

Sympathy and Empathy

Attentive to the complexities of human interaction, Smith
shows himself to be a splendid psychologist. In chapter after
chapter, he examines the manifold ways in which sympathy, no less than self-love, shapes our social and emotional
lives. And he sees in sympathy the foundation of our moral
sentiments.

In Smith's model, when we make moral judgments, we place
ourselves in the position of another, "we enter, as it were into
his body and become in some measure the same person, and
thence form some idea of his sensations" although in a much
weaker form. We must, of course, do this from without as "we
have no immediate experience of what other men feel" and so
"we can form no idea of the manner in which they are affected,
but by conceiving what we ourselves should feel in the like
situation" (Smith, p. 9). We then compare that imagined feeling with his feelings and judge whether they are appropriate.
Strictly speaking, Smith uses the term "sympathy" to mean
more than just pity, since we can sympathize with any feeling
whatsoever, including joy.[7]

---

7. See James R. Otteson, *Adam Smith's Marketplace of Life* (Cambridge University
Press, 2002), p. 18. Otteson's book defends the importance of *The Theory of Moral
Sentiments* as first-rate moral philosophy, offers a subtle analysis of its argument, and
suggests important connections between Smith's two masterpieces.

As we have argued, such sympathy is precisely what great literary works, and especially realist novels, are good at creating in the reader. Identifying with people unlike ourselves, we experience "pity and compassion, the emotion which we feel for the misery of others, when we either see it, or are made to conceive it in a very lively manner" (Smith, p. 9). And we experience joy, love, and ecstasy as well. In *War and Peace*, when Nikolai Rostov listens to his sister Natasha sing, he forgets all the cares on his mind and enters so deeply into the ecstasy she is conveying, her feeling of suspense about hitting the high note, and her sense of triumph when she succeeds, that he does not notice he is singing along with her. For Tolstoy, this is how great art works: we become "infected" with another's feeling.

Infection goes beyond mere sympathy because we share a character's experience from within, so sympathy (feeling along with) becomes empathy (in-feeling). And if the character herself experiences empathy for another, our own is doubled, as we feel it both for the other and for the character herself. A long novel makes practice in empathy extend over hundreds of pages. It becomes a skill we grow increasingly good at. More than any specific moral precept a given novel may contain, this experience is the genre's primary lesson in morality.

Theory as Anti-Theory

Part of the point of great novels is that sharing in the character's experience is a better guide to morality than any theory or combination of theories, now or to come. One reader of this manuscript suggested that we formulate, in philosophical terms, just what our theory of ethics is. At some times, the reviewer wrote, we sound like Kantians, at other times like consequentialists, and at still others as virtue ethicists. Perhaps so, and perhaps we resemble Jonathan Wight as pluralists in Isaiah Berlin's sense.

Or perhaps, like Toulmin, we do not lack a theory, but have an anti-theory. As Toulmin puts the point, it is a mistake to think that knowledge, to be real, must be theoretical. Practical wisdom is not some second-rate compromise. That, at least, is what Aristotle contended, and no one, we think, has thought of him as not offering a philosophical argument.

For Toulmin and Aristotle, some kinds of thinking are essentially practical and clinical. They are not just applied theory. For a biologist, individual cases are interesting only insofar as they contribute to a more general theory, but physicians work in the opposite way. They must use whatever tools they have to help a particular patient—and help her, moreover, in a timely manner. Timeliness is important, as it is not in theoretical reasoning. For these reasons, good clinical reasoning is never just applied theory, and any clinician who imagined otherwise would fail her patients. It is one thing to let a physician use your case as data for a study; it is quite another to allow yourself to be treated by someone interested only in the study and not in your particular case.

As discussed in chapters 1 and 6, these considerations led Toulmin to call for a revival of case-based reasoning. So long as it is not abused, as unfortunately it often was, case-based reasoning works from the particular up, not the theory down.[8] Principles are not laws, but at best tentative generalizations from past experience, useful only when, and to the extent that, a specific new case resembles old ones. Whether it does requires judgment and entails rebuttable argument. It is part

---

8. As Jonsen and Toulmin explain in *The Abuse of Casuistry*: "The rhetorical insults traditionally heaped on case ethics by its critics are therefore justified only when the method is misused. For this reason the title we have chosen for our book is drawn from the writings of the distinguished Anglican casuist, Kenneth Kirk; it embodies a deliberate play on words: 'The *abuse* of casuistry is properly directed, not against all casuistry, but only against its *abuse*'" (p. 16). Typically, casuistry was abused as a form of special pleading, a way to excuse someone worth exonerating by whatever tortured reasoning was at hand.

of the very nature of practical reasoning that judgments are always open to rebuttal, depending on circumstances, which is not the case, for instance, with mathematical propositions. Practical reasoning, to use Aristotle's favorite phrase, is a matter of "on the whole and for the most part"; however, anyone who thought the Pythagorean theorem was true "on the whole and for the most part" would not just be wrong but would demonstrate a failure to grasp why mathematical and moral (in Aristotle's terms, "rhetorical") reasoning differ. What makes one a better moral reasoner is, above all, experience reflecting on many cases.

Smith examines casuistry at length and with considerable sympathy before finding it wanting.[9] Like Toulmin, he favors a vision recognizing how much more complex people and moral questions are than any theory allows. Smith is given to formulations stressing the ineffable complexity of things: "It is impossible, indeed, to express all the variations which each sentiment either does or ought to undergo, according to every possible variation of circumstances. They are endless, and language wants names to mark them by" (p. 328). Smith likes to use words like "delicate," "exact," and "nice," in the older sense of a fine distinction. Ultimately, he cautions, language itself, which must choose general names, fails us. "It is impossible by language to express, if I may say so, the invisible features of all the different modifications of passion as they show themselves within" (p. 328).

Indeed, Smith's main objection to casuistry is that it seems to forget this very fact, on which it is based, and resort to rules. No less than their opponents, casuists, too, have attempted "to direct by precise rules what it belongs to feeling and sentiment only to judge of. How is it possible to ascertain by rules the exact point at which, in every case, a delicate sense of justice

---

9. For the discussion of casuistry, see Smith, *The Theory of Moral Sentiments*, pp. 329–342.

begins to run into a frivolous and weak scrupulosity of conscience? . . . with regard to all such matters, what would hold
good in any one case would scarce do so exactly in any other"
(Smith, p. 339). In other words, the casuists themselves are
insufficiently casuistical!

Smith is right about the need for fine distinctions among
unrepeatable experiences. Indeed, that is precisely why realist
novelists sought to examine moral questions by drawing cases
of much greater complexity than any casebook and by developing techniques for sharing the experience of inner psychological processes and moral reasonings. The logic of Smith's
argument looks forward to the genre just over the horizon as
he was writing, the psychological realist novel.

Smith the Novelist

Stressing "the invisible features of all the different modifications of passion as they show themselves within," Smith
laments that "there is no other way of marking and distinguishing them from one another, but by describing the effects
which they produce without, the alterations which they occasion in the countenance, in the air and external behavior, the
resolutions they suggest, the actions they prompt to" (pp. 328–
329). And indeed, in Smith's time, one could show the modifications of inner feelings only from "without."

Wouldn't it be helpful to our moral imaginations, then, if
we could somehow come closer to experiencing what another
experiences? If we could project ourselves into her feelings,
and sense them from within, as well as imagine what our
own feelings would be in her condition? That is precisely the
point of the technique referred to in chapter 6 as "free indirect
discourse," which Bakhtin called "double-voicing," and illus-
trated with a quotation from *Anna Karenina*. Bakhtin called it
double-voicing because it allows us to sense and compare both

the other's feelings and what our own would be in like circumstances, which is just what Smith's theory calls for.

In the discourse of the realist novel, readers trace a character's thoughts from within and do so in a way that illuminates the potential dialogues those thoughts might provoke if shared by others. The point is to allow a better understanding of psychological and moral processes that, as Smith noted, remain invisible to others in real life. Regardless of what we call this technique, the first novelist to use it consistently, as the guiding principle of an entire novel, was probably Jane Austen, where it forms the basis for such masterpieces as *Emma* and *Pride and Prejudice*. Austen's six great novels appeared between 1811 and 1818, that is, about a half century after *The Theory of Moral Sentiments* (1759).

The technique Austen developed became the trademark of the psychological realist novel and may indeed be taken as its defining formal characteristic. It develops Smith's psychological and moral insights in the direction Smith himself was going.[10] That is why the novel came to offer a way of thinking about psychological and moral questions that stressed identification and empathy. To really understand a novel and apply what one learns to life, one must experience from within what others feel, and experience the complexity of others' moral problems as if they were one's own. One must do so not theoretically—with the particularities abstracted out, as philosophers and social scientists tend to do—but practically, with a recognition that moral judgment cannot be reduced to any theory. Of course, that is itself a sort of theory.

10. The connection between Smith and Austen in terms of sympathy has occurred to a few recent critics. See Cecil E. Bohanon and Michelle Albert Vachris, *Pride and Profit: The Intersection of Jane Austen and Adam Smith* (Lexington Books, 2015); and Shannon Chamberlain, "The Economics of Jane Austen," *Atlantic*, August 3, 2014, http://www.theatlantic.com/business/archive/2014/08/the-economics-of-jane-austen/375486/. In addition, we would stress how Austen developed a technique for doing what Smith wished for but thought impossible, experiencing another from within.

Negative Pluralism

The theory (or anti-theory) implicit in the realist novel is indeed a version of pluralism, but of a special sort. It is not a positive pluralism, born of confidence in bringing many approaches together, but what might be called a negative pluralism, born of a suspicion of any theory, perhaps even of any combination of theories, as not supple enough. The great novelists have a keen appreciation that even the best theories lend themselves to misuse by our tendency to self-deception.

In *Middlemarch*, George Eliot devotes a chapter to the way in which the evangelist banker Bulstrode has managed—as many of us do—to think well of himself while rationalizing, or arranging not even to see, the evil he does. Eliot describes a psychological drama of immense complexity, a drama of dodges, subterfuges, and deceptions practiced on ourselves. At first, she allows readers to imagine that the problem lies in the outmoded religious doctrine Bulstrode has chosen, only to turn on them and say that *any* doctrine, including those we ourselves favor, entails the same risk:

> This implicit reasoning [of Bulstrode's] is essentially no more peculiar to evangelical belief than the use of wide phrases for narrow motives is peculiar to Englishmen. *There is no general doctrine which is not capable of eating out our morality if unchecked by the deep-seated habit of direct fellow feeling with individual fellow men.*[11]

When doctrine and direct fellow feeling conflict; when sympathy runs counter to ideology; when abstract theory threatens to overwhelm basic decency; in all these cases, we must give special weight to decency, sympathy, and direct fellow feeling. We may sometimes go wrong, but not so far wrong as risked by the opposite error of favoring theory over basic

---

11. George Eliot, *Middlemarch* (Modern Library, 1984), p. 591 (chapter 61). Italics added.

decency. What Eliot recommends will work only if we make a "deep-seated habit" of cultivating such feeling and reflecting on the mistakes to which it, too, may lead.

The narrator of Tolstoy's story "Lucerne" observes:

> What an unfortunate, pitiful creature is man, with his desire for positive decisions, thrown into this ever moving, limitless ocean of good and evil, of facts, conceptions, and contradictions!... Men have made subdivisions for themselves in this eternally moving, unending, intermingled chaos of good and evil: they have traced imaginary lines on that ocean, and expect the ocean to divide itself accordingly.[12]

Ultimately, he concludes, we have but one guide: "the universal spirit which inspiring each and all of us, implants in every individual a craving for what ought to be; that same Spirit which causes the tree to grow toward the sun ... and bids us instinctively draw closer together" (Tolstoy, p. 330).

This feeling, the "original passion" of sympathy, is instinctual, but it, too, can lead to error and must be educated. It must become a habit, something we do without thinking, and then it must be practiced until we develop the second habit of reflecting on the processes and results of the first. That cultivation of habit and reflection is the fundamental moral idea of the realist novel. The very reading of works like Austen's, Eliot's, or Tolstoy's is designed to create these habits. In so doing, the realist novel extends Smith's moral ideas.

Rethinking the Invisible Hand

The realist novel can also help us see the inner connection between Smith's two masterpieces, a question that has come to be called "the Adam Smith problem." How are the works

12. Leo Tolstoy, "Lucerne," trans. Louise and Aylmer Maude, in *Leo Tolstoy: Short Stories*, ed. Ernest J. Simmons (Modern Library, 1964), pp. 329–330.

consistent, or are they inconsistent? Thinkers have, of course, found links between *The Wealth of Nations* and *The Theory of Moral Sentiments*. Wight is correct when he contends that the former sees economic self-interest as necessary but not sufficient. He is also correct to see both volumes as studying "the invisible forces" that hold a society together.[13] James Otteson persuasively suggests that "Smith's general notion of a market forms the background for the conception of human actions in both TMS and WN."[14] We would add one more parallel.

Both of Smith's books evince a deep suspicion of human reason. The famous passage about the invisible hand derives from the sense that no rational planner could ever coordinate activity as well as an unconscious "invisible hand." But it is usually missed that *The Theory of Moral Sentiments* reasons in a similar way. Otteson calls our attention to Smith's discussion of "the man of system" who, in his hubris,

> seems to imagine that he can arrange the different members of a great society with as much ease as the hand arranges the different pieces on a chessboard ... to insist upon establishing, and establishing all at once, and in spite of all opposition, everything which that idea may seem to require, must often be the highest degree of arrogance. It is to erect his own judgment into the supreme standard of right and wrong. It is to fancy himself the only wise and worthy man

---

13. Jonathan B. Wight, *Ethics in Economics: An Introduction to Moral Frameworks* (Stanford University Press, 2015). Wight notes: "Although much has been written about Smith's two books (including the allegation that they represent contradictory theories), a late-twentieth-century revival of scholarship on Smith shows that his writings reflect a consistent philosophical view" (p. 153). In a footnote, Wight continues: "One important clue in support of this consistency is that Smith continued to edit both books throughout his life, completing the sixth edition of TMS a few months before his death" (p. 249, n14). In both studies, of course, Smith is trying to investigate "the invisible forces that held a society of persons together and enabled it to grow and prosper" (p. 153).

14. Otteson, *Adam Smith's Marketplace of Life*, p. 7.

in the commonwealth, and that his fellow-citizens should accommodate themselves to him and not he to them.[15]

Such systems are morally wrong precisely in their presumption that they get it all morally right, as no theory or "system" ever can. People are too different, their "principles of motion" are too different, and so the surest way to reason wrongly is to make a rational system the sole moral standard.

For much the same justification as guides Eliot and Tolstoy, *The Theory of Moral Sentiments* treats reason as an insufficient basis for morality. In this respect, it resembles skeptical thinkers of Smith's own time and their heirs, the great novelists to follow. A deep skepticism of reason famously belonged to Smith's close friend, David Hume, and was to shape Edmund Burke's suspicion of theory-based political reasoning. Critiques of reason, as well as celebrations of it, were characteristic of the Enlightenment. Hume contended that reason judges matters of facts and the relation of ideas, but cannot provide the least impulse to action or volition. "Nothing can oppose or retard the impulse of a passion, but a contrary passion," Hume contends, and reason aids only by showing us "causes and effects" and therefore means.[16] This is the sense in which Hume means the most famous sentence he ever wrote: "Reason is, and ought only to be the slave of the passions."[17]

Smith contends:

It is altogether absurd and unintelligible to suppose that the first perceptions of right and wrong can be derived from reason, even in those particular cases upon the experience of which the general rules are formed. These first perceptions,

---

15. Smith, p. 234. See Otteson's discussion of this passage in *Adam Smith's Marketplace of Life*, pp. 211–215.

16. David Hume, *A Treatise on Human Nature*, 2nd edition, ed. L. A. Selby-Bigge (Clarendon Press, 1978), p. 415.

17. Hume, p. 415.

as well as all other experiments upon which any general rules are founded, cannot be the object of reason, but of immediate sense and feeling.[18]

Like Hume, Smith sees reason as a means but powerless by itself:

Reason cannot render any particular object either agreeable or disagreeable to the mind for its own sake. Reason may show that this object is the means of obtaining some other which is naturally either pleasing or displeasing.... But nothing can be agreeable or disagreeable for its own sake, which is not rendered such by immediate sense and feeling. If virtue, therefore, in every particular instance, necessarily pleases for its own sake, and if vice as certainly displeases the mind, it cannot be reason, but immediate sense and feeling, which, in this manner, reconciles us to the one, and alienates us from the other. (p. 320)

How ironic, then, that those who have grasped the logic behind Smith's skepticism about central planning should have missed his broader skepticism of human reason! The last thing one would expect from Smith would be a theory explaining all of human behavior in terms of rational choice. Smith could only wonder at Becker.

The sort of thinking that takes economics as sufficient, rather than just quite helpful, for decision making does what Smith says cannot be done; that is, it builds a system of what ought to be done on reason alone. We need the insights that such economics provides so long as we do not imagine, as Smith

18. Smith, p. 320. Wight takes the point a step further and points out that Smith writes the same about the biological instincts of survival and propagation. He cites Smith's observation that "it has not been intrusted to the slow and uncertain determinations of our reason, to find out the proper means of bringing them [these biological functions] about," which nature has entrusted not to reason but to "original and immediate instincts" (Smith, pp. 77–78). In *Ethics in Economics*, Wight discusses Smith's suspicion of reason on pp. 154–157.

did not, that they are *all* we need. In short, nothing could be further from Smith's thought than the idea that it is possible to develop a hard social science, substituting mathematics for all narrative, reducing human motivation to self-interest alone, and starting from the assumption of total human rationality.

Smith was a fox, recommending a foxy understanding of both economics and morality. We understand him better if we see him as the forerunner not only of *Freakonomics* but also of *Pride and Prejudice*, *Middlemarch*, and *Anna Karenina*.

What Humanists Can Learn from Economists

So where does that leave our understanding of the value of modern economics?

We have arrived at a place where we are prepared to argue that, as economics can learn from the humanities, so the humanities, as usually practiced, can learn from economics. Sometimes, when the humanities fall short, economists do better. The liberal arts curriculum should ideally demand work both in literature and in economics.

In the social sciences, one must engage opposing arguments. As the old Yiddish proverb goes, "assertion is no proof." "I feel" is not evidence. Moreover, there is considerably more difference in point of view to be found in most economics departments than in English departments. As pointed out in chapter 6, Mill argues that it is important for an honest thinker to hear arguments for the other side "from persons who actually believe them; who defend them in earnest, and do their very utmost for them. He must know them in their most plausible and persuasive form" (Mill, *On Liberty*, p. 44). But that is scarcely possible in most literature departments today.

As a start, it would be helpful if more humanists came into contact with economic thinking. Sometimes market solutions can actually be better, even from an ethical point of view! It does not make sense to dismiss such ideas as "neoliberalism" without knowing the basics of economics to begin with. Chekhov never tired of pointing out that intellectuals who posture about helping the poor themselves waste resources. If poverty is bad, then wasting resources that might alleviate poverty is bad. To be sure, as we have argued throughout this book, efficiency is not as simple a concept as economists sometimes assume. It may suggest a particular goal when other goals are possible.[19] Nevertheless, regardless of what goal is chosen, it pays to achieve it without excessive waste. There is a moral argument for efficiency, and insofar as market solutions are efficient, one must presume that they cannot be rejected out of hand.

Morson once attended a meeting of humanities department chairs at Northwestern. Knowing that the chairs had stressed the importance of improving the pay of nontenure track instructors, the dean asked them how she should divide the money available for raises. How much should go to the nontenure track faculty, whose interests the chairs had advocated, and how much to the tenure track faculty, which included the chairs themselves and the people who had, for the most part, selected them?

The question obviously put the chairs in a tight spot because it involved a trade-off between their self-interest and their professed principles. If they chose the former, their high-minded declarations would be revealed as hypocritical; but if they chose the latter, they would themselves suffer. What would they do? Anyone who knows how many humanists argue will not be surprised. After a long pause, one chair declared forcefully, "We reject this false choice based on the notion that resources are limited."

It would have been pointless to reply that, regardless of what goals one might choose, resources are limited. No mat-

---

19. This is the point Wight makes repeatedly in *Ethics in Economics*.

ter how big the dean's pot for raises, the amount was finite. To reject the idea of scarce resources is to reject reasonable thought altogether. And yet such objections are not ones that carry much weight for many humanists. Even before the advent of postmodernism, literary scholars were prone to reject logical argument as somehow contrary to the spirit of poetry itself.

Economists could learn from humanists the complexity of ethical issues, the need for stories, the importance of empathy, and the value of unformalizable good judgment. But humanists could also learn from economists how to think about scarce resources, about the nature of efficiency, and the importance of rational decision making.

Our theme here, of course, it that we can all profit from such a dialogue of disciplines. But just as some diehard humanists will undoubtedly chafe while reading about how we think the approach they take in practice often reduces the value of their discipline, some economists will complain that we are talking about a strawman version of mainstream economics. Hasn't behavioral economics, for instance, already incorporated the theories and methods of other fields in a meaningful way? In some ways, yes, but not the ways we have in mind.

Humanism and Behavioral Economics

When we have discussed our idea that economics could benefit from the humanities, we have repeatedly heard the response that behavioral economics is doing just that. In fact, behavioral economics could also use insights from the humanities. It is worth explaining why.

Behavioral economics challenges mainstream economics' core assumption of rationality. It has offered proof that at times people behave irrationally, by which they mean differently from the way standard rational choice models would predict. They have called attention to complexities in human decision making that mainstream economists had either not considered important or not considered at all.

From a humanist perspective, it might seem that this would be an improvement. And in some respects it is. But by and large behavioral economics repeats, and sometimes magnifies, the shortcomings of rational choice models. It is not helpful to give the impression of improvement without the substance. Whatever else it might do, behavioral economics does not represent a way to humanize mainstream economics.

For a humanist, the finest parts of behavioral economics derive from the distinction it draws between how people should behave (according to rationality models) and how they do behave—or, to use Richard Thaler's terms, between "Econs" (wholly rational economic agents) and "Humans" (real people, as determined by laboratory experiments).[20] Unfortunately, "humans" as behavioral economists understand them bear little resemblance to actual people.

At their best, mainstream economists follow Milton Friedman's advice and offer their view of individual choice as a useful fiction to be justified by the predictions it enables. In that case, they neither endorse nor reject the view that people actually make their choices rationally. Behavioral economists offer no such qualification.[21] They claim to describe how individual agents behave. In that case, the objection that their view of human beings is shallow has real bite, as it would not for a mainstream economist careful to follow Friedman's advice. Only if you claim to do something can you be faulted for failing.

20. Richard Thaler, *Misbehaving: The Making of Behavioral Economics* (Norton, 2015). There is consequently a gap between "experienced utility" and "decision utility." For a superb review of the state of behavioral economics, see Raj Chetty, "Behavioral Economics and Public Policy: A Pragmatic Perspective," Richard T. Ely Lecture, *American Economic Review: Papers and Proceedings 2015*, May 2015, pp. 1–33.

21. An important exception is Chetty, cited previously and discussed subsequently.

By distinguishing between ideal and empirical behavior, the behavioral economists properly address an ambiguity present in rationalist utilitarian models from the start. Are they describing how people should behave or how they do behave? Often enough, economists have assumed there is no difference between the two, since rationality is defined as acting according to one's best interest and it is inconceivable someone would knowingly do anything else.

This conflation of "should" and "does" goes all the way back to the beginning of utilitarianism. Jeremy Bentham's *Introduction to the Principles of Morals and Legislation* famously begins:

> Nature has placed mankind under the governance of two sovereign masters, pain and pleasure. It is for them alone to point out what to do. On the one hand the standard of right and wrong, on the other the chain of causes and effects, are fastened to their throne. They govern us in all we do, in all we say, in all we think: every effort we make to throw off their subjection, will serve but to demonstrate and confirm it. In words a man may pretend to abjure their empire: but in reality he will remain subject to it all the while. The principle of utility recognizes this subjection, and assumes it for the foundation of that system, the object of which is to rear the fabric of felicity by the hands of reason and law. Systems which attempt to question it, deal with sounds instead of sense, in caprice instead of reason, in darkness instead of light.[22]

The phrase "standard of right and wrong," the stated goal of rearing "the fabric of felicity," and, indeed, this very plea to adopt utilitarian ethics all suggest that Bentham is telling us how we *should* behave. One should behave rationally and not any other way, and society should be reconstructed

---

22. Jeremy Bentham, *An Introduction to the Principles of Morals and Legislation* (Beacon, 1955), pp. 1–2.

according to the principle of utility rather than continue as it is. But Bentham's insistence that the "chain of causes and effects" ensures this behavior, his contention that no other behavior is possible, and his closing remark that one cannot even coherently question that people behave according to the principle of utility all suggest that he is describing how they *do* behave. There is a logical confusion here, which Bentham does not recognize. It is a confusion that has persisted.

The normative formulation is what allows Bentham to offer social recommendations: to prescribe one course of action rather than another. But the statement that all actions fit the criteria by definition switches to a tautology: whatever one does is by definition rational. In that case, recommendations, including the recommendation to adopt utilitarianism, make no sense.

Over the past two centuries, a common solution to the normative/descriptive question has been to argue that people do indeed behave according to what they think will provide the most pleasure and least pain but that they are often mistaken. They are led astray not by emotion, or by pursuing goals other than utility, but by cognitive errors. In that case, "should" does have a meaning. We suffer from innate cognitive confusion, which we would do well to recognize and counteract. This is the model adopted by behavioral economics.

If the problem is cognitive, then irrationality is as predictable as rationality would be and we still have the hard foundation for a predictive science. We also have the possibility of making recommendations to correct the irrationalities to which people are prone.

One could conceivably make two sorts of recommendations. We could try to educate people, as a tradition of social reform dating to John Locke would presuppose. If only people understood their true rational interest, they would necessarily follow it; so we need scientific research to determine biases and educational lessons to correct them. Alternatively, one could use government policy to counteract the biases.[23] "Choice architects" might "nudge" people by setting default options that are best for them and letting inertia ensure that most will not choose something else. In either case, irrationality is intelligible, predictable, and corrigible.

But does such a utopian picture really make sense? Are the sources of "irrationality" so easy to determine? Does irrationality perhaps come in various kinds, and if so, how many? For that matter, is it always irrational to behave differently from the way rational choice models predict? Assuming they are known, are the sources of "error" usually correctable by designing institutions that counteract our irrational tendencies—without unintentionally introducing new irrationalities? Life would be so easy if that were so!

We see at least three objections to these ideas. They concern the neglect of culture, the thin sense of a person, and the existence of genuine irrationalities.

The Neglect of Culture

Most strikingly, culture is entirely neglected by behavioral economists. To be sure, a number of economists in recent years have indeed tried to come to terms with culture, at least where historical questions are at issue and, in some cases, have made considerable progress in the direction we favor. But they remain a minority, as Eric L. Jones argues in his insightful study *Cultures Merging: A Historical and Economic Critique of Culture*. Jones begins: "Economists agree about many things—contrary to popular opinion—but the majority agree about culture only in the sense that they no longer give it much thought." In the 1960s and 1970s, he continues, the hope faded that "a strong relationship would be found

---

23. See Richard H. Thaler and Cass R. Sunstein, *Nudge: Improving Decisions about Health, Wealth, and Happiness* (Penguin, 2009).

between economic and cultural change."[24] Most economists adopt a position Jones calls "cultural nullity," which presumes that cultures are so "marginal to economic concerns that they may be safely ignored ... the professional culture of economists prevents most of them from seeing that culture matters at all" (Jones, p. 5). Jones does not remark on the irony that economists' denial of culture is itself culturally based.

The opposite position, which tries to minimize the role of economic factors in favor of cultural ones, is of course most popular among those in other disciplines. We may suppose the view that culture matters most is especially popular among anthropologists and adherents of "cultural studies." Are we to attribute this popularity to cultural or economic factors (or to both)?

The idea that culture matters gained adherents among economists trying to understand history. What made the industrial revolution and continuing technological innovation happen in the West? Why did it happen when it did? These very questions already constitute a departure from standard economic theory, which tends to presuppose an environment where the groundwork of a market economy is taken for granted. When economics and market economics become synonymous, cultural factors seem irrelevant.[25]

As mentioned previously, Douglass North pioneered one route for understanding economic historical questions when he proposed that institutions were a key factor, an approach

24. Eric L. Jones, *Cultures Merging: A Historical and Economic Critique of Culture* (Princeton University Press, 2006), p. 3.

25. The late economist Aron Katsenelinboigen liked to say that naming the discipline "economics" is using a misnomer, since it deals with only one of several economic systems. Katsenelinboigen, who began his career as a planner of the Soviet economy, suggested it be called "market economics."

that has proven fruitful for many.[26] Avner Greif developed an approach to institutional analysis that expanded it to combine economic factors with cultural and social ones. Particularly interesting is his concept of "private order," that is, "situations in which order prevails despite the lack of a third-party enforcer."[27] His approach tries to explain not only how institutions shape economic development but also how and why they themselves change.

Institutions seem at least relatively "hard," but what about the sort of "soft" things that humanists like to discuss, like values and beliefs? And doesn't culture, in some mushier sense, have to be invoked?

In his recent book, *A Culture of Growth: The Origins of the Modern Economy*, one of the heroes of chapter 5, Joel Mokyr, presents a carefully reasoned approach to culture's role.[28] He

26. In addition to North's work cited in chapter 5, see Douglass C. North, *Institutions, Institutional Change, and Economic Performance* (Cambridge University Press, 1990), and Douglas C. North and Robert Paul Thomas, *The Rise of the Western World: A New Economic History* (Cambridge University Press, 1973). For a comprehensive review of recent literature on the relationship between culture and institutions, see Alberto Alesina and Paola Giuliano, "Culture and Institutions," *Journal of Economic Literature*, December 2015, pp. 898–944. They conclude that culture and institutions interact and evolve together, with feedback between the two. Guido Tabellini argues that culture has an important causal impact on economic development, at least in the context of European history. If he is correct, individual values and beliefs matter and help explain some of the puzzles we laid out in chapter 5 on differential growth rates. See Guido Tabellini, "Institutions and Culture," Presidential Address at the European Economic Association, Budapest, August 2007, which appeared in the April–May 2008 issue of *Journal of the European Economic Association*, pp. 255–294. See also his "Culture and Institutions: Economic Development in the Regions of Europe," *Journal of the European Economic Association*, June 2010, pp. 677–716.

27. Avner Greif, *Institutions and the Path to the Modern Economy: Lessons from Medieval Trade* (Cambridge University Press, 2006), p. 8.

28. Joel Mokyr, *A Culture of Growth: The Origins of the Modern Economy* (Princeton University Press, 2017). For another pathbreaking effort at introducing culture into the analysis of why growth rates differ, see the remarkably insightful book by David S. Landes, *The Wealth and Poverty of Nations: Why Some Are So Rich and Some So Poor* (W. W. Norton, 1998).

offers a rigorous consideration of something inherently fluid. "If economists admit that economic history cannot do without institutions," he argues, then "it cannot do without a better understanding of culture. They like things, however, clear-cut, precise, and if possible formally modeled and testable. This is a daunting task" (p. 12).That may be too much to ask with culture, but that does not mean that nothing of value can be known.

In the course of his analysis, Mokyr, among other inquiries, boldly explores the relation of institutions to beliefs; examines culture as a matter of beliefs, preferences, and values; stresses the important but highly complex roles played by religion; examines the contributions of individual "cultural entrepreneurs" like Bacon and Newton; formulates a quasi-evolutionary model of cultural change; and stresses the inherently contingent nature of events. Nothing is inevitable, but much is understandable.

Where there is contingency, there is choice, and where there is choice, there are alternative possible paths. It is this insistence on genuine alternatives that shows Mokyr taking culture, and with it human agency, seriously. Presumably, that is why his study begins with a quotation from David Hume: "There is no subject, in which we must proceed with more caution, than in tracing the history of the arts and sciences; lest we assign causes which never existed, and reduce what is merely contingent to stable and universal principles. Those who cultivate the sciences in any state, are always few in number: The passion, which governs them, limited: Their taste and judgment delicate and easily perverted: And their application disturbed with the smallest accident. Chance, therefore, or secret and unknown causes, must have a great influence on the rise and progress of all the refined arts" (Mokyr, p. vi). Or as Mokyr observes, "History is neither fluke nor necessity, but somewhere in between. Individuals mattered ... even if their impact was in the end constrained by the environment" (p. 67).

Mokyr's account approaches the humanities more closely than the others who have incorporated culture—culture as a humanist would approach it—into economic explanation. As a humanist would see the matter, it is natural for a social scientist to create a model as a form of explanation. The more the model can account for, the better. It is best if the model is itself economic, but if not, some other model, for example, institutional or game theoretical, will do. Not surprisingly, sometimes ideas from economic modeling, like equilibria, reappear. Greif, for example, explains:

> The perspective adopted here departs from viewing institutions from either a structural, cultural perspective (as common in sociology) or an agency, functionalist perspective (common in economics). Instead, it combines the structuralist and agency views. It emphasizes the importance of studying institutions as equilibrium phenomenon in which they constitute the structure that influences behavior, while the behavioral responses of agents to this structure reproduce the institution. (p. 14)

If economic and sociological models by themselves are inadequate, using them in combination may lead to a better outcome. This sort of pluralism, as Greif handles it, works reasonably well.

But culture as a humanist, and many historians, would see it begins where the models end. Recall from chapter 5 Herbert Butterfield's comment in *The Whig Interpretation of History* that "the thing which is unhistorical is to imagine that we can get the essence apart from the accidents."[29] The particularities that do *not* fit a model are precisely what is "historical."

By much the same token, the realist novel works from the assumption that, while individuals and cultures shape each

---

29. Herbert Butterfield, *The Whig Interpretation of History* (1931, reproduced in Norton, 1965), p. 69.

other, neither is reducible to the other or to anything else. As the titles of novels like Eliot's *Middlemarch*, Trollope's *Barchester Towers*, or Henry James's *The Bostonians* suggest, the realist novel does not portray cultures and societies as an inert backdrop against which characters act. Rather, they are complex webs of relations with an aura impossible to define precisely but that exert an active role on events. The norms and practices of these cultures change subtly over time, sometimes even within the span of a single novel, and never in a way that seems preordained or arrives at a resting point. There is no equilibrium, though there is considerable stability.

As the realist novel describes cultures, they shape the individuals who participate in them, which is one reason personalities can never exactly repeat from age to age. A miser, an officer, or a lover in eighteenth-century England does not resemble one in nineteenth-century Russia, and such variations indeed constitute the theme of many novels about cultural difference. But while the culture shapes the individual, the individual can never be described solely in terms of the culture. There is a strong sense that culture goes only so far and that individuality begins where social and cultural categories leave off. Those categories may be adequate for minor characters and mere satiric types but not for psychologically rich heroes and heroines. Or as Bakhtin paraphrases the view implicit in realist novels: "He ... cannot become once and for all a clerk, a landowner, a merchant, a fiancé, a jealous lover, a father, and so forth. If the hero of a novel actually becomes something of the sort—that is, if he completely coincides with his situation and fate (as do generic, everyday heroes, the majority of secondary characters in a novel)—then the surplus of humanness is realized in the main protagonist."[30]

---

30. Mikhail Bakhtin, "Epic and Novel" in M. M. Bakhtin, *The Dialogic Imagination: Four Essays*, ed. Michael Holquist, trans. Caryl Emerson and Michael Holquist (University of Texas Press, 1981), p. 37.

By "the surplus of humanness inherent in the human condition," Bakhtin means each person's real humanness, which is the most valuable thing about him or her. People do not "coincide" with their situation, that is, they "exceed" (have a "surplus") that goes beyond all models. In fact, people even exceed themselves because whatever they are, they could be and could have been something else. Human beings include their might-have-beens because they are constituted not only by the facts about them but by their "unrealized potential" as well.

Bakhtin famously concludes:

> An individual cannot be completely incarnated into the flesh of existing sociohistorical categories. There is no mere form that would be able to incarnate once and forever all of his human possibilities and needs, no form in which he could exhaust himself down to the last word.... There always remains an unrealized surplus of humanness ... All existing clothes are always too tight, and thus comical, on a person.... Reality as we have it in the novel is only one of many possible realities; it is not inevitable, not arbitrary, it bears within itself other possibilities. (p. 37)

If this view is correct, then what we need is not only a model but also a sense of where models fail. Indeed, even a combination of models falls short: we need as well a sense of individuality and particularity beyond the reach of models. And that is what the humanities are best at teaching.

Models are most likely to fail with individuals, which is why social science modelers prefer to assume them away or factor them out. So it is especially impressive that Mokyr does quite the contrary. His treatments of Bacon and Newton—he indicates several other individuals whom it would pay to treat this way—show his belief that both models and a sense of individuality are required. So does his cautious combination of an evolutionary model with a stress on

sheer contingency. Reality, as he describes it, is indeed neither "inevitable" nor wholly "arbitrary" and "it bears within
itself other possibilities."

Not surprisingly, we love this foxy approach and wish it
were more widely accepted not just among economic historians but among all economists, especially those who purport to
explain human behavior.

Why Behavioral Economics Is Not Enough

To return to behavioral economics, its adherents (and their
laboratory experiments) take no more account of culture
than do those mainstream economists who entirely neglect
it. Their portraits of decision making show how people—any
people—make biased decisions. If they attempt an explanation of such irrationalities, they leap directly to evolutionary
psychology or neurobiology. Culture is implicitly regarded
as immaterial.

From a humanist perspective, this is decidedly odd. Since
we are dealing with people, rather than organisms, a literature
scholar or cultural anthropologist would ask, why go first to
the organic? Why not begin closer to the starting point, that
is, with culture? If one was trying to understand why Swedes
or Saudis get married and why they separate or divorce, and
if one was unsatisfied by the sort of explanation Gary Becker
would use, one might first inquire about the differences
between Swedish and Saudi culture, about a Lutheran heritage among mostly irreligious people on the one hand and a
Wahabi Muslim culture on the other, before one invoked neurons and evolution.

Mainstream economists like Becker try to circumvent culture because of their aspiration to scientific status. If scientific
status entails mathematicization, then culture is an impedi-
ment because one cannot mathematicize culture. So economists try to show that what look like cultural causes can really
be described in terms endogenous, that is, internal, to eco-

nomics. It is illuminating to see how far this method can work (perhaps more often than humanists think), even if it does not work everywhere.

Behavioral economist Dan Ariely asks, "Wouldn't it make sense to modify standard economics, to move it away from naive psychology (which often fails the test of reason, introspection, and—most important—empirical scrutiny)?"[31] A humanist might suppose that empirical scrutiny would lead to examining the role of culture, even if doing so entailed surrendering scientific predictability. But behavioral economics does nothing of the kind. The model of a decision maker changes but remains just as acultural. And people remain just as predictable, as they would not be if something as complex as culture were taken into account.[32]

A humanist might identify a fallacy not limited to behavioral economists: what we call the *fallacy of abstraction*. The mistaken idea is that because cultures vary, nothing cultural can be essentially human. One can therefore understand what people essentially are by abstracting everything merely cultural from them. In the case of behavioral economics, we have a particular kind of fallacy of abstraction that might be called the *fallacy of the abstract person*.

The fallacy of the abstract person occurs in quite diverse fields. Consider John Rawls's highly influential book *A Theory of Justice*, which in our view offers several insights that could bring a moral perspective to economic ideas.[33] We agree that, as Rawls argues, people do have a tendency to forget they have not earned advantages with which they were born and that shape their views of justice. They somehow become sincerely convinced that justice and their own advantages coincide.

---

31. Dan Ariely, *Predictably Irrational: The Hidden Forces That Shape Our Decisions*, revised edition (HarperCollins, 2009), p. xxx.

32. Thus the title of Ariely's book, *Predictably Irrational*.

33. John Rawls, *A Theory of Justice* (Harvard University Press, 1971).

And economists tend to forget that reaching equilibrium has nothing to do with reaching a moral state of affairs. A "fair" market price simply means it is the amount that a knowledge-able, willing, and unpressured buyer would pay to a knowledgeable, willing, and unpressured seller. Markets clear, but the only thing necessarily "fair" about that is the word used to describe the transaction.

Nevertheless, Rawls purports to establish what a "just" society would be by beginning with people outside "the contingency of social circumstances," including, but not limited to, all of culture. He asks, what sort of society would people choose if they did not know what place they would occupy in society?

And so Rawls imagines agents beginning in a position of "absolute equality," which means they have no distinguishing characteristics to distort their conception of fairness. They lack class position, social status, assets and liabilities; they have no idea what their intelligence, strength, or other personal qualities will be; "I shall even assume that the parties do not know their conceptions of the good or their special psychological propensities. The principles of justice are chosen behind a veil of ignorance" (p. 12). What's more, "they are conceived as not taking an interest in one another's interests" (p. 13), but only in their own—a view that evidently distinguishes Rawls's idea of the human from Adam Smith's. Given this starting point, they choose rationally, and this concept of rationality "must be interpreted as far as possible in the narrow sense, standard in economic theory, of taking the most effective means to given ends" (Rawls, p. 14).

With only one's own interest to consider, "no one has a reason to acquiesce in an enduring loss for himself" even if a small loss for oneself produced a large increase in the net satisfaction for everyone else. Reasoning about what "no one" or anyone would choose, Rawls arrives at his model of justice. The specifics of this model are less important than the fact that it is unique and unanimous. "It is clear," Rawls concludes, "that since the differences among the parties are unknown to them, and everyone is equally rational and similarly situated, each is convinced by the same arguments.... If anyone after due reflection prefers a conception of justice to another, then they all do, and a unanimous agreement can be reached" (p. 141). There is no room for difference of opinion, any more than there would be in determining the hypotenuse of a right triangle. And how could there be once everything pertaining to individuality and culture have been thought away?

In much the same spirit, Lawrence Kohlberg formulated a rationalist, acultural model of children's ethical development—the dominant model for decades. Just as Piaget had posited that children go through a series of stages in understanding the physical world, Kohlberg proposed they go through six stages in understanding the moral world. They at last reach the most sophisticated stage, and, as with physics, what is most sophisticated is a rational given.

A humanist would immediately note that the notion of rationality embraced by both Kohlberg and Rawls leads to the views already shared by modern American academic liberals. That seems a remarkable coincidence. Since those views run counter to those of most cultures today, almost all past societies, and indeed many people in our own society, it would seem much more likely to have turned out otherwise. Is there not something suspect about the conclusion? After all, people everywhere regard their own ethics as superior, or they would not be their ethics in the first place. And it is always easy enough to begin with assumptions that allow one to derive the conclusions one has already planted.[34]

---

34. For a recent critique of the Kohlberg school and its rationalist approach, see Jonathan Haidt, *The Righteous Mind: Why Good People Are Divided by Politics and Religion* (Pantheon, 2012).

Both Rawls and Kohlberg have constructed a system that allows them simply to dismiss other moral and political preferences as irrational or immature. One can take it as a general rule about situations with contested social issues: the more abstract reason seems to endorse one's own position, the more one should suspect that the deck has been stacked in determining "reason." Rawls, for instance, does not seem to recognize that the way he has constricted the essential, precultural person presumes unqualified individual egoism as rational.

The underlying problem for a humanist lies in the initial assumption itself, the "precultural fallacy." Just because cultures vary does not mean that culture can be abstracted from humanness or that the essentially human is precultural. One might as well argue that because languages vary, the essentially human is either mute or prelingual like a chimp. Cultures differ, but all people belong to some culture. Culture is essential to being human in the first place. To think away language and culture is not to arrive at, but to bypass, the human.

In an autobiographical essay, Isaiah Berlin recalls how he shared rationalist assumptions of many social scientists and philosophers that, as in the hard sciences, "all genuine questions must have one true answer and one only, all the rest being necessarily errors" and that "the true answers, once found, must necessarily be compatible with one another … we could then conceive what the perfect life must be."[35] Berlin abandoned this view when he recognized that cultures may be genuinely different and that sets of values may indeed be incompatible with each other. He became a fox and a "pluralist," holding "the conception that there are many different

---

35. Isaiah Berlin, "The Pursuit of the Ideal," *The Crooked Timber of Humanity: Chapters in the History of Ideas* (Knopf, 1991), pp. 5–6.

ends that men may seek and still be fully rational, fully men, capable of understanding each other and sympathizing and deriving light from each other, as we derive it from reading Plato or the novels of medieval Japan" (p. 11).

The more novels we read and the more cultures we read them from, the less likely we are to commit the fallacy of the abstract person, as Rawls, Kohlberg, and behavioral economists do.

The Thin Sense of a Person

A humanist is also struck by how often she is moved to say in response to some discovery, "You mean, you had to prove that?"

We are told of discoveries such as the following:

Sunk costs matter. If a person bought an expensive theatre ticket, but on the evening of the play would rather do something else, she might "irrationally" choose not to "waste" her purchase.

People use reference points to determine what is a good purchase, so establishing a different reference point may affect the decision. It is concluded that since only one of these decisions can be rational, the other must be irrational.

It matters how you frame a decision: if you want to charge two different prices (say, one if a charge card is used and another for cash), you will encounter less resistance by calling the lower price a discount than by calling the higher price a surcharge.

People are more likely to expend a given amount of effort to save money on a small purchase than to save the same money on a large purchase. That is, a person who would travel fifteen minutes to save $10 on a $25 coffeemaker will not travel the same distance to save $10 on a $500 suit or a $30,000 car. But since it is the same effort for the same number of dollars, that (according to the behavioral economist) is irrational. Such a person "is not valuing time consistently" (Thaler, *Misbehaving*, p. 21).[36]

None of these insights seems remarkable to a humanist or, a humanist might think, to anyone with introspection. For that matter, they do not seem surprising to anyone who shops. After all, it is obvious that marketers take advantage of these psychological dispositions by, let us say, claiming that a given price is a markdown from some other price. Call it a bargain and people are more likely to buy it. Place an item at the end of a supermarket aisle where bargains are usually placed but don't lower the price, and people are more likely to buy it. Who has not noticed that merchants price products at $19.99 rather than $20, as if that penny made more of a difference than, let us say, a penny off of $19.50? If marketers and their customers are all aware of these facts, how can they be a discovery? Or, returning to the topic of enrollment management, practitioners have realized that a $10,000 discount off the sticker price often has a larger enrollment impact if labeled "merit aid" than if it is called "need-based aid." Students, and their parents respond better if told the reduced price results from academic talent, not financial neediness. Surprised? We doubt it.

What's more, behavioral economics notwithstanding, it is not clear that these reactions are all irrational. Someone familiar with novels might imagine one describing a person buying a car. The person, who was not born yesterday, has a specific story that, let us say, has led to reluctance to spend large sums.

---

36. The introduction to Nick Wilkinson's textbook *Introduction to Behavioral Economics* (Palgrave Macmillan, 2008) poses four puzzles that behavioral economics can solve, including versions of the ones above and this one: "Why are people delighted to hear they are going to get a 10% raise in salary, and then furious to find out that a colleague is going to get 15%?" (p. 7). What must someone's sense of a person be if this requires explanation?

She has just gone through a day, described at length, in which she has quarreled with her spouse, suffered from a mildly upset stomach, been trapped in stop-and-go traffic and then forced to speed to make up for lost time, and, shortly before going into the showroom, has heard distressing news on the radio. She is no expert on automobiles and knows she is at a disadvantage in negotiations. Would it really be wise for her to worry about $10 in price as she would when buying a coffee machine? After all, attention is a limited resource, and it would be foolish to spend it on something so small in proportion to the entire purchase. One might risk overlooking something much more significant, as one would not with a coffeepot. Indeed, a less than scrupulous automobile salesman might try to distract a potential buyer from important issues precisely in that way, by raising less significant ones.

Some supposed irrationalities, in short, prove quite rational when one considers that attention is itself a resource in short supply. This behavior is not misbehavior we would be wise to correct. Indeed, it is readily handled by a mainstream economic model that accepts attention, like time, as a limited resource.

For the same reason, it is sometimes rational, not predictably irrational, to make a habit of trusting to habits and a rule of using rules, even though on particular occasions they may lead to a suboptimal outcome. We may be, and often are, aware that such suboptimal outcomes happen and, even when they are clearly recognized, may choose to follow the rule so as not to establish the need to think through future choices. You can't just follow a rule, you have to make a rule of doing so, as anyone on a diet knows. The standard behavioral economics examples of irrationality seem to overlook why, given human nature, they are rational accommodations to human limitations. We are not always fully attentive, undistracted, with only the task at hand on our mind, willing or able to be at our best.

Culture, as well as human nature, may also shape how and whether one can properly negotiate, how much one should value money saved, and many other aspects of a transaction. More is involved in an exchange than the exchange itself. We are always monitoring our self-image as well as the transaction. Our self-image is shaped by cultural values. And what is irrational in one culture may be entirely rational in another. Or rather, *reasonable*, for, as Toulmin liked to say, it is sometimes not reasonable to be rational (and vice versa).

Consider the issue that Richard Thaler calls "the gift paradox": "Lee's wife gives him an expensive cashmere sweater for Christmas. He had seen the sweater in the store and decided that it was too big of an indulgence to feel good about buying it. He is nevertheless delighted with the gift. Lee and his wife pool all their financial assets; neither has any separate source of money."[37] Thaler regards this as economically irrational because "Lee feels better about spending family resources on an expensive sweater if his wife made the decision, though the sweater was no cheaper" (*Misbehaving*, p. 21).

If one steps back, it seems decidedly odd that any discipline studying human beings would be puzzled by the difference a gift makes. Gift giving would seem to be a cultural fact that would be impossible to ignore. It is hardly surprising that in the history of cultural anthropology, gifts, and their complex roles and meanings in different cultures, have figured prominently, at least since Bronislaw Malinowski's 1922 anthropological classic *Argonauts of the Western Pacific* and Marcel Mauss's 1925 *The Gift*.[38] As Mauss's subtitle suggests, it turns out that the market system of barter or purchase belongs to a larger category of

37. Thaler, *Misbehaving*, pp. 20–21. Wilkinson poses this puzzle as one it takes behavioral economics to solve: "Why is someone unwilling to pay $500 for a product, but then delighted when their spouse buys him the same product for the same price using their joint bank account?" (Wilkinson, p. 7).

38. Bronislaw Malinowski, *Argonauts of the Western Pacific: An Account of Native Enterprise and Adventure in the Archipelagoes of Melanesian New Guinea* (Dutton, 1961), and Marcel Mauss's brilliant, *Essai sur le don: Form et raison de l'échange dans les societies archaïques*, translated as *The Gift: The Form and Reason for Exchange in Archaic Societies*, trans. W. D. Halls (Routledge, 1990).

exchange types, involving groups as well as individuals, different concepts of honor, and, above all, various expectations of reciprocity. Malinowski makes a point of showing how "the economic standpoint" fails to capture what is involved in Trobriand Island gift giving, "since there is no enhancement of mutual utility through the exchange" (p. 175). For example, "it is quite a usual thing in the Trobriands for a type of transaction to take place in which A gives twenty baskets of yams to B, receiving for it a small polished blade, only to have the whole transaction reversed in a few weeks' time" (p. 175). For that matter, gifts, which we all regard as in some way different from purchases, play a prominent role in our own culture, as everyone from earliest childhood knows by experience.

If Lee's feeling better requires explanation, then so do Christmas stockings, birthday and anniversary presents, gift certificates, and countless other behaviors that make up our daily lives. Indeed, we might regard someone who could not understand gifts as deficient in humanness, and we would wonder apprehensively what else to expect from him.

Thaler notes that "economic man" "would be perplexed by the very idea of gifts" because he would know that cash is the best possible gift "since it allows the recipient to buy whatever is optimal" (*Misbehaving*, p. 6). Then why do close friends not routinely give cash, and why do many regard such a gift as insensitive? To see what this perspective leaves out, one does not need to turn to the psychology of perception and misperception, neurobiology, or any of the "misbehaviors" studied by behavioral economists. One needs to understand one's culture, which one cannot grasp by looking at the brain. One might instead turn for insight to literature, beginning with Dickens's *Great Expectations*, the gifts Raskolnikov receives from his mother in *Crime and Punishment*, or even the useless but immensely valuable gifts in O. Henry's sentimental tale "The Gift of the Magi."

Lee might appreciate the gift not because he uses a different mental accounting for gifts (as a behavioral economist might explain) but precisely because it came from his wife. She thought enough to get it and to anticipate what he might like. The main currency here is not money but care, which is why the fact that they share a bank account does not matter in the least. Indeed, gifts often have no economic value at all, which means no cash could buy them. One might cherish a bad drawing done when one's son was eight precisely because at age eight he thought enough to make and give it. It's not available on eBay. Where is the puzzle?

Behavioral economists might reply to the query "you mean, you had to prove this?" by explaining that this might be obvious to a humanist but not to an economist. And if that were all that behavioral economists were claiming, who would object? But it is not. They are as imperialist as Becker, only in a different way.

If they were only reasserting a truism that everyone but mainstream economists knows, why seek support in laboratory experiments or neurology? One does not prove that the sexes are attracted to each other, that people are capable of aggression, or that taste in food and art differs by doing fMRIs. On the contrary, one would sooner suspect the usefulness of fMRIs if they showed anything else. And if they were only supplying economists with news to them alone, why claim to be remaking the social sciences generally, or offer suggestions on issues of public policy, or indeed give advice to people about their social lives? "By the end of this book," explains Ariely in *Predictably Irrational*, "you'll know the answers to ... questions that have implications for your personal life, for your business life, and for the way you look at the world.... My goal ... is to help you fundamentally rethink what makes you and the people around you tick" (p. xxii). The result, he says, will be a method "for improving decision-making and changing the way we live for the better" (p. xxx). The subtitle of Thaler and Sunstein's book *Nudge: Improving Decisions about Health, Wealth, and Happiness* also suggests far-reaching applications.

Nothing here indicates that the "fundamental rethinking" is restricted to hard-core mainstream economists. Quite the reverse; in both cases the ambitions are expansive.

Ariely, in fact, writes an advice column for the *Wall Street Journal* where he answers a broad range of questions from readers. If this is intended, as it seems to be, to demonstrate the usefulness of behavioral economics, one can only be struck that some of his advice is (from a humanist's perspective) astoundingly simplistic.[39] He suggests that if you want to see whether you will like having kids, arrange to take care of a friend's kids for a week, and then do the same with other friends who have kids of a different age.[40] A reader confides that he has been in a relationship with a woman for six years, and is comfortable with her, but that the passion of the first days "when oxytocin levels were extremely high" has passed. In reply, Ariely cites an economist who has shown that people have a tendency "to take the comfortable, safe, and predictable path all too often.... So, perhaps, this is a good opportunity to give up your comfort and give pleasure a chance."[41] Or maybe, instead of turning to a behavioral economist, read *Anna Karenina*.

The Existence of Genuine Irrationalities
The "irrationalities" and "misbehaviors" cited by behavioral economics do not represent the sort of irrationalities that spring to a humanist's mind. They are simply examples of poor cognitive intuition, a sort of cognitive equivalent to the optical illusions we all know. These illusions and biases exist, of course. But there are other irrationalities.

39. Some of these columns are collected in Dan Ariely, *Irrationally Yours: On Missing Socks, Pickup Lines, and Other Existential Puzzles* (Harper, 2015).

40. *Irrationally Yours*, pp. 114--115. If you do not want to do this experiment, Ariely adds, it can only mean that you have either made up your mind or that you are too lazy to put in the effort.

41. *Irrationally Yours*, pp. 68–69.

For example, sometimes we seem to act according to a will not our own. As mentioned earlier, the military uses this tendency to bind soldiers in a group they would die for, the phenomenon historian William McNeill called "muscular bonding."[42] Politicians at mass rallies exploit it, too. People get swept up and do what they would not otherwise do and what they wonder at later. It happens at some college football games. In the Middle Ages, this was thought of as possession because it seemed as if an alien will were in control. Social psychologists do not, of course, invoke the devil, but they do consider the fact that people are by nature not just individuals but also members of groups, and that sometimes their "hive switch" is activated.[43]

In his classic 1841 study, *Extraordinary Popular Delusions and the Madness of Crowds*, Charles MacKay traces a variety of phenomena, from the South Sea and Tulip Bubbles to witch manias, where people are caught up in a sort of frenzy they later recognize as madness.[44] It seems that, for a while, a person's will ceases to be his own and is shaped by "the madness of crowds." The will becomes double, partly the person's own, partly that of the crowd acting within him. Afterward, these people can't fathom why they did what they did or, as we say, "what possessed them."[45] This seems to be one of the vulnerabilities entailed by our essentially social nature.

No less interesting, we sometimes deliberately act against our self-interest precisely to show that we can be unpredict-

---

42. William H. McNeill, *Keeping Together in Time: Dance and Drill in Human History* (Harvard University Press, 1995).

43. Haidt, *The Righteous Mind*, pp. 221–245.

44. Reprinted as Charles MacKay, *Extraordinary Popular Delusions and the Madness of Crowds* (Wilder Publications, 2008).

45. The great literary work on this theme is Euripides's *Bacchae*. Agave and the Maeneds in a frenzy tear apart Agave's son Pentheus, and the mother only recognizes what she has done when the frenzy passes and she returns to herself. Dostoevsky's novel *The Possessed* [more literally, *The Demons*] sees revolutionary violence in much the same terms.

able. As discussed several times in the book, that is the theme of Dostoevsky's *Notes from Underground*. Under this spell, one may take pride in one's own degradation or act deliberately to cause oneself harm, a phenomenon Dostoevsky calls "lacerations." If this sort of behavior is admitted, rational choice economics has, for such cases, met its match. But behavioral economics does not even imagine it.

Human intentions are much more complex than behavioral economics allows. For example, it is commonly supposed that before one can do something, one must have chosen to do it (whether rationally or irrationally). In fact, we often do things without deciding at all. One might, for instance, enter a dream state or a sort of long-term trance, stupor, or other debilitating mood. Or one might just keep options open. In *Crime and Punishment*, Raskolnikov does both and winds up killing the old pawnbroker woman without ever having decided either to do so or not to do so.

What's more, people may deceive themselves about their wishes before they act on them. Self-deception by its very nature involves a double intentionality. It is also very hard to explain from any rationalist perspective because it might seem that if you know you are trying to deceive yourself, you would automatically detect the deception. And yet it happens all the time. Psychological novelists have detailed the processes by which self-deception takes place.

If we begin with mainstream economics, we can describe a great deal of human behavior. After all, people often do act rationally. Even when individuals don't, market forces may produce in the aggregate what rational individuals would have chosen. For all practical purposes, that may amount to the same thing.

Mainstream economists, when careful, can avoid the accusation of psychological naiveté by adhering to the Friedman rule: do not claim to be describing real people, only to be constructing a useful fiction. That fiction is meant to be judged not by whether it accords with what actual individual people do but by the general predictions it yields. This stance, if adhered to, makes the objections raised by behavioral economists against mainstream economics, namely, that real individuals behave irrationally, largely beside the point.

By contrast, behavioral economists rarely adhere to the Friedman rule. Their experiments on individuals are offered as showing what individuals really do, and claims about individual psychology are made. If they claim to be describing real individual psychology, they leave themselves open to objections that they are not doing a very good job at it. The failure to consider culture, for instance, becomes a major problem. Making claims that a Friedman-inspired mainstream economist would avoid, they have gone further from, not closer to, a humanist perspective.

But this is not an error that behavioral economists are bound to make. They could observe the Friedman rule as well. In that case, the insights they derive from introspection, laboratory experiments with individuals, or anything else would be offered not as adequate descriptions of individuals but as prompts for predictions about economic behavior on the same scale, but different from, those generated by mainstream economists.[46] Their only claim would be that those predictions are sometimes superior to those of mainstream economics.

That is just what Raj Chetty does in the article "Behavioral Economics and Public Policy: A Pragmatic Perspective," cited earlier in this chapter. A pragmatic approach, as Chetty describes it, avoids arguing that behavioral economics is theoretically superior or a more accurate description of individual behavior. Instead, it "starts from a policy question … and incorporates behavioral factors to the extent that they

---

46. In *Thinking Fast and Slow* (Farrar, Straus and Giroux, 2011), Daniel Kahneman stresses that when he and Amos Tversky were developing the insights leading to behavioral economics, they relied heavily on introspection.

improve empirical predictions.... This approach follows the widely applied methodology of positive economics advocated by Friedman, who argued that it is more useful to evaluate economic models on the accuracy of their empirical predictions than on their assumptions" (p.1). In that case, behavioral economics would turn out not to be a frontal assault on mainstream economics but a "natural progression" from it. "In this sense," he explains, "behavioral economics is better viewed as part of all economists' toolkits" (p. 29).

After offering several examples of the contributions behavioral ideas can make to specific policy decisions and indicating how they might be justified empirically, Chetty concludes that "the applications reviewed in this paper show that an updated reading of the 'as if' approach to economic modeling advocated by Friedman—traditionally one of the main arguments used to defend neoclassical models—calls for incorporating behavioral economics" insofar as it "can offer more accurate and robust predictions for optimal policy" (p. 29).

Viewed this way, behavioral economics stands on the same ground as mainstream economics so far as its claims are concerned. If either school is understood as Friedman proposed—not as a plausible description of individual behavior but as justified by the success of its predictions—then it may, when appropriate, be supplemented or corrected by insights from the humanities, both psychological (for descriptive accuracy) and moral (since policy recommendations are never of strictly economic concern in their intended or actual effects).

That is exactly what we have tried to do in this study.

Chapter 8

Humanomics
A Dialogue of Disciplines

> To live means to participate in dialogue.... In this
> dialogue a person ... invests his entire life in discourse,
> and this discourse enters into the dialogic fabric of
> human life, into the world symposium.
> —Mikhail Bakhtin[1]

Our hope was to produce a volume that speaks to both
economists and humanists. We have tried to stress the many
strengths of each approach, to spell out what in our view are
their weaknesses, and to argue that they are stronger together.
A dialogue between the two might yield fruitful and unexpected results.

Our students regularly ask us to provide a list of takeaways.
In fact, they often insist on it! While we loathe long summaries
and extended conclusions—if we had something important to
add, we would have included it in the preceding chapters—we
nonetheless want to stress a few points.

To begin, even when economists focus on subjects that are
very much in their wheelhouse, their work could be both more
effective and more just if infused with humanistic approaches

---

1. Mikhail Bakhtin, "Toward a Reworking of the Dostoevsky Book," *Problems of
Dostoevsky's Poetics*, ed. and trans. Caryl Emerson (University of Minnesota Press,
1984), p. 293.

and ways of thinking. Examples abound. Economists know a great deal about the consequences of reducing government subsidies on basic food products, how to evaluate the efficiency of a health intervention or the implications of storing toxic waste, how to implement enrollment management tools to minimize unnecessary price discounts, how to create a market for human organs, how to anticipate how people will react when prices and incomes change, and much, much more. But knowing how to do something does not tell us whether to do it. Ethical considerations by their very nature lie outside the economists' narrow expertise.

As tempting as it is to think that bread riots, abandoned health programs, dumping waste into areas with already high mortality, underhanded college pricing schemes, and a market solution for meeting an excess demand for organs, among many examples, can be justified on purely economic grounds, there are far-reaching implications that should not be ignored. Some of those implications are best understood through stories.

Where human beings are concerned, stories are an indispensable way of knowing. Whether it is gaining insight from speaking with talented high school students who confound our models by not selecting the colleges they "should," or learning the history, reading the literature, and studying the culture of places that, despite the best efforts of economic planners, don't develop the way we expect, there is much to be gained from qualitative approaches. In a world of contingency and narrativeness, stories are essential. Econometric methods and mathematical models teach us so much, but *only* so much.

Sometimes economic approaches shed light on noneconomic topics. But when economists venture outside their normal subjects of analysis, they need not do so in an imperialistic manner. Too often, when economists talk about exploring subjects usually within the purview of other disciplines, they don't mean learning from these fields or taking them seriously; they mean taking them over. They approach these disciplines as if they were bastions of unscientific fluff and vagueness, ready to be replaced with economists' scientific certainties.

But it doesn't have to be that way. There can be real dialogue. When economists are serious about incorporating the wisdom from psychology, philosophy, sociology, anthropology, the sciences, and, of course, the humanities, their analyses become much richer. They must not only speak to other disciplines but let them speak back.

When economists delve into far-flung issues, check their bibliography: Is it just economists talking to economists, or, for example, do the authors at least acknowledge the insights from psychology and sociology in developing behavioral models, or from philosophy and literature in deciding which policy is more just? And of course, even citations are not enough. Is there a genuine attempt to integrate the wisdom from other fields into economic analyses? We have offered numerous examples of such efforts throughout the book. They should be celebrated both for their sincere outreach and for the humility their authors show in acknowledging that the truth is messy and that answers pretending otherwise are fraught.

We recognize that academe needs its hedgehogs. Without them, we would miss important principles they have discovered. Suitably "de-universalized" and judiciously reformulated, those principles can become useful additions to our toolbox of concepts. Whether it is Diamond in geography, Becker in economics, or Rostow in development theory, the energetic formulation of big truths and broad patterns can capture the imagination of many others. And those who respond to the hedgehogs, whether to confirm or refute them, often unearth still more truths that would have otherwise remained invisible. Critics may justly demur at statements such as "The economic approach is a comprehensive one that is applicable to all human behavior" or "This book attempts to provide a short history of everybody for the last 13,000 years," but sometimes it takes bold analyses to disturb our complacency and to expand the literature in dynamic ways.

On the other hand, we need foxes to come closer to the real truth about contingent beings and cultures. When hedgehogs rule alone, they may mislead; when they inspire foxes, they may shed light. Hedgehogs are prickly, foxes cunning. We need our foxes to formulate models, make predictions, and develop policies that reflect the nuances of real life. Foxy approaches are far less sexy, but they are more likely to be right.

To be sure, humanists may act as if they do not believe in the wisdom of their own disciplines. Sometimes they seek to imitate their more prestigious cousins by creating some purported literary science, based in linguistics or evolution or neurobiology or computer science or, we predict, whatever other field starts gaining attention and stealing enrollments. At other times, they turn to theories that deny the very existence of great literature or adopt approaches that preclude real, empathetic engagement or the discovery of wisdom. But the wisdom is still there, and many humanists still find and teach it.

So let us summarize a few ways economists can learn from the study of literature. A serious engagement with great writers includes living into their perspectives and the perspectives of their characters. One comes to sense from within what it is like to feel like someone else and to think like someone else. We overcome our natural tendencies to presume that everyone is like us or that, if they are not, they are benighted. In many ways, literature liberates us from the prison houses of self, of our culture, and of our historical period.

Literature thereby teaches us to be humble about our own knowledge. When it comes to human beings, things are always likely to be much more complex than they seem. In the hard sciences, Galileo was right to imagine that most times real simplicity lies behind apparent complexity, but with human beings, apparent simplicity usually conceals underlying complexity. Due to a sort of intellectual optical illusion, which filters out

what does not fit, we easily miss all those nuances, particularities, psychological idiosyncrasies, and cultural contingencies
that make people what they are.

Given the role that contingency plays in human affairs, narrative explanation is often essential. Mathematicization can
provide a good start; after that, we need to recognize narrativeness. The great novels can educate us not only about human
psychology and other worldviews but also about explanation
itself. They demonstrate why and when we require stories.
Economists need to stop excluding from their field of vision
what stories alone can explain. That includes behavioral economists who, despite the promise of their models, have taken
just baby steps toward narrative. Whether we are speaking of
economics or any other field examining real people, the neat-
ness of models is neither proof of nor substitute for truth.

Perhaps above all, one needs the humanities when ethical
questions are involved, as they are likely to be whenever economists make policy recommendations. There are various ways
to do an end run around complex ethical questions, but doing
so also entails ethical problems. Those problems are no less
real for being unseen. There is no place where the complexity
of ethical questions is appreciated more than the great novels,
unless it is in other literary forms. What looks like a cogent
abstract argument needs to be examined for its likely effect on
particular people, and we have no better achievement for such
examination than great novels. They provide an education in
ethical thinking that can be applied to newer questions they
have never addressed.

To be sure, humanists have a lot to learn from economists
as well. When resources are limited, the efficient use of them
is itself a moral as well as an economic issue. We need to recognize that choices entail costs as well as benefits. We need to
be more wary than humanists often are of counterexamples
and confirmation bias. We have mentioned only a few ways in

which the dialogue can go in this direction because that is not the topic of this book—but those ways are real.

Two cultures; a common aim. To build a world in which we not only draw upon economics, medicine, engineering, and science in order to lead longer, healthier, and more prosperous lives, but also never forget that it is the humanities and the arts that make those lives worth living. Let's supplement the quantitative rigor, the focus on policy, and the logic of economics with the empathy, judgment, and wisdom that defines the humanities at their best.

Impossible? Maybe not.

We conclude with a reprise of the Sam Cooke classic: "What a wonderful world this would be."

Index